£50.00

ANTHONY CROSLAND

Also by David Reisman

ADAM SMITH'S SOCIOLOGICAL ECONOMICS
ALFRED MARSHALL: Progress and Politics
ALFRED MARSHALL'S MISSION
CROSLAND'S FUTURE: Opportunity and Outcome
THE ECONOMICS OF ALFRED MARSHALL
GALBRAITH AND MARKET CAPITALISM
MARKET AND HEALTH
THE POLITICAL ECONOMY OF HEALTH CARE
THE POLITICAL ECONOMY OF JAMES BUCHANAN
RICHARD TITMUSS: Welfare and Society
STATE AND WELFARE: Tawney, Galbraith and Adam Smith
THEORIES OF COLLECTIVE ACTION: Downs, Olson and Hirsch

Anthony Crosland

The Mixed Economy

David Reisman

First published in Great Britain 1997 by
MACMILLAN PRESS LTD
Houndmills, Basingstoke, Hampshire RG21 6XS and London
Companies and representatives throughout the world

A catalogue record for this book is available from the British Library.

ISBN 0–333–65928–7

First published in the United States of America 1997 by
ST. MARTIN'S PRESS, INC.,
Scholarly and Reference Division,
175 Fifth Avenue, New York, N.Y. 10010

ISBN 0–312–15950–1

Library of Congress Cataloging-in-Publication Data
Reisman, David A.
Anthony Crosland : the mixed economy / David Reisman.
p.   cm.
Includes bibliographical references (p.   ) and index.
ISBN 0–312–15950–1 (cloth)
1. Crosland, Anthony, 1918–1977.   2. Economists—Great Britain–
–Biography.   3. Legislators—Great Britain—Biography.
4. Economics—Great Britain—History—20th century.   5. Socialism–
–Great Britain—History—20th century.   I. Title.
HB103.C7R45   1996
320.5'312'092—dc20   96–1509
[B]   CIP

This book is printed on paper suitable for recycling and made from fully managed and
sustained forest sources.

10   9   8   7   6   5   4   3   2   1
06   05   04   03   02   01   00   99   98   97

Printed in Great Britain by
The Ipswich Book Company Ltd
Ipswich, Suffolk

Contents

Acknowledgements

The author and publishers wish to thank the Estate of Anthony Crosland and Jonathan Cape Ltd for permission to quote from *The Future of Socialism*, *The Conservative Enemy* and *Socialism Now*, all by C.A.R. Crosland. They would also like to thank Susan Crosland for permission to reproduce unpublished material from the Crosland Papers, in the British Library of Political and Economic Science, and Dr Angela Raspin and her colleagues at the Library for their interest and support.

1 Introduction

The Future of Socialism was a work of moderation born into a world of consensus. A rigorous reappraisal of the scope for the State, it established itself almost immediately as British Labour's most influential manifesto since Durbin's *Politics of Democratic Socialism* in 1940 if not since Tawney's *Equality* in 1931. Anthony Crosland's important contribution to the theory of the middle ground was published in 1956. Two decades later *The Guardian* was still describing it as 'a great seminal work which ... remains the main intellectual fount of modern British democratic socialism'[1] and *The Economist* was treating it as a classic that had stopped the clocks at the moment of its birth: 'To a shaming extent, the Labour party (or at least its moderate wing) has been living off the intellectual capital of *The Future of Socialism* ever since.'[2]

The Future of Socialism is a political economist's analysis of the proper balance between the individual and the collectivity, the market and the State. It is not the only attempt that was made by the Oxford economist turned Member of Parliament to shed light on the crucial relationship between the self-reliance of exchange and the guiding hand of authority. Anthony Crosland, public figure as well as prolific author, took opportunity after opportunity to develop and expound his vision of a pragmatic Centre-Left, neither too greedy nor too stifling. The result is a remarkable body of insights and theories in which the *Summa* of the *Future* is joined by *The Conservative Enemy* (1962) and *Socialism Now* (1974), by articles in *The Sunday Times* and the *Tribune*, *Socialist Commentary* and *Encounter*, by Fabian Tracts and academic papers, by interviews in the media and speeches in the House, by unpublished letters kept in Oxford and unpublished manuscripts kept in London. Seldom has a philosopher-ruler devoted more time and effort to the formulation of the philosophy that would legitimate the rule.

The ideas are dispersed but still the vision is one. That vision is the subject of this book and of its sister-book, *Crosland's Future: Opportunity and Outcome*. Uniting those books is the contention that the disparate parts are not random *ad hocs* but rather the inter-dependent pieces of a unified whole. Anthony Crosland was a systemic thinker who recognised that there could be no middle way without a reliable map. It is the task of this book and of its sister-book to demonstrate that Anthony Crosland did

1

indeed have in mind a system and a schema – and that even pragmatism was to be situated in its context and guided by principle.

Crosland's Future: Opportunity and Outcome is concerned with equality, welfare and growth. Its theme being political engineering and social development, its character is affirmative and its rallying-cry the demand for more. The present book is about the mixed economy. The focus being production rather than redistribution, property rather than culture, the tone is more damped, the recommendation more muted. Crosland went on the offensive where the need was to eradicate poverty and to reduce social distance. With respect to the economy, however, Crosland was quick to leaven his proposals for reform not with a pinch but with a whole handful of *festina lente*.

Yet proposals for reform there undoubtedly were. These are considered in Chapter 5 (on Control) and Chapter 4 (on Ownership). Changes being ambiguous in the absence of a baseline, the material and intellectual setting is the subject of Chapter 3 (on The World of the Revisionist), the politician-theorist's life and career the subject of Chapter 2 (on Anthony Crosland). Chapter 6 concludes the book by accepting that the story of Anthony Crosland on the mixed economy is unlikely to frighten merchant bankers or put currency speculators off their lunch. Chapter 6 does not take issue with Colin Welch's description of Crosland as a man who many years ago had done his best 'to make socialism seem respectable, undoctrinaire and safe, clearly the most sensible and humane, if not the only way of running our affairs.... It was painless socialism, socialism without tears; or so it said.'[3] Chapter 6 observes, however, that Crosland's socialism is a playing-field for intellectual discourse even as it is a specified set of objectives and goals. Crosland's socialism implies that the future of the mixed economy is a future of interminable seminars, detailed documentation and case-by-case reasoning. The banners and the slogans were more exciting in their day. No doubt they were – but, stranded on the middle ground, we start from here.

2 Anthony Crosland

Charles Anthony Raven Crosland was born at St Leonards-on-Sea, Sussex, on 29 August 1918. His background was that of the work ethic, the strict moral code, the intense Christianity of the Plymouth Brethren. Later he rebelled: when made a Privy Councillor in 1965 he chose to affirm rather than to swear the Christian oath. The Christianity may have worn off but not the commitment to work (he spent 12 to 15 hours a day on *The Future of Socialism* and when a minister, unlike a great number of his colleagues, himself shared in the drafting of major State papers). Nor did the high moral standards: what his lifelong friend Philip Williams once said of Hugh Gaitskell may with equal justice be said of Crosland himself, that 'if all politicians are either bishops or bookmakers, Gaitskell the public man sat firmly on the episcopal bench'.[1]

Crosland's father, politically a Liberal, turned down the knighthood which was offered as a matter of course to so highly-ranked a civil servant in the War Office. Just as the Brethren eschewed the pleasures of ice-cream and newspapers on Sunday, so they were opposed to ostentation and honours so great as to constitute a barrier between God's creatures, all equal in the Creator's sight. Tony Crosland was thus brought up in a well-to-do household which, in spite of the nannies and the servants and the cook, was by no means cossetting (only after his father died was a radio allowed) or snobbish (the clergyless Brethren emphasising strongly that all men must be accorded equal respect since God alone held the mandate to lead). Crosland's socialism of cultural homogenisation through consumption and affluence is no doubt indicative of a tension with the duty-bound asceticism of his formative years that John Vaizey perceptively identified when he wrote of the ideologue of restraint and licence that 'he was a puritan seeking to be a hedonist'.[2] Crosland's often-cited impatience with the views of his intellectual inferiors may well betray a vision of the philosopher-ruler that, arguably at variance with that of the Brethren Protestants, is more in line with the condescension and the arrogance that *The Observer* once imputed to Crosland and to Gaitskell alike: 'Both were egalitarians in the same sense of treating everyone else as slightly less clear-headed and principled than themselves.'[3] In some respects Crosland moved on from the uncompromising Gospels of his father's house. In other respects he did not. The democratic egalitarianism that was the core of his political

philosophy unquestionably owes much to the strict Christianity of a
happy childhood.

Crosland's mother, Jessie Raven, was a lecturer in French at Westfield
College, in the University of London. Her speciality was medieval literature. Earlier in contact with Bloomsbury intellectuals such as Lytton
Strachey, always interested in the Continent and its culture, her love of
books and of Europe was passed on to Tony, a voracious reader who as a
politician and a minister would habitually go on holiday to France or Italy
(usually on his own) with a suitcase full of promises and adventures.
Included were *Clochmerle*, *Myra Breckenridge*, Kingsley Amis, Iris
Murdoch, Günter Grass, Turgenev, a whole string of E.M. Forsters, plus
the latest political biographies (of Macmillan, Wilson, Truman, Keir
Hardie, Baldwin, Montgomery, John Strachey), plus Ngaio Marsh and Len
Deighton for occasional light reading. His diaries meticulously document
his reactions. These range from moderate surprise concerning D.H.
Lawrence ('Hadn't realised D.H. Lawrence died at 44') to something
stronger when putting down Christopher Lasch's book on Eleanor
Roosevelt: 'One can see how intolerable she must have been to live with
for gay character like FDR, & why he *had* to find relaxing mistress as well
as this permanent nagging conscience: simply to have female company
without being *badgered* all the time.'[4] A conscientious tourist never far
from his guidebook, he was equally good about writing down his impressions of places such as Moret-sur-Loing ('How does flat France come to
have all these wonderful rivers, & we don't?') and, of course, Albi:
'Marvellous place ... Red-brick cath. stupendous ... xxxx ... Considerable
difficulty over lunch, mainly but not entirely at wk-ends.'[5] Crosland's
roots were in puritanism and equality. They were in books and Europe as
well.

The family's comfortable circumstances made possible an independent
education in the privilege and exclusivity of Highgate School. Tony
finished school as a day-boy rather than a boarder, the Croslands living at
46, Sheldon Avenue, just around the corner. Even in London N6 the
Depression and the dictators made themselves felt. By 1934, aged 16,
Anthony Crosland had made up his mind that the perpetuation of class-
based capitalism was not for him. He joined the Labour Party and soon
thereafter the Left Book Club as well. The Left Book Club, founded by
Victor Gollancz with John Strachey and Harold Laski, was then very close
to the Communist position. At the same time Crosland was clearly reading
the works of the Labour moderates as well. While still at school he submitted an essay entitled 'Bread for the masses, cake for the few'. In 1935
Dalton had written that capitalism was morally reprehensible precisely

because 'it gives cake to a few, while many lack bread.'[6] Crosland had evidently made it his business to learn about the Marxists and the moderates alike even before he went up to Oxford in 1937 to read classics at Trinity.

Crosland remained at Oxford from 1937 to 1940. Already highly political, he became involved with extreme left-wingers such as the young Denis Healey, Andrew Shonfield and Iris Murdoch in the pro-Soviet Oxford University Labour Club that enjoyed considerable influence in the turbulent years of the *Anschluss*, the Munich appeasement and the Spanish Civil War. Roy Jenkins, reading PPE at Balliol, recalls of Crosland that 'before the war he was an active and orthodoxly Marxist member of the Labour Club'.[7] The Rippentrop–Molotov Pact, the Soviet invasion of Finland, the growing threat to Britain herself, had the effect of returning Crosland to the middle ground. With Roy Jenkins (and a mature student, Ian Durham), he was instrumental in setting up the Oxford University Democratic Socialist Club as an anti-communist alternative to the more militant mainstream. This is unlikely to have been the only time in his life that he contemplated the possibility of abandoning the Labour Left in order to defend the core Labour message. Roy Jenkins ultimately did more than simply contemplate the possibility of a split in the uneasy coalition: with David Owen, Bill Rodgers and Shirley Williams, he was a member of the 'Gang of Four' that brought the Social Democratic Party into being in 1981, four decades after the war of the Clubs and four years after Crosland's death.

Big Business and Wall Street, Soviet full employment and Soviet planned development, ceased to figure prominently in Crosland's worldview by 1939. Not so the need to react and respond to the methodology and predictions of the Marxian model. Few British non-Marxists have taken more trouble to incorporate Marx as a benchmark and a sounding-board:[8] Tawney, Titmuss and T.H. Marshall, to mention but three, seem barely to have been aware of Marx's existence. In an unpublished manuscript dating from 1940 Crosland observes that Marx was wrong to neglect the growing subdivision both of labour (into skilled, professional, manual and other grades) and of capital (due not least to the unexpected survival of the small business): 'The fact is that the class division of modern society is not so simple or clear-cut as Marx thought it would become with the development of capitalism.'[9] In the same manuscript he proposes that Labour should become a classless party with a socialist vision that transcends the partiality and the bias of the proletariat alone: regrettably, he writes, the middle classes 'have felt that the Labour Party was concerned soley with winning concessions for the working-classes at their expense, without putting forward a constructive Socialist programme in which they could see a place for themselves.'[10] Revolution is a logical eventuality where repression closes off the parliamentary option: 'It was thus no accident that the one Socialist Party which remained completely loyal to Marxist principles was the Russian Party, which could not have obtained power by any other than revolutionary means.'[11] Revolution is not, however, either necessary or sensible where political democracy allows men and women of good will to reform the economic basis in accordance with their morals and ideals: 'In this country it is particularly relevant to emphasise the fact that the present Liberal Party, and indeed a tiny section of the Conservative Party, is composed of people who are sincere democrats in that they are anxious to see the government of the country taken out of the hands of the present ruling-class and invested in the representatives of the great mass of the population; they are in fact prepared to go a considerable way towards nationalising major industries.'[12] Social consensus, political democracy, economic restructuring – Crosland may have been promulgating a volitional alternative to historical materialism but at least he knew precisely which intellectual system it was that he was seeking to stand on its head.

Crosland in the 1940s had decided that 'the hard core of beastliness' in the Soviet Union ('to-day there is far less freedom than pre-Revolution') had rendered completely unacceptable to him the 'out-of-this-world and Utopian' thrust of Leninist theory that had opened the door to the inevitability of Stalinist abuse. Soviet Communism, he said, had moved beyond the pale because of 'the intense political repression, the growth of a self-perpetuating ruling-class, the extent of social & economic inequality, sacrifice of all international ideals, the prostitution of art, the absence of workers' representation, the element of pure aggrandisement in Soviet foreign policy',[13] much else besides that all socialist democrats (in the sense of liberty-loving majoritarians who 'are democrats first, Socialists second')[14] could only regard with the deepest distaste. Watching the British election of 1945 from his billet in Austria, Crosland wrote to Philip Williams that he believed in the innate benefits of socialism but also in the *sine qua non* of the validation by vote: 'God knows we need a Labour victory. This constant competition in bloody-mindedness between the extreme Right (de Gaulle) & the extreme Left (Tito, Lublin, Moscow) is wearing one down a bit: & if one European country doesn't very quickly prove that you can be both Socialist & democratic at the same time, I shall drown myself.'[15] Marx and Lenin would have sung a different tune; and so would the hard-core Left in the Oxford University Labour Club of the 1930s. By 1939, however, Crosland had made his home on the middle ground. Chairman of the Oxford University Democratic Socialist Club, ably supported by Roy Jenkins as his Treasurer, his notes and letters contain the embryo of *The Future of Socialism* while his determined jockeying for Oxford influence may indicate a conscious decision to go later for greater prizes still. Not all future leaders have been so involved in Oxford Labour. Hugh Gaitskell (at New, from 1924–27) was not, and Harold Wilson (Jesus, 1934–37) wrote it off as 'a bitter disappointment'.[16] But Crosland from the start was a political animal – and a Party man.

Never a pacifist, Crosland volunteered for war service before completing his degree. Five and a half years of active engagement, first in the Royal Fusiliers, then in the Royal Welch Fusiliers, then in the Parachute Brigade, meant that he saw bloodshed and death in Italy and North Africa such as most intellectuals only learn about in the news. His defiance in the face of adversity was apparently not directed exclusively at the enemy without: 'I made a thoroughly bad start by omitting to remove my pipe from my mouth during a mock bayonet charge.'[17] His fellow-officers did not always approve of him, one of them noting officially that he was 'intelligent, but inclined to be lazy and casual, & generally too critical.'[18] The free spirit for his part was delighted to return their reservations with interest: 'The main snag is my fellow-officers.... These are depressingly British, beer-drinking, & female-conscious.... I am gradually ferreting out the relative intelligentsia of the place.'[19] Military service gave Crosland his first extended exposure to the less-privileged classes who had been conspicuous by their absence at Highgate and Oxford. Never inclined to idealise the proletariat or to exaggerate its political acumen, Crosland found that on a human level he was able to interact comfortably with men from a variety of backgrounds without appearing to be patronising or relapsing into that snobbery that so commonly separated the officer-class from the below-stairs ranks. Tawney (who, refusing a commission, had gone as a private to the front) had been schooled by a similar experience when he came face-to-face with the typical Englishman – 'Henry Dubb' – in the trenches and the hospitals of the First World War.

In 1945 Crosland returned to Oxford to complete his degree. He converted to Politics, Philosophy and Economics (obtaining his First in 1946), was elected President of the Union, and then, in 1947, began his career at the age of 29 by replacing his tutor, Robert Hall (just beginning a 14-year stint as Economic Adviser to the Government) as economics lecturer at Trinity College. He was to remain in that post until 1950. Roy Jenkins has consistently emphasised how much Crosland, 'extravagant and dashing',[20] came to stand out from the rest in an Oxford that respected charisma and recognised a star: 'Crosland was an imposing undergraduate, apparently self-confident, irreverent, and even glamorous, with striking good looks, intellectual assurance, a long camel-hair overcoat and a rakish sports car. Later, as a young don, he with one or two contemporaries formed something of a cult group, of which the distinguishing characteristic was the unusual combination of hard intellectual endeavour and undisciplined, even rather riotous, relaxation. Crosland was, and remained, a puritan.... shot through with strains of self-indulgence.'[21] Bill Rodgers first met Crosland in the summer of 1950. He too sensed that he was in the presence of a personality quite unlike any other: 'He was an immensely attractive figure, handsome, clever and politically informed. To a young undergraduate, his reputation for having fought with the 1st Airborne Division and for girls who left his college rooms at dawn was an irresistible combination.'[22] Women were drawn to him and he was never oblivious to them. Hilary Sarson met him in 1948 and married him in 1952. They separated in 1953 (divorcing quietly in 1956): she was apparently not prepared for serial infidelity when she had expected monogamy. Crosland's second marriage in 1964 to Susan (Watson by birth, Catling by marriage, Barnes for convenience, Crosland by re-marriage) was more successful. Her support and intelligence made it possible for him to bear the great burdens of State that were to fall upon him in the succeeding years. They had no children of their own although he took a warm and fatherly interest in her two children from her previous marriage. A journalist and writer by profession, she is the author of an important biography, *Tony Crosland*, as well as of a political novel, *Ruling Passions*, in which a principal character, Andrew Harwood, bears more than a superficial resemblance to her late husband. Andrew Harwood is a socially-conscious Member of Parliament (a man of whom a staunch right-winger observes that 'he could go far if he quit bleating about how we should anoint with perfumed oil every layabout and murderer and black')[23] who becomes a socially-conscious Minister of Defence ('Andrew relinquished a tiny part of his Defence budget on an understanding with the Chancellor that it would go to the meagerly funded Housing Minister')[24] and ultimately a socially-conscious Foreign Secretary. He is also, incidentally, a Conservative of the middle ground.

Crosland's most famous student in his years as an Oxford don was probably the Hon. Anthony Wedgwood Benn, later Lord Stansgate, still later Tony Benn ('Anyone would think from your wealth of aliases', Crosland commented to the reluctant aristocrat, 'that you were hiding from the police').[25] When Benn was contesting the 1950 Bristol by-election and told his former tutor that he was determined to lose the stigma of being an intellectual, Crosland warned him that he might be 'putting the cart before the horse': 'The thing is to get the stigma first, and then worry about getting rid of it'.[26] Later, both of them in the Commons, the one Labour Right, the other Labour Left, Crosland said of 'Jimmy' that there was 'nothing the matter with him except he's a bit cracked';[27] and that 'we all know he occasionally lies, but no one doubts his sincerity in seeing himself as a Messiah'.[28] 'Jimmy' had his own reservations about the advocate of *festina* very *lente* whom he suspected of confusing *Match of the Day* with much-needed socialist reforms: 'For him, informality is a sort of substitute for radicalism and it amuses him.'[29] In spite of their differences Tony Crosland and Tony Benn managed to remain friends.

An academic for only three years, Crosland at Oxford cannot be said to have proceeded far down the road to excellence. There was a theoretical paper on 'Prices and Costs in Nationalized Undertakings' in the *Oxford Economic Papers* for 1950 and an applied contribution on 'The Movement of Labour in 1948' in the *Bulletin of the Oxford Institute of Statistics* (another respected journal) for 1949: the former concerned with marginal cost pricing and plant-level administration, the latter showing a fluency with the tabulation if not the re-calculation of data, both reveal intellectual promise (unsupported, interestingly, by diagrams or mathematics) but also a less-than-detached concern with current affairs. There was a stream of more polemical, more partisan, more politicised articles that foreshadow his later contributions to the *New Statesman, Encounter* and *Socialist Commentary*: 'Has Profits' Taxation Reached Its Peak?' and 'Sharing the National Income', both published in the *Tribune* in 1949, illustrate the kind of topics which he sought to explore with a wider audience than that of scholars alone. There was a generous personal interest in the preparation of Ian Little's *A Critique of Welfare Economics* (a book which Crosland subsequently reviewed in the *Universities Quarterly* in 1951): Ian Little (who succeeded him at Trinity from 1950–53 before moving on to Whitehall to join Robert Hall, by then Sir Robert Hall, at the Treasury) later read through the sections on economics in two at least of Crosland's own books. Overall, however, Crosland at Oxford cannot be said to have made the single-minded assault on economic scholarship that he might have done had he intended to be a career academic and nothing else.

In 1950 Anthony Crosland entered the House of Commons as the Member for South Gloucestershire. Hugh Dalton had played an important part in his selection. Dalton was a great talent-spotter for the Labour Right: Gaitskell had been one of his 'colts', and he had also helped to find seats for such members of the 'Class of 45' as George Brown, Jim Callaghan and Christopher Mayhew. A former London School of Economics academic (1920–36), a former Labour Chancellor (1945–47), the elder statesman had a private list of young politicians who were to be given automatic access to him. Arthur Bottomley, Barbara Castle and Alfred Robens were on the list; and, as Ben Pimlott reports, 'there were later additions. Lord Trend remembers the Chancellor returning from a visit to the Oxford Union early in the summer of 1946. "Make a note! Make a note! Name's Crosland! I want him here!" Shortly afterwards the young Anthony Crosland, still an undergraduate, visited No. 11 Downing Street and his name was put on the list.'[30]

In 1947 Dalton and Crosland met again: the occasion was a dinner organised by Nicholas Davenport at Hinton Manor to celebrate Dalton's sixtieth birthday. Davenport remembered well the impact on the Member for Bishop Auckland of the young Fellow in the bright red sports car: 'As he drove away, I could see in Hugh's eyes the rekindling of his romantic love for gallant and handsome young men.'[31] Dalton at the time made the following entry in his Diary: 'He is an attractive and promising young man and in a year or two should be sufficiently experienced to begin to be useful as a Socialist Economist.'[32] By 1950 he was recording the following: 'Am thinking of Tony, with all his youth and beauty and gaiety and charm and energy and social success and good brains–and a better Economist and a better Socialist than Kaldor, and with his feet on the road of political success now, if he survives to middle age…. I am more fond and more proud of that young man than I can put into words.'[33] That page, torn from Dalton's diary, was found in Crosland's papers after Crosland's death. Dalton probably sent it to him in a mood of extreme sentimentality. In Susan Crosland's words: 'The protégé he loved best was Tony.'[34] Tony was aware of how Hugh felt about him. Perhaps, as Pimlott speculates, Tony saw in the older man a substitute for the father he had lost when only 17. Perhaps, less charitably, he understood about patronage and recognised the main chance.

The election of 1950 approaching, Dalton made a determined effort to find a seat for Crosland. He visited South Gloucestershire to lobby for his first choice and actively discouraged others from entering the ring. An approach from Roy Jenkins was apparently turned down with the comment: 'No, no. That wouldn't suit you at all. South Gloucestershire would be a very good seat for Tony.'[35] Tony, Jenkins wrote almost forty years later, was 'very much the apple of the eye of Hugh Dalton': 'Dalton was always friendly and helpful provided a choice did not have to be made between Crosland and me; when it did, I was nowhere with him.'[36] Once Crosland was in Parliament, Dalton began to intrigue for his advancement. In 1951 he wrote to Gaitskell, then Chancellor of the Exchequer, recommending (unsuccessfully) that Crosland be promoted despite the fact that he had less than two years' experience in the House: 'He is amazingly able and astringent, and is becoming as good a politician as he is an economist. I get much more mental stimulus out of him than out of any of the others. On sheer ability, and knowledge of the subject, and personality, he, of course, ought to be the next Treasury Junior Minister.'[37] In the same year he had a quiet word with Attlee when Bevin stood down as Foreign Secretary: Attlee listened with respect but concluded that Crosland was young and ought to wait. In 1955, when Crosland lost his seat at South Gloucestershire, Dalton buttonholed Eden about a peerage for Morgan Phillips Price in order to create a vacancy in the pro-Labour West Gloucestershire constituency. Dalton was not instrumental in Crosland's adoption as the Labour candidate for Grimsby in 1959, but he lost no time in contacting the Party Leader to welcome the good news: 'So now this most gifted political problem-child, this all-but-statesman already at 40, so outstandingly able, astringent, brave, integral, quick, gay – such fun to have about – is on the high road up. Great success, given a flick of luck, is easily within his powers.'[38] Three years earlier Dalton had not been quite so confident: writing in his Diary at the time of *The Future of Socialism*, he expressed the fear about the book that 'it may yet make trouble for him at a Selection Conference.'[39] In fact, it did not.

Dalton like Crosland was a trained economist and a lapsed academic. He cannot have failed to have been flattered by Crosland's obvious appreciation of his *Practical Socialism*, of his *Public Finance*. Ben Pimlott describes the intellectual linkages in the following words: 'Crosland's *The Future of Socialism* contained much of Dalton, whose name appeared more often in the text than that of any other individual, with the exceptions of G.D.H. Cole and Karl Marx. Indirectly, there was the influence of works like Evan Durbin's *The Politics of Democratic Socialism*, which had developed Dalton's pre-war ideas. Directly there was the impact of Dalton's personal tutelage. Significantly, Dalton was one of only four people (and the only politician) to read and criticise the full manuscript in draft.'[40] Dalton, earlier, had also read Crosland's first book and made detailed comments on its text. He liked *Britain's Economic Problem* but expressed some concern about the burden that Crosland's proposals would impose on the Chancellor. He suggested devolution of responsibility (perhaps to two junior ministers) and warned that good planning is crucially dependent on good staff. Crosland in exchange was able to assist Dalton in a variety of ways. At the beginning there was the unsigned article in the *Tribune* of 11 February 1949 that defended Dalton's Chancellorship. At the end there was the position of literary executor that safeguarded Dalton's reputation when the elder statesman at last passed from the scene in 1962. In between there was the intriguing and the in-fighting of the 1950s that, when the smoke had cleared, had produced a Labour programme with which the moderate Dalton, a moderniser and not a militant, was proud to be associated. Crosland was a man with a deep personal commitment to the middle ground that Crossman once dispar-aged as 'furious moderation'[41] but that *The Economist* correctly identified as the self-perceived radicalism of a centrist by conviction: 'He became a Labour MP in 1950 because he was just old enough to have been deeply stirred by the emotions of the 1930s, while still young enough to realise that some of those emotions are now out of date.'[42] Dalton in the 1950s must have been very pleased indeed to have found in the trained econ-omist and lapsed academic a younger Dalton who would continue his crusade.

Crosland was an intellectual who wanted to see results. At once an ivory-tower philosopher and a hands-on reformer, 'he enjoyed', in the assess-ment of a former Chairman of the Fabian Society, 'the rare satisfaction of the "ideas man" who is capable of translating his ideas into action'.[43] Oxford would have given him the opportunity to think out his theoretical system in an atmosphere of tranquil investigation. Westminster seemed to offer something more. The ideas man at Oxford would spend his life in pure thought. The ideas man at Westminster would in contrast have a chance to get involved in the shaping of events. Personal ambition no doubt played its part as well.

Crosland presented himself to the selection meeting at South Gloucestershire as a man of conviction who wanted to enter Parliament because he had concluded 'that Tory capitalism was unjust, immoral & ugly', because Tory capitalism 'was founded on privilege & inequality'.[44] Inefficiency too was a problem – but a less pressing one. The debate, Crosland said, had moved on from the crisis theories and the economic planning of the 1930s. The outcome of the developments had been that the future of socialism was more and more a matter of right relationships, less and less a synonym for tractors and hydro-electric plants: the 'ultimate ideal of Soc. seems to me essentially a *moral*, & *not* a material one. It is nothing to do with nationalisation of means of production, nothing to do with any one particular economic policy. It is something to do with a just and moral and equal society, in wh. it's no longer true that half the people live in cramped ugly houses & the other half in spacious beautiful ones, in wh. half the people leave school at 15 to go into factories & the other half have all the advantages of Eton and Oxford.'[45] Talking like a bishop when the pound was being devalued from $4.03 to $2.80, concentrating on Eton and Oxford when the local constituency had more immediate concerns on its mind, Crosland was in a sense fortunate that the selection meeting did not suggest politely that an unprincipled opportunist would be more likely to speak for the electors on taxes and subsidies than would a man of conviction in hot pursuit of the New Jerusalem.

Selected in 1949, elected in 1950, re-elected in 1951, Crosland appears not to have taken to the House of Commons like a duck to water. Unlike some Members who get a positive thrill from the games-playing and the cut-and-thrust, Crosland was clearly disappointed with the low level of political debate. As he said to Richard Crossman when rebuked for being drunk in Parliament: 'How else is one to endure being here?'[46] Life in Cabinet was later on to provide no guarantee against boredom and mediocrity. Witness the following comment on an 'interminable' session spent as a minister with Mrs Castle: 'Barbara never stopped talking in Cabinet.... I can understand about macro-economics, I can understand about sex. What I *cannot* understand is the desire of human beings to hear their own voices.'[47] The honourable members did not fail to notice his poor attendance in the House, the paucity of his speeches and questions, his absence on a study-tour of the United States at a time when Parliament was in session. Douglas Jay (who was equally unhappy with Roy Jenkins's attitude to the routine burdens of the democratic process) put on paper what many others must have thought: 'Their attendances in the House were infrequent and Crosland and Jenkins had the reputation of being "aloof".'[48] Crosland is unlikely to have won many friends when, entering Parliament in February 1950, he seized the opportunity of his maiden speech at 5:40 on 19 April to censure the Chancellor for exaggerating the threat from inflation: 'We have not had the Budget we should have had.... He has erred very seriously on the side of excessive caution.'[49] The new boy then proceeded to inform the Chancellor that it would have made more sense not to expand income-tax relief but rather to eliminate purchase tax levied on household necessities: 'If I am right in supposing.... that the dominant problem in 1950 will be the wages problem, then I believe that this £70 million to £75 million should have been used not on tax reliefs but to influence the cost of living and prices. I think that if the money were used in that way, and not to reduce taxation, there would be more chance of the general restraint on the wages front being continued.'[50] Crosland in his maiden speech was advocating the socialist package deal that would later be known as the socialist social contract. Interesting though this was in itself, the fact remains that he was breaking with the tradition that a maiden speech ought not to be controversial – and that he was criticising a Chancellor (Sir Stafford Cripps) who was a member of a *Labour* Government – and that he was doing so at a time when a second general election in two years appeared unavoidable. Self-willed individualists were just another species of harmless eccentric in the Oxford of the 1950s. At Westminster, rocking an already rocking boat, they were somewhat less acceptable to the foot-soldiers and the backbench-men who were clever enough to glimpse the danger of being too clever by half. There is no reason to think that Anthony Crosland was a popular figure in the Houses of Commons of 1950–51 and 1951–55.

Crosland in this period continued to publish extensively, sometimes on class and politics, more frequently on industry and trade. Reading his essays on 'Tomatoes and Cucumbers' (*Tribune*, 1950), 'Legislating against Monopoly' (*Socialist Commentary*, 1951), 'My Budget' (*News Chronicle*, 1952), 'This Would Be My Socialist Budget' (*Reynolds News*, 1953), 'The Case against Take-over Bids' (*The Listener*, 1954), 'The Future of the Labour Party' (*The National and English Review*, 1955), the reader is consistently impressed by the clarity of Crosland's exposition. Had he not seen himself as an intellectual in politics, the status of intellectual in journalism on the model of Andrew Shonfield in the 1950s and Samuel Brittan at a later date would have been an option that he could most successfully have pursued.

Britain's Economic Problem, published in 1953, established Crosland's reputation as an applied political economist. Ranging widely over the dollar shortage (a problem Crosland had already addressed in 1950 in the Fabian Tract *Independence by 1952?*) and the Sterling Area, the balance of payments and the terms of trade, the exchange-rate and the price of gold, the need for restructuring and the re-nationalisation of steel, the author's relative indifference to textbook microeconomics ('I do not think', Vaizey charitably observes, that 'Crosland ever had a deep knowledge of, or interest in, pure economic theory')[51] is more than offset by his obvious strengths in respect of description and inference. Of particular importance was his insistence, frequently reiterated in his other publications, that the State was able to plan without the need for it first to nationalise.

Crosland's commonsensical analysis was almost universally acclaimed, not least because it was 'pleasantly easy to read'[52] and provided the layman with 'a healthy antidote to excessive concentration on remote theoretical possibilities'.[53] Douglas Jay wrote that 'it is the best book since the war on the British struggle for solvency'.[54] Nicholas Kaldor said that its 'sober and admirably lucid analysis deserves the most serious attention'.[55] Accompanying the talk of 'comprehensible and comprehensive',[56] of 'attractively written',[57] of 'excellent',[58] accompanying the suggestion that the author of the little book ought realistically to be regarded as a potential President of the Board of Trade or a future Chancellor, there were also the critical comments of socialists like John Strachey and

Thomas Balogh. John Strachey objected that if Crosland had been serious about socialism he would have assigned pride of place to exchange-controls: 'The cutting edge by which socialist principles must be applied to our problem of national survival is by comprehensive and effective controls over all foreign transactions.'[59] Thomas Balogh observed that it was an unacceptably unsocialist explanation of the British problem to assign no blame at all to the capitalist class and its speculative institutions: 'Mr Crosland has written an extremely able economic brief without paying sufficient attention to the political, sociological or psychological background, either in this country or abroad. It is the tale without the real villains, unlikely to provide a workable solution of our problems.'[60] Despite the possible thinness in the area of socialism (or, arguably, precisely because of its apparent impartiality), the little guide to the balance of payments was in general quite well received.

Crosland in any case had already begun work on a major contribution to British socialism. The idea had come early to him, and even before his war-service the precocious undergraduate had written to Williams that he knew where he was going: 'I am engaged on a great revision of Marxism, & will certainly emerge as the modern Bernstein.'[61] Crossman's *New Fabian Essays*, in 1952, had given Crosland an opportunity, in his paper on 'The Transition from Capitalism', to put on record his conviction that, given the managerial revolution and in view of the interventionist State, the evolution of socialist thinking had regrettably lagged behind the dynamism of the economic reality: 'Capitalism is undergoing a metamorphosis into a quite different system', he wrote in 1952, and 'this is rendering academic most of traditional socialist analysis.'[62] Working from his armchair at 19, The Boltons, Crosland in the mid 1950s set out quite consciously to bring up to date the intellectual framework of the democratic Left. *The Future of Socialism*, published in 1956, was the result.

In the election of 1955 Crosland lost his seat in the House. Aware that new boundaries had made South Gloucestershire a marginal constituency (and aware too that there would very probably be a national swing against Labour), he decided to seek greater security at Southampton Test. It was a miscalculation: Southampton Test on the day went Tory through an even larger swing than at South Gloucestershire.

Out of Parliament, he completed his book on the *Future* and expanded his list of papers, articles and tracts. Notable in this period were his critical reception to Galbraith's paternalism (*The Listener*, 1958), his conspicuous reservations about industrial democracy (*Encounter*, 1959) and his scholarly contribution to E.S. Mason's *The Corporation in Modern*

Society (1959) in which he demonstrated, almost a decade away from Oxford, that he was still capable of arguing an academic's case. He also served from 1956–58 as Secretary (actually writing the Report) to the independent Commission of Inquiry into the Co-operative Movement that Hugh Gaitskell had been asked to chair. It was apparently because of his incipient involvement in the work of the Commission that Crosland made a deliberate choice to say as little as possible about Rochdale mutual aid and its latter-day successors in his big book on *Socialism*. The Preface to the 1956 edition explains the exclusion of the Movement in the following words: 'This Movement, on account of its size, its democratic principles, and its non-profit-making character, must clearly have a large part to play in furthering socialist ideals in Britain. But I have reluctantly decided that I must delete all references to Co-operative problems and policies, lest I should seem to pre-judge the findings of the Commission.'[63]

Not *all* references were in fact deleted. Nor are the references that remained necessarily all that enthusiastic about fraternalistic economics by means of low-level collectivism. In one place Crosland seems to be implying that New Lanark is an anachronism in an era of big-is-beautiful: 'Small-scale cooperative units are not practicable under modern conditions.'[64] In another place he seems to be indicating that Swedish entrepreneurship ought not to be confused with British conservatism: 'In Sweden the most spectacular examples of competitive social enterprise have come from the Co-operatives rather than from the Government. The British movement has perhaps been somewhat less venturesome.'[65] Such reservations may explain why, even after the Commission had completed its deliberations, he never wrote an extended appreciation of the cooperative model or explained its relevance to Britain. The nearest Crosland ever came to producing the missing assessment was his decision to reprint Chapter 2 of the 1958 Report as pp. 228–36 of his *Conservative Enemy*. The Chapter concludes with a defence of 'the Co-operative share of total economic activity': 'Our recommendations have the one object of increasing this share to the greatest possible extent.'[66] Perhaps because of a fear that syndicalist tendencies were a threat to democratic politics, perhaps because he simply never found the time, the fact remains that Crosland never really redeemed the promise which he as Secretary of the Commission had penned in 1958.

In 1959 Crosland re-entered the House of Commons as the Member for Grimsby. It was no secret to the local Party that Hugh Gaitskell thought highly of him and wanted him in Parliament. Grimsby in 1959 was by no means the safe Labour seat that it was under Crosland's 18-year stewardship subsequently to become. The dockers, railwaymen and factory-workers voted Labour but the fishermen had a tradition of voting Tory. In 1959 there was a further national swing against Labour and Crosland's majority was only 101 votes. The Grimbarians took to him and his majority was to increase over the years. One reason is that he strove actively to represent his grass-roots constituency as well as to agitate in the national forum for a democratic-socialist Britain. His pro-North Sea stance in the Cod Wars with Iceland is likely to have been especially popular with the floating voters in his port.

Labour was in opposition in the 1959–64 Parliament. It had been in opposition since Atlee's defeat by Churchill which had put an end to the reforming Governments of 1945–51. There was 1951, there was 1955 and then (in the only campaign ever mounted under Gaitskell's leadership) there was 1959 – Crosland re-entered the House of Commons at a time when a demoralised Labour was wondering if it would ever return to power. Crosland played a leading part in the soul-searching of the early 1960s. He argued strongly for a centrist image in his Fabian pamphlet *Can Labour Win?* of 1960 and in two articles, 'The Future of the Left' and 'Radical Reform and the Left', which were published in *Encounter* in the same year.

Those three occasional pieces, together with 13 others, were reprinted in 1962 in a collection of Crosland's essays entitled *The Conservative Enemy*. Crosland, maintaining that he had 'a temperamental preference for non-flamboyant titles',[67] had wanted to call the book something like *Left and Right Conservatism, Socialism in the Sixties, Socialism and Democracy* or *Essays in Socialism*. G. Howard Wren at Jonathan Cape in London is not known to have had strong feelings about the title. T. Herzl Rome at Schocken Books in New York appears to have been less willing to miss out on sales through gentlemanly reticence: 'While I quite agree that the title of your book need not be flamboyant', T. Herzl Rome wrote to Crosland, 'I do hope that we can find one that is more expressive of the essential quality of your thought than *Essays in Socialism*. I think that we would be doing a disservice to the book's potential on the American market by presenting it under a title so bland. For example, Dan Bell's *The End of Ideology* would, I fear, have attracted very little attention as "Essays".'[68] The American publisher's reference to Daniel Bell was a tactful one: Bell (who shared many of Crosland's assumptions) had written one of the very few reviews of *The Future of Socialism* to have appeared in the United States,[69] where the book by the end of its print-run had sold less than 1000 copies. Schocken Books had only become involved when The Macmillan Company had decided that it did not want to be the American co-publisher of Crosland's subsequent venture: the

volume sounded 'too English', they said to Cape. It was, in the circumstances, rather adventurous on the part of T. Herzl Rome to express an
interest in Crosland's new book.[70] It was also, in the circumstances, rather
likely that Crosland would accept the suggestion and re-think his title.

The *Enemy* did not in the event sell much better in the United States
than had the *Future*, but at least the new title gave a good indication of the
message that Crosland was trying to communicate. Innovation, experimentation and novelty were closely linked to the desirable objectives of economic growth, social reform and personal development. Conservatives of
the Left retarded progress through their adherence to out-of-date ideologies such as Marxism in support of out-of-date panaceas such as nationalisation. Conservatives of the Right retarded progress through their
commitment to class barriers that were indifferent to merit, and idle wealth
that augmented no productivity. In the middle was the dynamism of
progress – the radical moderation of the forward-looking mould-breakers
who alone held the key to growth and meritocracy in combination with
compassion and dignity.

The *Conservative Enemy* was intended by its author as an attack on the
stuck-in-a-rut and a blueprint for affluence with equality. The conservative
enemy for its own part replied that the author had exaggerated the polar-
ities in order to make himself sound more original. Richard Crossman
worked through the reprints and reported that the Left could hardly brand
as controversial new proposals which were in fact little more than agreed-
upon positions: 'What strikes me in re-reading them is the contrast
between the flat, middle-of-the-road programme he advocates and the
polemical tone in which it is dressed up. In actual fact all the policies he
recommends are quite acceptable to the Left, reflecting as they mostly do
the official compromises achieved in the recent policy documents drafted
by the National Executive and approved by Conference.'[71] *The Economist*
compared Crosland's socialism with Macmillan's capitalism and concluded that the Conservative Party was on no reasonable reckoning to be
regarded as the Conservative Enemy that Crosland had wanted to con-
front: 'He departs from realism because on almost every second page he
feels compelled to shout reassurance at himself that the Conservatives are
congenitally incapable of adopting policies which everybody knows that
they have really been adopting – with surprising apparent willingness – for
years.'[72] Both Left and Right seem to have been in relative agreement that
Crosland had tried too hard to show that they were the Conservative
Enemy that the radical moderates had had no choice but to rout.

The *Conservative Enemy* did not attract the media-coverage of *The
Future of Socialism* and was not commercially an outstanding success.

One reason was the curious date of publication: whereas *The Future of Socialism* appeared in October, at the height of the conference season, *The Conservative Enemy* was rushed out in the run-up to Christmas, when most people were thinking of parties but less frequently of political ones. Suspecting that a General Election might be called in spring 1963, the Gaitskellites had encouraged Crosland to publish before the campaigning began in earnest. Crossman and *The Economist* had written as if consensus politics, convergent Butskellism and the end of ideology had deprived *The Conservative Enemy* of its cutting edge. The Gaitskellites, on the other hand, saw correctly that Crosland's collection was simply not to be written off as 'a perfectly packaged tranquilliser for top minds'.[73] Critical of Galbraith on demand-manipulation and of Raymond Williams on popular culture, hostile to the quasi-Marxians of class-conflict and to the dodo nationalisers of Clause IV, *The Conservative Enemy* can reasonably be called the work of 'Labour's Liberal'[74] and, less reasonably, the work of Labour's Conservative 'wet' – but it cannot be called the work of a man who was determined to paint out the differences and paper over the divides. English barricades are, however, more subtle than Continental barricades; and Crosland was every inch an *English* author. The Gaitskellites recognised just how great was the challenge that was implicit in Crosland's polite, under-stated essays. Not surprisingly, they encouraged the author to bring out his book in the season of good-will and not in the heat of a General Election. Then it might have attracted unwelcome publicity to old wounds – and to surviving splits.

The Conservative Enemy contained some reprints and some new essays. Crosland by the early 1960s had become so caught up in practical politics that he was finding it more and more difficult to make time for sustained scholarly activity. The future of *The Future of Socialism* was an especial problem for him: a cult volume with no obvious competitor, the *vade mecum* of the 1950s British revisionists, it was, not unnaturally, due for a moderate revision of its own if it was to retain its intellectual preeminence in the British democratic middle of the succeeding decade. Crosland by 1961 had apparently reconciled himself to the fact that even a moderate revision was not on the cards for the time being. Writing to Wren at Cape, increasingly a politician with ideas rather than a political intellectual *pur sang*, Crosland in January 1961 had to suggest to his publisher that new ink poured over old plates might in the circumstances be the best that could be managed: 'It is now quite clear that there is *no* hope of doing a proper revised edition of THE FUTURE OF SOCIALISM in the next three years. It would be a monumental task in view of the size of the book and the number of detailed facts which would have to be brought up to date. I therefore hope that you might see your way to reprinting the book as it now stands.'[75] Crosland was obviously not very receptive at first to the publisher's proposal, put forward in a letter dated 22 August 1960, for an abridged version of the book that, excising irrelevant statistics rather than updating them, could then be sold more cheaply in a paperback format. Later Crosland was persuaded. The shortened edition appeared in 1964. Slimmed from 540 to 368 pages, the references and footnotes radically cut back, a nervous 'even if' added on p. 148 where previously the author had confidently predicted the withering away of primary poverty, otherwise the new *Future* was essentially the same as the old *Future*. Crosland never again returned to his big book. And events moved on.

By the time of the new *Future* the tide had turned. In the election of October 1964 the Labour Party was returned to power and Harold Wilson became the first Labour Prime Minister since Clement Attlee 13 years before. Crosland's career in politics would undoubtedly have been very different had Hugh Gaitskell not died so suddenly and so unexpectedly of a mysterious *lupus erythematosus* on 18 January 1963, aged only 56 and with Downing Street at long last in view. Crosland respected Wilson but never liked him: 'Harold Wilson is a shit', he once said, 'but a *clever* shit'.[76] Wilson, Roy Jenkins reports, felt more or less the same about Crosland: 'Crosland was cleverer than I was and substantially more skilled in economics. But Wilson could never get on with him. Perhaps oddly, Wilson and I, when not locked in a dispute which made him suspicious, could get on. We liked talking to each other about minutiae which Crosland regarded as puerile: railway timetables or Wisden-like political records. More important, however, was Wilson's belief (or so I have been led to understand) that I had a command over the House of Commons that eluded Crosland, and that I was the more decisive of the two.'[77] Whatever his doubts – and his fears – Wilson at least was an opportunist who was astute enough to recognise talent too valuable to be wasted on the back benches. In all Crosland in his political career spent nine years in ministerial office and held six different posts. However great the temptation to deplore the personality-clash that blocked his access to the portfolios of Home Secretary and especially of Chancellor that he most coveted, it is important as well to keep in mind Crosland's very real successes alongside his undoubted frustrations in the 14 years that followed Gaitskell's death.

From October 1964 to January 1965 Crosland was the Minister of State in the Department of Economic Affairs. Headed by Wilson's Deputy Leader, George Brown, propelled by Wilson's commitment to the 'white heat of technology' that made all problems soluble, the new Department was regarded by the Labour leadership as an embryonic ministry of economic growth, separate from the Treasury and responsible for indicative coordination through a national plan. The permanent secretary, recalled at haste from his Washington posting at the International Monetary Fund, was Sir Eric Roll.

Crosland was to remain at the DEA for only four months. The failure of Patrick Gordon Walker to win a seat in the House, either in the General Election (at Smethwick) or in a hastily-arranged by-election (at Leytonstone), meant that Harold Wilson decided to drop his extra-parliamentary Foreign Secretary and to appoint Michael Stewart in his place. Anthony Crosland was invited to succeed Michael Stewart as Secretary of State in the Department of Education and Science. It was his first Cabinet-level position and his longest-single ministerial posting. He was at Education for just over $2\frac{1}{2}$ years, from January 1965 to August 1967.

Education interested him. Although he did not have the classroom background of ex-schoolmasters like Michael Stewart and Edward Short, he had, of course, himself been a university teacher; and he had also written extensively about educational policy in *The Future of Socialism*, *The Conservative Enemy* and elsewhere. As a man who did not suffer fools gladly, it must have pleased him that his Department was one of the more self-contained ministries: there was relatively little overlap with his colleagues' pet projects (save in the obvious sense of bidding for limited budgets) and relatively little interference in the formulation of policy (not least because Education was still regarded as a low-prestige Department, worthy but dull). At Education he was not afraid to rely on outside advisers such as Ian Byatt (on economics) and A.H. Halsey (on sociology). As Crosland put it: 'Academics are paid to have new ideas, civil servants are paid to administer.'[78]

Replacing Stewart as he did, it is hard to tell how many of the projects that Crosland brought to fruition were Crosland's own and how many were in draft when he arrived. That said, he is known to have moulded the policies even that he did not initiate and to have had a definite influence on Labour's internal process of goal-setting in advance of the 1964 Election. Crosland's tenure at Education was at any rate an eventful one. In 1965 the Social Science Research Council (the SSRC, later the ESRC) was set up to fund the investigation of economy and society: Crosland saw to it that his friend, Michael Young, was made its first Chairman. In the same year the eleven-plus examination and the grammar/non-academic divide were challenged by Circular 10/65, which employed the persuasive word 'request' rather than the directional word 'require' in its campaign to convert the local educational authorities to the comprehensive principle.

Bitterly opposed to the selective system ('If it's the last thing I do', he once declared, 'I'm going to destroy every fucking grammar school in England'),[79] his personal intervention in support of the word 'request' is an illustration both of his realism (the buildings to house the new-style comprehensives simply did not exist) and of his tolerance (since, rightly or wrongly, Britain has a long tradition of *local* involvement in the formulation of educational policy).

Critics who took his 'request' as a sign of weakness and an evasion of responsibility were no more satisfied with the solution he proposed to the problem of the public schools, expensive, exclusive and privileged. Crosland in *The Future of Socialism* had stated unambiguously that he regarded the superior private sector as, ethically speaking, a 'glaring injustice': 'This is much the most flagrant inequality of opportunity, as it is cause of class inequality generally, in our educational system.'[80] Justice and equality pulled him one way. Realism and tolerance pulled him back. The result was that the Secretary of State in 1965 decided to empanel a Public Schools Commission under Sir John Newsom to advise him on how to proceed. The economic situation, to be fair, hardly smiled on new departures in the period of Crosland's Secretaryship: cost was the reason, for example, why he had to shelve his proposal for the raising of the school-leaving age from 15 to 16. Even so, Crosland's critics contended, he ought to have done more as Secretary of State to attack in practice the aberrations that he had so eloquently castigated in print.

Crosland as Secretary of State presided over the creation in 1967 of the 30 new polytechnics that were upgraded out of existing colleges. He first announced the Government's commitment to the university/polytechnic divide in a speech in Woolwich in April 1965 (at a time, arguably, when he had not been at the Department long enough to stand up to his civil servants on the controversial issue of the 18+ stigma). The polytechnics were local and technical and flexible – important advantages to a socialist who wanted to expand student numbers and fill in the gaps in access. The polytechnics were also cheap. New universities were being constructed, austerity was in the air; and the Secretary of State may not in the event have been actualising a meritocratic ideal in the binary system so much as bowing before the inevitability of the second best.

In the reshuffle of summer 1967 Crosland was made President of the Board of Trade. Although an economics portfolio and as such a small step in the direction of the Chancellorship, he appears not to have welcomed the new challenge with open arms. On holiday in Cyprus, he complained to his diary about 'the horrible news that I'm to go to the BoT'.[81] Back home in England, he complained his way into Richard Crossman's diary as well: 'It had always been his nightmare that he might be pushed into this ghastly Ministry which was nobody's business.'[82] Pharmaceutical exports to Greece, imported chipboard, the rehousing of the Patent Office and the status of flat glass were evidently not his cup of tea, even if fish fillets and the weather off Iceland were presumably of greater interest to an elective Grimbarian. Once he had settled into his new office, however, Crosland made a conscientious attempt to immerse himself in the day-to-day detail of one of Whitehall's least theory-driven ministries. He also made a determined effort to champion both the consumer welfare that is secured through competitive markets and the consumer welfare that is made possible by economies of scale. Assigned as President unique powers to hold up suspect mergers, a member of a Government that was relying on its Industrial Reorganisation Corporation to rationalise small units into large ones, Crosland saw no contradiction between the emphasis on rivalry and the emphasis on productivity that he was expected simultaneously to promote: 'I see no inconsistency in showing concern about the possible detriment to the public interest of monopoly power, while at the same time working actively for stronger industrial units, because they are both means to the common end of industrial efficiency.'[83]

Speaking as President on the occasion of the second reading of the Restrictive Trade Practices Act of 1968, Crosland surveyed the British experience with monopolies and mergers and concluded that, irrespective of the party in power, 'throughout, the basis of the legislation has been pragmatic and not dogmatic': 'Throughout this process of evolution, the underlying objective has remained the same. It has been to check restrictions on competition and undesirable forms of market power, without at the same time hindering improvements in efficiency or necessary changes in industrial structure.'[84] Adaptable and discretionary rather mechanistic and inflexible, the basis of the legislation was a look-and-see attitude to results that Wilson's President was bound to find congenial: Crosland had, after all, gone into print as early as 1951 in support of the outcome-orientated approach that had been enshrined in 1948 in Labour's historic Monopolies and Restrictive Practices Act that had created the Monopolies and Mergers Commission as a calm British counterpart to the Americans' Anti-Trust.[85] The President of the Board of Trade in 1948, interestingly, had been Harold Wilson, aged 32.

The President of the Board of Trade in 1949 was still Harold Wilson, aged 33. As such the future Prime Minister had been personally involved in the 30 per cent fall in the parity of the currency in which a quarter of the world's trade was conducted. Atlee knew little of economics, Cripps was abroad, and the decision to devalue seems effectively to have been taken by Jay, Gaitskell and Wilson as the economics ministers on the spot. The experience of going back on a solemn promise not to devalue, of betraying the trust of the Overseas Sterling Area that had banked its reserves in pounds, of playing the fixed-rate game and then appearing to cheat, of providing an opportunity for foreign speculators to make money through selling sterling short, must inevitably have left its mark on all who were involved. It is bound to have contributed significantly to Wilson's subsequent conversion to the proposition that the pound must be kept out of politics.

As early as the early 1950s, by then the Shadow Chancellor, Wilson was committing socialism to a fixed peg. As late as the mid-1960s, become the Leader of the Opposition, he was publicly staking his personal and political reputation on the pledge that he and his party would not for a second time be responsible for cutting the British currency down to size. When Labour came to power in October 1964 the new Prime Minister was informed that the payments deficit was officially expected to be double the figure that outsiders were predicting. An immediate devaluation, blaming the economic situation on the 13 years of Tory rule, was an obvious possibility. It was a possibility which the former President and experienced '49er simply refused to contemplate. The consequence, as Crosland saw it, was a period of economic waste and socialism foregone: 'Growth was consistently sacrificed to the balance of payments, notably to the defence of a fixed and unrealistic rate of exchange.'[86] The pain was not crowned with gain. On 18 November 1967 the pound was devalued from $2.80 to $2.40. Some blamed foreign spivvery and gnomes in Zurich. Crosland had a different explanation: 'Everybody knew the pound was over-valued. Everybody except the Labour government, I should have said.'[87] Everybody, in other words, except the Labour Leader. A member of the Labour Cabinet since 1965, the President of the Board of Trade in the eventful period from August 1967 to October 1969, Crosland was in a strong position to know who had wanted devaluation at an early date – and who had stubbornly made up his mind to buck the market at the cost of growth.

Crosland on the Labour Right preferred a devalued or a floating pound to the depressing alternative of domestic deflation and public expenditure cuts. So did Crossman on the Labour Left, who in August 1965 made the following note on the need to move quickly: 'Failing to defend the pound would not mean the end of everything; we have already paid far too high a price in the effort to bolster it up .... Defending the pound by frantic cuts and then in the end finding one has to devalue makes no sense at all ... Tony Crosland is passionate about this.'[88] Passionate in his discussions with Richard Crossman, Crosland was passionate as well in his discussions with George Brown, his Secretary of State at the DEA. George Brown in 1964 had shared the Prime Minister's conviction that the parity of the pound could not be challenged. By 1965, as Ben Pimlott explains, he had recognised the sacrifice and switched his allegiance: 'Brown had departmental reasons for supporting devaluation. If the alternative was to be a harsh deflation, it would be impossible for the DEA to promote the industrial expansion and economic growth which was the department's supposed purpose.'[89] Pimlott says that the trained intelligence of Crosland (and of Roy Jenkins) was instrumental in helping to convert the trade unionist Brown to the idea that the rate of exchange is always a means and never an end: 'This was a potentially deadly combination, because it brought together proletarian fervour and the best of Frognalite expertise.'[90] At one point George Brown threatened to resign if Wilson opted for deflation: while he made such threats at regular intervals (Marcia Williams, eloquently described in the *People* as Wilson's faithful 'Monday-to-Sunday Girl Friday', kept a special file exclusively for the Deputy Leader's proposed resignations), this shows nonetheless just how seriously he took the question of cuts. A graduate not of Oxford but of the shop-floor, Brown knew from personal experience the truth of Crosland's dictum that 'cuts put people out of work who can't get jobs'[91] as well as starving society of vital public services.

Barbara Castle and Tony Benn joined the others in criticising the abandonment of the Plan, the rise in unemployment, the incomes-freeze that became necessary, one after another, in the attempt to stem the pressure on the pound. The Chancellor of the Exchequer, importantly, did not. Jim Callaghan is known to have wavered throughout but to have allowed himself to be swayed by the superior knowledge of the Prime Minister: 'I had to put another backbone into the Chancellor today',[92] Wilson would say in the mid-1960s. Despite his reservations, Callaghan invested his credibility in Wilson's pledge. He for that reason felt honour-bound to resign (on the precedent of Cripps) when the people who had believed him ended up in effect with 14.3 per cent less of sterling as their reward. Crosland had been active in the Cabinet's Steering Committee for Economic Policy and had been as consistent as he had been passionate in the controversy that had at last been resolved. Deputising for the absent Chancellor in the difficult days following the devaluation, he must have thought that the Exchequer was finally within his reach.

Crosland led for the Government in the debate on the economic situation that took place on 21 November 1967.[93] His exemplary performance in the House combined with his effortless mastery of economic issues (a command that was all the more remarkable for the fact that he had until August been in charge of Education) impressed even Harold Wilson. Crossman wrote that Crosland 'made a very able speech, as he always does',[94] that he is 'becoming quite a statesman these days',[95] that he had 'become a definite addition to the Cabinet because he has a mind of his own'[96] – and that the Prime Minister was not one to allow a 'balanced statement'[97] to go unappreciated: 'He now thinks highly of Tony Crosland and regards him as wholly reliable. Tony looks to me like the man booked for the Treasury.'[98] It was not to be. What happened instead was that Callaghan exchanged positions with Roy Jenkins. Callaghan went to the Home Office, Jenkins became the Chancellor – and Crosland stayed where he was.

The experience was a disheartening one for Crosland, who, in Roy Jenkins's assessment, was 'dismayed and depressed': 'It was a devastating blow to him that I became Chancellor.'[99] Lifelong friends and lifelong rivals, the events of November 1967, as Roy Jenkins remembers them, drove a wedge between the two moderates which had implications of its own for the future of British politics: 'It would be idle to pretend that these events of November 1967 did not leave a scar on Crosland which had the effect of crucially damaging the cohesion of the Labour right over the next eight or nine years. Had he and I been able to work together as smoothly as did Gaitskell and Jay or Gaitskell and Gordon Walker a decade before it might have made a decisive difference to the balance of power within the Labour Party and hence to the politics of the early 1980s.'[100] It might have made a decisive difference and it might not have made a decisive differ- ence – it is impossible to resolve the multiple *what ifs* that surround the four decades of 'sibling rivalry'[101] between Hugh Gaitskell's two favourite sons. This much, at least, can be said with confidence, that the eternal bridesmaid, eight years on still being introduced by Barbara Castle as 'the Chancellor-in-waiting',[102] was making clear to Richard Crossman two years after November 1967 that the bitterness and the disappointment had yet to wither away: 'Tony has never forgiven Harold for making Roy Chancellor and has never lost hope that if Roy goes he will be Chancellor in his place. His best chance would be the breaking up of this Government and Callaghan's taking over.'[103] Frustrated and left out, his work appears to have suffered. The Prime Minister, in Crossman's assessment, was not unaware that his President was retreating into himself like an also-ran: 'He is infuriated by Crosland and I must say that Tony's behaviour at the Board of Trade has been more than usually irritating. He has been inefficient but nonchalant and cavalier, just not seeming to mind. He seems thoroughly browned off, sick at not being Chancellor, sickened by the Chancellor's policy and, having failed to become Chancellor, he now seems to have got into that peevish frame of mind which I believe is one of the bases of leaks.'[104] There were few things that Harold Wilson disliked more than leaks unless it be Anthony Crosland. However serious the implications for the Labour Right of the decisive wedge that was driven between Roy and Tony, there was an additional consequence of November 1967 which, looking back, was no less a threat. Anthony Crosland in October 1969 was very nearly dropped from the Cabinet.

The reshuffle took place, and Crossman's instinct proved reliable, that very nearly is as good as a mile in politics: 'Crosland? Well, he has not proved himself a good Minister, he is too dilettante, too much of an intellectual. But somehow he is such an able man that it would be impossible for Harold to get rid of him.'[105] Moved but not removed, the keen macro-economist and disappointed Chancellor became Secretary of State at the Department of Local Government and Regional Planning, from October 1969 until June 1970. Involved in transport, housing, location of industry, devolution of function, the new job may not have been a first-choice but nor was it lacking in interest for a politician who, accustomed to thinking big, could appreciate the intricate social interdependencies that were the focus of the high-profile umbrella ministry. Crosland's new Secretaryship was in any case but a winter-and-spring one. The victory of the Conservatives in the election of June 1970 brought to an end the $5\frac{3}{4}$ years of Wilson Governments that had begun in 1964.

In opposition from 1970–74, with Edward Heath the Prime Minister, Crosland continued to shadow his old portfolio, by then given the new name of Environment. He also used his time to write extensively on 'what Labour really stands for in the 1970s'.[106] Fabian Tracts on *A Social-Democratic Britain* and *Towards a Labour Housing Policy* (both 1971) reiterated his core message about equality and growth, market freedom and social priorities, adequately redistributive taxation and decent public services. Speeches were delivered on education, articles on housing appeared in The *Guardian*, a piece on the environment was published in *The Sunday Times*. No substitute for a major original treatise on the future of the middle way in an age of uncertainty, these publications at least demonstrate that Crosland was still capable of mobilising abstract ideas in support of practical policies.

The best of Crosland's later essays found their way into a collection of reprints (similar in that respect to the *Conservative Enemy* of 1962) which, edited by Dick Leonard (then Labour Member for Romford and Crosland's Parliamentary Private Secretary), was published in 1974 under the title *Socialism Now*. The collection was introduced by a long survey chapter in which Crosland attempted to indicate in what way his *Future* was still sound, in what way his *Socialism* might be in need of revision. With respect to the fundamentals he made clear that the Good Society remained precisely where it had stood: about meritocratic opportunities and more equal outcomes, about pragmatism in State ownership combined with sensitive regulation to put right a market failure, the social philosophy of welfare socialism and managed capitalism appeared to him no less attractive, no less relevant in 1974 than it had done at The Boltons when a radio was still a wireless. In respect of the details, however, he was prepared to concede that social problems had all-too-frequently proved surprisingly resistant to social engineering: 'Extreme class inequalities remain, poverty is far from eliminated, the economy is in a state of semi-permanent crisis and inflation is rampant.'[107] Ideologically speaking, the doctrinaire and militant Left was back in business: 'There has indeed been a revival of semi-Marxist thought in Britain ... asserting that a new and sinister crisis of capitalism is upon us, which can be resolved only by a massive programme of public ownership.'[108] In the arena of industrial relations the powerful unions, the backers of the Labour Party, were veiling power and not only countering it: 'Some of the commanding heights of the economy are now to be found in union headquarters in Euston Road.'[109] The rule of law was openly being challenged by the Clay Cross councillors, the delinquent student demonstrators, the violent striking anarchists, who seemed not to have learnt the lesson of history, that 'the law has been the means by which the weak obtained redress against the strong'.[110] British democracy itself seemed at risk from the malaise of apathy: 'The turn-out at the 1970 General Election was the lowest since 1945, and lower than in nearly every other comparable democracy.'[111] Much could clearly be done to patch up the rents and tears in the socialist fabric: development land could be taken into the public sector, for instance, and educational spending targeted still more selectively at priority areas. Much, on the other hand, appeared to Crosland a black hole of confusion and doubt – and, in 1974, a cause of an uncharacteristic pessimism as well.

Slow growth, even zero growth, naturally drove a coach and horses through a non-confrontational welfarism that relied on the positive-sum increment to fund reform without breeding divisiveness. In the last interview he ever gave (it took place on the Thursday before the stroke on the Sunday and contained the prescient and unprompted summing-up 'what a marvellous life it's been'), Crosland discussed the stumbling-block of insufficient growth with Ivan Rowan. Rowan reports the exchange of views on *The Future of Socialism* in the following words: 'It is the nation's failure to prosper that has led some of Crosland's critics to declare his thesis null and void. He said: "I don't share this view. If one were to re-write it, one would amend a great number of things".'[112] If one were to re-write it, one would presumably add an economist's explanation of how, precisely, to accelerate the expansion in the national dividend – together with, presumably, a philosopher's analysis of how, precisely, to make redistributive justice electorally acceptable in a hard-luck economy that is hibernating in stagnation. Amendments such as these would strengthen Crosland's *Future* and would do so without materially detracting from the thrust of Crosland's *Socialism*.

Importantly, Crosland had chosen not to use the opportunity afforded him by the extended introduction to *Socialism Now* to suggest a radical new recipe that would cause the cake more rapidly to rise. Complaining as he does of the deplorable under-performance that was 'due to the deflationary policies which stemmed inexorably from the Labour Government's obsession with a particular parity for sterling',[113] the reader wonders why in 1974 he was still harking back to 1967 rather than showing convincingly that uncaged demand could *in the future* exercise a magnetic pull on national productivity without at the same time unleashing a ruinous inflation. Turning from the economics to the politics of slow or zero growth, Crosland in 1974 had not been much more of a pioneer in extending his synthesis to the fully-squeaked pips of an altruism that had had enough. Crosland in *Socialism Now* said the obvious, that scarcity was abundant and that socialists in Government had to weigh carefully the alternatives: 'We must ruthlessly select priorities. We must prepare in advance a limited programme of radical measures which do not promise more than we can actually perform.'[114] Crosland in *The Future of Socialism* had been infinitely more casual about allocation and welfare in the post-rationed era of growing abundance: 'With personal consumption rising by 2–4% a year and likely to double in 20 years, it will really not much matter a decade from now whether we plan to produce rather more of this and less of that, or exactly what prices are charged for this commodity or that.'[115] Crosland exactly 20 years later was writing in The *Guardian* that choices and sacrifices were back on the agenda: 'Economists have said for years that there are no free school meals; at last, politicians and the public are beginning to take note.'[116] Crosland in the same eventful year of 1976 was writing in the *Socialist Commentary* (the paper, entitled 'Equality in Hard Times' and originally delivered as the John Lewis Memorial Lecture in Merthyr Tydfil, was the last he ever published) that the haves would have to cede to the underdogs when insufficient growth placed a cap on public spending: 'We must and will give priority to better housing for the worse-off, rather than to roads used by the better-off. Social services should have priority over leisure services.'[117] Crosland in 1977 was telling Ivan Rowan that slow or zero growth did not invalidate the broad thesis that he propounded – but that there was an undeniable need nonetheless to 'amend a great number of things'. Crosland in 1974 had in *Socialism Now* acknowledged that the economy was letting him down. Sadly, he had chosen not to use the opportunity afforded him by his extended essay to develop either an economic *how to* of rapid growth or a political *how to* of redistribution without unpopularity. Perhaps he felt that he had made his contribution by outlining the problem and that it was down to the next generation to add some value of its own.

Socialism Now in certain places betrays a certain pessimism. With hindsight, however, there was one storm-cloud on the horizon which even in a mood of uncharacteristic pessimism the mixed-economy moderate simply failed to spot. *Socialism Now* is critical of the New Left and the student demonstrators. *Socialism Now* is silent about the New Right and the privatising marketeers. With hindsight, Crosland would appear to have underestimated the strength of the *Conservative* enemy.

Socialism Now, to be fair, is a selection from the early 1970s that is indicative both of what was happening at the time and what had been happening in the past. Looking at the Conservatives under Heath, Crosland in 1973 wrote in *The Observer* that the Selsdon Men were growing up and the fanatical libertarians were calming down: 'The Government have, predictably, moved towards the centre; the era of confrontation ... is past; and we are back to a Macmillan-style Toryism.'[118] Looking at the Conservatives under Churchill, Crosland in 1950 had said something equally sanguine to a Fabian conference concerned about the mixed economy should the reaction be voted in: 'I am sure the essential framework will persist even under Tory Govts. – the Butlers and Stassens, for all the wild men in their parties, will eventually win through.'[119] Crosland was right in 1950 and right in 1973. What he failed to predict was Mrs Thatcher. A year after *Socialism Now* he had to admit to the Grimsby Labour Party that one of the two major parties had irresponsibly deserted the middle ground 'in favour of a narrow class-based approach': 'The Conservative Party is now launched on a crusade in the cause of reaction; the Tories have been taken over by their extremists.'[120] The Socialists, fortunately, had not been. Speaking to the Tonbridge Labour Party, he was able to reassure his listeners that convergence and consensus lived on in the coalition of Dalton and Gaitskell: 'Travelling about the country, [the] average local Labour Party [is] much as it has always been. It has a Left-wing, yes, a Right-wing, yes; and – usually by far the biggest group – a Centre.'[121] *Socialism Now* concedes that there is indeed a conservative enemy preaching antediluvian nationalisation within a Labour Party that ought not to listen. What it does not anticipate is that there might soon be a real and a *Conservative* enemy that would within five years be questioning the future of Butskellism from the very Cabinet Room to which Harold Wilson had returned in triumph only one month before the publication of *Socialism Now*.

Appearing when it did, Crosland's compendium attracted considerable attention. Booksellers in the Charing Cross Road had exhausted their stocks by the afternoon of the first day and a 5000-word extract was published in *The Sunday Times*. Not all of the interest was from serious students of democratic socialism. A senior Labour front-bencher, a potential Chancellor or even something more, Crosland was turned to by journalists, bankers, members of the general public for guidance on the probable policies of the incoming administration. Theoretical works by socialist politicians were thin on the ground: Roy Jenkins specialised in political biography, Richard Crossman never produced the philosophical treatise that the former don and published Platonist had occasionally promised, and the list of prominent competitors comes at that point precipitately to an end. It was not the first time that coincidence had worked to Crosland's advantage. One of the reasons why *Time*, *The New York Times* and a significant number of other American journals had reviewed *The Conservative Enemy* when they had ignored *The Future of Socialism* was because of a growing realisation that Gaitskell might soon be the British Prime Minister, Crosland in the foreseeable future Britain's socialist Chancellor.

Socialism Now was reviewed widely and generally rather favourably. *The Financial Times* called it 'lucid and constructive', 'enjoyable and stimulating', 'a substantial and thought-provoking piece of work' and (despite the fact that Crosland's socialism 'has some very sharp teeth') 'an invaluable guide to the policies a Labour Government may introduce if it can remain in power for long enough'.[122] *The Economist* said that, in most matters save the levelling of outcomes, the thinking non-socialist would be able to follow Crosland 'with understanding, and occasional lively enthusiasm'.[123] Dick Taverne (writing in *The Times*), Anthony King (writing in *New Society*) and Neil Kinnock (writing in *Tribune*) all attempted a more ambitious assessment. Recognising that the *Now* was respectable but still not the equal of the *Future* that a full-time intellectual could have produced and a front-bench spokesman could not, they wisely decided to evaluate the whole of the edifice and not just the latest brick.

Dick Taverne was in no doubt that the middle had met its master: 'Anthony Crosland is the leading philosopher of social democracy in Britain.'[124] Anthony King was not disposed to disagree: 'Anthony Crosland is probably the most important socialist thinker Britain has produced.... Only Tawney is in the same class as Crosland.... Crosland combines Tawney's creative moral vision with a much greater intellectual command than Tawney had of the relevant social sciences, especially economics. We are accustomed to reverencing the giants of the past; we should not overlook the giants of the present.'[125] Then there was Neil Kinnock, in those days a red-blooded Foot-soldier and not yet the Party Leader who was to take on the Militant Tendency. Neil Kinnock criticised Crosland for trying to do the impossible, for erroneously assuming 'that we can have a capitalist bakery and eat our socialist cake': 'In a time when major capitalist enterprises are sustained by state dole in the parliamentary archipelago and by assassins and secret police elsewhere, when multinational conglomerates form, as François Mitterand says, "a sort of Government of the world", the social democrat still equates free enterprise with freedom.'[126]

Neil Kinnock admitted that Crosland's cocktail was 'civilised' and that almost all the right platitudes were there ('only motherhood is missing'). The problem, he said, is that there was far too much of the *Now* and not nearly enough of the *Socialism*. Arguing that Crosland-type social democracy 'is merely a middle way and never a different way', Kinnock went on to maintain that poverty and inequality *could not* be eliminated within the framework of the capitalist system for the very reason that they were functionally necessary to ensure its survival: 'Poverty and inequality are the essential penalties and rewards of capitalism. The system can thrive only where they exist and without them and the exploitation and subservience, greed and bullying which they spawn the system would die. And even if social democrats don't (or won't) understand that, capitalists and their apologists like Margaret "Right to be Unequal" Thatcher do.'[127]

Insisting that the welfare services and the mixed economy only alleviate social evils that they cannot eliminate, demanding the nationalisation of the means of production and the conduits of finance, the Neil Kinnock who took on the philosopher-ruler was most unlikely to find himself described in *Time Magazine* as a detached democrat in favour of industrial efficiency accompanied by American-style classlessness. *Time Magazine* was somewhat kinder to what it clearly saw as a user-friendly centrist. *Time Magazine* referred to Crosland as 'a philosophical socialist who never lets himself be led by party doctrine. An Oxford man and ex-paratrooper, Crosland affects a languid academic aloofness that enrages the militant left almost as much as his cheerful argument that socialism has no magic technique for speeding up economic growth, and in his equally candid concession that capitalist nations do not do too badly.'[128] The *Tribune* on the one hand, *Time Magazine* on the other, Harold Wilson in the middle – it is just as well that Anthony Crosland had his home and his hobbies to divert his attention.

Edward Heath came in by a fluke and went out by a fluke. In 1970 Heath ensured the lead by convincing the floating voter that the Conservatives knew how to cut price-inflation (widely misinterpreted to mean a cut in the price-level) and to do so 'at a stroke'. In 1974 Heath accidentally created the Labour Governments of 1974–79 first by imposing a three-day week to punish the nation for the miners' strike and then by calling an election to demonstrate the popularity of what he had done. Even Harold Wilson is unlikely to have expected to have power re-thrust upon him quite so quickly. The Heath interregnum lasted only three years and eight months. Its second most lasting contribution to British economic and political history was the selection of Margaret Thatcher to replace the revolving-door Heath as the Leader of the Conservative Party. Its principal and most permanent contribution was the successful negotiation of Britain's entry into the European Communities that finally occurred on 1 January 1973.

Harold Wilson, once again Prime Minister, created his Cabinet. Anthony Crosland was asked to remain with the portfolio he had shadowed, serving as Secretary of State at the Department of the Environment from March 1974 to April 1976. The regulatory influence that Crosland exercised over controlled capitalism in this capacity (as in his earlier and shorter attachment at Local Government) provides a useful insight into the constructive symbiosis between market and State that he wished as an intellectual in politics effectively to bring about. It is discussed in more detail in Chapter 5.3.

Meanwhile, there was Europe. In 1967 Labour under Wilson had applied in vain for membership. In 1972–73 Labour under Wilson had tried in vain to block Britain's entry under Heath. In 1974 Labour under Wilson was once again under pressure to review the New Zealand lamb and the Common Agricultural Policy, the Atlantic Community and the foreignness of foreigners – and to make up its minds.

Anthony Crosland was never a committed pro-European to the extent, say, that Roy Jenkins was. Nor, however, was he ever actually anti-Europe on the model of Tony Benn. Basically in favour of more formal ties but unprepared to regard the union as a pill for every ill, Crosland early on became a yes-but European and never wavered in his tepid support.

Economically, he was never really persuaded. In 1962 he favoured entry despite Gaitskell's opposition; but he also made clear that he had not been convinced by the theories of trade creation and dynamic expansion that he at one point dismissed as 'the claptrap being expounded by my pro-European friends'.[129] Late in life he was able to describe himself as having consistently been 'amongst the more sceptical of the "Pros" in this country' and therefore not personally to be blamed for the disappointment of unrealistic hopes: 'Total exports to the Community have risen, but total imports from the Community have risen more.... The notion that membership constitutes the magical key to a British economic miracle was and is a myth.'[130] Crosland believed that there was no clear-cut economic case to be made either in favour of the EEC or against it; and he even harboured fears that the obsession with Europe would divert attention from the bigger issues of housing, education, growth and equality. Economically, he tended to a position that was only slightly more positive than total indifference. Hugh Gaitskell at his most enthusiastic had taken a similar sort of stance: 'To go in on good terms would, I believe, be the best solution.... Not to go in would be a pity, but it would not be a catastrophe.'[131]

Hugh Gaitskell, accepting that 'the thing is there', rather regarded the issue of the European Community as 'a bore and a nuisance'.[132] Anthony Crosland, on the other hand, was never less than welcoming towards the 'thickening of contacts and cooperation'[133] that the new openness was bringing in its train: 'Our future as a nation lies with Britain as a member of the European Community.'[134] The difference is to be explained not with reference to the economic arguments (on which Gaitskell and Crosland were in broad agreement) but in terms of the cultural and political advantages that to Crosland were the real gains that stood to be reaped from membership.

Culturally, Crosland styled himself 'an instinctive European' not least because he believed that Britain's conservative traditionalism would be agreeably weakened 'if we link our destinies with a dynamic and resurgent Europe.'[135] It would be a mistake to underestimate the inward-looking Englishness (even, in extreme cases, the downright xenophobia) of significant sections of British society, Left and Right, at the time when Crosland was active. Michael Postan recalls of two of Britain's most distinguished reformers that Durbin was resistant to holidays abroad whereas Gaitskell spoke fluent German and loved travel: 'Yet although Gaitskell used to chide Durbin for his insularity, he invariably placed his own socialist ideas and his visions of the future in a purely English setting.'[136] Once, when Tawney was speaking (as he habitually did) of his 'fellow Englishmen', Postan asked Gaitskell if he would not himself have said 'fellow human beings' instead: 'But Hugh, after a brief pause, confessed that he would have used the same words. He had reasoned himself into international socialism, but his vision of the future was one of England's Jerusalem.'[137] Crosland's own work (despite the occasional comparison he draws with the United States) is by no means free of parochialism, castigated by the author as 'the besetting sin of the British character'.[138] A greater openness to the variant practices of the different cultures would presumably, shaking things up, do much to force the blinkered and the protected to look again at the complacency of their assumptions.

Politically, Crosland was an early advocate not only of 'the full acceptance of our obligations under NATO' but also of something more – 'an abatement of national sovereignty, in the long run in favour of world government, in the short run in favour of Europe'.[139] Crosland was not an idealist or a dreamer who, remembering Coventry and Dresden, expected rapid progress towards a European federation. He was careful in the 1960s not to speculate on the distant possibility of a European defence policy at a time when the British were content with the American special relationship and the French had only recently rejected the European Defence Community. He was careful in the 1970s not to cite a common foreign policy but rather an effective trading environment when he sought to persuade his fellow countrymen that the British lion would roar louder if it roared in Europe: 'As a member of the Community we can make our own strong contribution to the Community's growing power and influence.'[140] At a dinner held in December 1976 to mark the historic appointment of Roy Jenkins as the first British President of the EC Commission, Crosland reiterated his point about political strength – and extended it from trade treaties to embrace wider issues such as human rights and the North – South dialogue: 'These are precisely the kind of issues on which we as Democratic Socialists have something distinctive to say to the world; but if Britain simply says it in her own small voice, no-one need listen.'[141] Careful in the 1960s and the 1970s not to make haste too quickly, there can be no doubt that Crosland, looking to the future, was greatly attracted by the political influence that Britain could continue to exercise as a part of the wider regional order.

Tony Benn in 1975 forced a referendum on the issue of membership: he was confident (mistakenly, since 67 per cent voted in favour) that the British people shared his opposition to Europe and would, given the chance, express themselves overwhelmingly for withdrawal. Crosland supported the idea of a referendum, believing that it would help to resolve the issue once and for all. Benn is right to say that Crosland in 1975 was not especially enthusiastic about the union: 'He was an agnostic, skeptical about large markets, but he thought there were strong arguments for staying in.'[142] So persuaded was he by the force of the cultural and the political if not by the economic arguments that he became a Vice-President of the Labour Campaign for Britain in Europe and lobbied actively, insisting that there was no longer any alternative. Harold Wilson marginally renegotiated the terms of entry, the House approved them – and thus it was that Labour rose to the occasion and made up its minds.

More controversial than in 1975 had been Crosland's attitude to Europe in 1971. The Conservative Government under Edward Heath had negotiated a treaty of membership. The Labour Party under Harold Wilson had voted against it in the House. Sixty-nine Labour pro-Europeans like Roy Jenkins had defied the Whips and voted with the Tories. Twenty Labour MPs like Anthony Crosland had defied the Whips and not voted at all. The Government's majority in the division was 112 because of the 89 Labour rebels who did not vote as they were told.[143]

Crosland appears to have abstained on the grounds that the issue, by dividing the Labour Party, was likely to prolong the tenure of the Conservative Government. While the split obviously did the Party no good, it is hard to see how a Shadow Secretary of State and a member of the Shadow Cabinet can have convinced himself that the Party could be kept together if he remained in his room. The upshot of his inaction was that the Parliamentary Labour Party accused him of disloyalty, the pro-Europeans accused him of cowardice, and no significant group was much impressed by a gesture that even his admirers, disillusioned, were tempted to describe as equivocation in a good light, foolishness in a bad one. Crosland's abstention in 1971 was an important reason why he stood no real chance of being elected Deputy Leader in 1972. Edward Short was chosen instead.

In March 1976 Harold Wilson announced unexpectedly that, at 60, it was time for him to stand down. A successor had to be found and six names emerged: Benn, Foot, Crosland, Jenkins, Healey and Callaghan. Crosland finished bottom out of the six, winning the support of only 17 of the 314 voting members. Even his friend Roy Hattersley switched his allegiance to Jim Callaghan as the man most likely to keep the Party Leadership out of the hands of the Left.

Callaghan thought well of Crosland and shared much of his philosophy. Callaghan knew that Crosland wanted to be Chancellor and had indeed recommended Crosland for the post in November 1967. Disappointed as he must have been at his own poor performance in the poll, Crosland at least could console himself with the probability that Wilson's successor would be more receptive to Crosland's arguably under-used potential.

The new Prime Minister did not appoint Crosland to the Exchequer. Whatever might have occurred in the next reshuffle, Callaghan opted initially for continuity in the form of the incumbent, Denis Healey. Crosland was offered the Foreign Office. It was a promotion and a step up. It was also the only one of the three great offices of State that he was destined to hold – and then for less than a year. Anthony Crosland was Foreign Secretary from April 1976 until February 1977.

The position was not an obvious one for a political intellectual whose strengths lay in egalitarianism and economics rather than diplomacy. Crosland lacked the background of Jim Callaghan, his predecessor, who had been Shadow Foreign Secretary, or of David Owen, his successor, who was already the Minister of State and had previously been at Defence. Interested in international socialism and international trade, Crosland was, at least at first, surprisingly insular with respect to the international blow-by-blow which he clearly found more difficult than, say, education or housing to situate in the moral philosophy of equality and welfare. A professional, as Roy Jenkins records, he did his best to learn: 'He was unacquainted with the intricacies of the nuances of the foreign policy game. He knew foreign sociologists rather than foreign statesmen. Yet, after a hesitant start, he impressed most of his officials and his foreign colleagues by his authority, his wit and his intellect.'[144]

Most, perhaps, but certainly not all. Civil servants were unaccustomed to a Foreign Secretary who (like Aneurin Bevan, Michael Foot and the 'common man') was reluctant to wear the white tie and tails on formal occasions. Ambassadors found it unusual to be told that they would have to wait because the Foreign Secretary could not be disturbed during *Match of the Day*. The press sometimes wondered if he was not deliberately marking time in his high-profile posting before swapping jobs with Denis Healey six months down the road: 'There were occasions when unsympathetic journalists feared his interest in foreign affairs was confined to international football.'[145]

Then there was Henry Kissinger, his American opposite-number. Kissinger wanted to discuss Rhodesia, not the Cod Wars. Crosland, however, managed to give the impression that he was up-to-date in foreign policy on nothing save British trawlers being escorted by Navy frigates into Icelandic waters. Kissinger (who once said of him that 'Tony is an acquired taste') came away unenlightened about the African crisis: 'I realised he could master the subject. I didn't know if he wanted to.'[146] Later relations between the two intellectuals in politics were to thaw and a certain mutual respect was to develop. One reason is likely to have been Kissinger's growing awareness that the public school flippancy and the donnish self-indulgence were a modest man's means of concealing a Plymouth assiduity in collaboration with a First Class shrewdness.

The most pressing challenge facing Britain in the summer and winter of 1976–77 was in any case not fish and not Africa but the balance of payments. On 29 September 1976, when the pound had fallen to $1.64 and threatened to fall further, the Government announced the intention of borrowing £2300 million from the International Monetary Fund. November 1967 was back again. The new Prime Minister cannot have failed to appreciate the coincidence.

The economic crisis was in the first instance the responsibility of the Prime Minister and the Chancellor of the Exchequer. It was not in the first instance the responsibility of the Foreign Secretary. A socialist economist, a believer in public spending, Crosland cannot have wanted to be out of the country so frequently at a time when Callaghan and Healey seemed on the point of repeating all the old mistakes. He was distressed and embarrassed to find himself a senior minister in a Government that was courting foreign loans through cutting British budgets. A member of the Cabinet but stranded in a non-economic ministry, the Foreign Secretary grew increasingly concerned at the Labour Chancellor's 'relapse into total ec. orthodoxy'.[147] Equally frustrating was the realisation that he was all but alone in his defence of first principles. A note to himself from July 1976 shows him in despair at the lemming-like passivity of his colleagues: 'Healey had v. easy ride in Cab.: partly [because] I was away *and* muzzled, partly [because] Cab. now v. conservative and orthodox.'[148] A note to himself from August of the same year shows him brooding about resignation and deciding it would do no good: 'Wd. have looked damn silly to resign *alone* when Foot and Benn did not.'[149] In the 1975 spending round, still at Environment, he had threatened resignation and meant resignation: 'In the end did reasonably well: but only after slamming papers together in gesture of resignation and scaring Harold. A cut in housing investment *wd.* have been a resigning issue.... My first ever *near*-resigning issue since 1964.'[150] Yet 1976 was a crisis whereas 1975 was only a round; and the Foreign Secretary was all-too-aware that even a socialist's resignation would not stop Callaghan and Healey in 1976 from delivering the austerity that the IMF was known to expect.

Crosland in 1953 had set the pattern of a lifetime by dismissing the IMF as a Moaning Minnie, a congenital complainer which 'played no useful or constructive role ... confining itself mainly to giving petulant and unhelpful advice at ill-chosen moments.'[151] The essence of that advice seemed to be that deflation, unemployment, even zero growth were not too high a price to pay for price-stability and a fixed exchange-rate. It was a message which Anthony Crosland throughout his career made it his business to challenge. In 1953 his target was the economic myopia of monetary restriction: 'Dear money means low investment, and low investment means an unprogressive economy.'[152] In 1965 he added the alienation of the labour-force and the scuppering of a voluntary incomes-policy to the list of reasons why even an unavoidable reduction in domestic demand ought not to be dramatic: 'Such a policy of deliberate deflation would be wholly unacceptable.'[153] In 1966 he argued strongly that a rise in prices ought not to be contained at the cost of welfare services and infrastructural investment: 'He didn't want to see us once again combatting inflation by cutting public expenditure.'[154] In 1968, accepting that devaluation had not ended the debate, he made the point that public programmes 'represent just as legitimate a form of spending as any other'.[155] He stressed in 1968 that demand-deflation could equally well be brought about through a rise in targeted taxation (an increase, say, in the employers' contribution to superannuation funding) and not through the cuts in public expenditures with which the IMF appeared to be all but obsessed: 'Tony Crosland said very vigorously, as he always does, that he didn't want to assume in advance that it was preferable to cut £250 million from expenditure rather than to raise it in tax.'[156] In 1976 he expressed the fear that austerity could imperil the new cooperativeness of the social compact and accelerate the pace of cost-inflation through a return to the collective bargaining free-for-all: 'Outstanding success of last 2 yrs. has been implication and involvement of T.U.s in nat. ec. policy. If this survives, will struggle through: If not, disaster.'[157] Even good race-relations could be put at risk through the insecurity and the hopelessness that austerity is bound to create. In 1976 as so often before, it is clear, Crosland was arguing that austerity was not the answer and that more constructive solutions should be sought. In 1976 as so often before, he was fighting a losing battle and was doing so all but alone.

Desperate to find an alternative to deflation, Crosland in 1976 took an interest in the proposals for import-controls that were then being advanced by Wynne Godley and his colleagues at Cambridge. Crosland had himself explored the possibility of a managed solution in the Hugh Gaitskell Memorial Lecture that he had given at the University of Nottingham in 1965. Crosland at that time had said that 'the right policy for a balance of payments deficit' would have to be 'to operate directly on the balance of payments, whether by import-restriction or export-promotion, thus giving time for longer-term policies to increase efficiency to take effect'.[158] Crosland was prepared to operate directly in 1965. In 1976 he appears to have had an open mind: anxious about 'even bigger cuts in pub. exp.', concerned that the proposals emanating from Cambridge were supported by 'v. little informed pub. op.', he made a note to himself in July not to reach an immediate conclusion but instead to 'think and consult hard in Sept.'[159] Crosland in 1976 appears to have been unsure: 'Import Controls prob. nec. to ease *political* situation, tho' doubt if it will make much difference to the reality.'[160] Unsure or not, at least he took the trouble to assess the alternatives and to form new impressions. His search is particularly creditable when one reflects just how low the probability must have been that the Foreign Secretary would be successful in persuading the Prime Minister and the Chancellor to refuse the medicine that was being prescribed by the IMF.

Searching for alternative stabilisers, isolated in Callaghan's Cabinet, Crosland looked around him and saw everywhere the 'breeding of illiterate and reactionary attitude to pub. exp. – horrible.'[161] In public he was still insisting that the Left stood for spending and justice, that the Thatcherite monetarists were in the circumstances completely unelectable: 'Against this background, the competitive individualism of the radical right has little popular appeal.'[162] In private, on the other hand, he was increasingly prone to recording in his commonplace-book that he genuinely believed the wind to have changed: '*Is* general swing to Right of "informed" & pub. op. in W. world: New Conservatism, monetarism, anti-egalitarianism, free market economy, anti-W. State, acceptance of unemp. & deflation, reaction v. prog. of comp. edn., etc.... Esp., strong reaction v. high pub. exp.: Schmidt, Giscard & Ford all sermonise abt. it: *is* feeling of fat & waste.... Keynesian args. appears much weaker: entire Press on Govt.'s side.... Good socialist policies *not* electorally popular.'[163] A Cabinet Minister himself in just another of the Governments that had gone in for cuts, Crosland in 1976 had to admit that, in Britain as in other countries, the Left was 'now totally demoralised': 'No sense of direction & *no* priorities: only pragmatism, empiricism, safety first, £ supreme' – what it all added up to was the 'demoralisation of decent rank-&-file: Grimsby L.P. ... And N.B. of much of revisionist intelligentsia.'[164] The future of socialism had seemed so different from the foothills of 1956.

Keeping up with fish and Africa while also keeping up with stop-go and spending, Crosland in his final year had occasion to demonstrate his capacity for hard work. The red boxes followed him from Lansdowne Road in Notting Hill to his week-end cottage at Adderbury, near Oxford, to Dorneywood, which came with the job. As Foreign Secretary he was required to travel extensively, often for quite short meetings: he told Tony Benn that, enjoying the post, still 'it is a bore having to go abroad so much'.[165] The strain took its toll; and sometimes it showed. Answering questions on 2 February 1977, for example, Crosland accompanied his answers to the House by warning it that, 'in my rather tired condition, I am not sure that I have remembered all four questions'.[166] The previous night, thanks to a late-night sitting and vote, he had got to bed at 5:30. Simultaneously dealing with crises in Rhodesia and the Falklands, he was also involved in the EEC, as President of the Community's Council of Ministers. The smoking and the drinking cannot have done him much good. Nor could the excess weight, the high blood pressure and the lack of time for exercise.

Anthony Crosland died in the Radcliffe Infirmary on 19 February 1977. He was 58 – almost the same age as Gaitskell at the time of his death. The immediate cause was irreversible damage resulting from a stroke suffered on Sunday the 13th. Two days before that he had been to the Radcliffe Infirmary in a different role, to visit Philip Williams, also felled by a stroke. Crosland's ashes were scattered by Susan in the Humber off Grimsby on 4 March 1977. Three days later a Memorial Service was held in Westminster Abbey. By then the Prime Minister, speaking in the House, had already said what needed to be said – that the Radcliffe Infirmary was miles away from Westminster and a ten-minute walk from Trinity. Recalling his first meeting with Crosland in the late 1940s, Callaghan reminded the Commons that an intellectual in politics has a very different life from an intellectual in a university: 'I wondered how he would go down in politics, and I asked him tactfully whether he was sure that he would feel at home away from the Oxford atmosphere.... He always carried the aura of the university don even into his local Labour club.'[167] Torn between two cities, it may be that Crosland would have made a greater contribution to the future of socialism if he had remained with his books and not opted for the rainbow of action.

Crosland chose to be an intellectual at Westminster because he wanted to get things done. Spending as he did nine years in six ministerial positions, no one could accuse him of lacking the ambition, the determination or the ability to proceed upwards from the back benches to the Cabinet rooms where the real power is exercised. On the other hand, it is undeniable that he was repeatedly overlooked for the Chancellorship that he was known to want; and that the Party showed a conspicuous reluctance to make him either its Leader in 1975 or its Leader's Deputy in 1972. It is never safe to pass a final judgement on a career that was brought prematurely to a close: Crosland would almost certainly have succeeded Healey as Chancellor in summer 1977, he would almost certainly have stood against Foot when Callaghan gave up the Leadership in 1980, he might even have led a social-democratic Labour to victory over Mrs Thatcher in 1983. All of this is possible. Somehow, however, it is not all equally likely. What is probable is that Crosland would, more than a decade in the wings, have come into his Chancellorship just after his 59th birthday – and that the Party and the nation would thereupon have decided that enough was enough for a clever outsider who didn't really fit in.

Crosland was not universally liked; and one reason was his uncompromising refusal to be ingratiating in the cause of advancement. As Dick Leonard writes: 'At an early age he had acquired a reputation for being sensationally rude.... He was an intensely private man, surprisingly shy for somebody who had revelled in an extrovert reputation. His charm, his infectious gaiety, his loyalty and concern for his friends, was known only to a relative few: his public reputation was of a formidable but not particularly warm personality.'[168] Abnormally abrasive and abnormally thin-skinned, he could be too passionate to be calculating, too committed to be diplomatic. Many found him 'hostile or arrogant', and not least, as Lord Donaldson explained at the Memorial Service, because he had the academic puritan's intolerance of triviality: 'He was extremely exclusive and he cared only for serious issues. He could not bear small talk or social gossip.'[169] In the boys'-school atmosphere of Commons clubbability, an unwillingness to conceal boredom or to rein in petulance is unlikely to generate much loyalty on the part of people who might one day be useful.

Roy Jenkins himself had recognised in the 1950s that his good friend had much in his make-up that gave him the unpredictability of a loose cannon: 'We had already decided that, close though we were, it was better to see Crosland only on his own. Famous for his flounces and his unconcealed disapproval of those he might be asked to meet, he was too hazardous a guest for dinner parties.'[170] Crosland evidently put Jenkins in mind of his own father, charismatic and volatile if also considerably less temperamental: 'He had a capacity, comparable oddly enough in my experience only with that of Anthony Crosland, to infuse a small gathering with either exhilaration or gloom according to his mood. Happily benignity was about five times as prevalent with him as with Crosland, and social sulkiness was almost wholly absent.'[171] Like Leonard, like Donaldson, Jenkins had had the opportunity to probe beneath the prickly exterior of a complex of contradictions, at once aggressive and vulnerable, solitary and gregarious. Undeniably a risk and often a liability, Crosland, Jenkins indicated in 1988, was badly served by those who took his superficial acerbity to be the sum total of a multi-layered identity: 'Not only was his character engaging, his personality was dazzling and his intellect was of very high quality. He had maddening streaks of perversity ... but was the most exciting friend of my life.'[172]

Jenkins had had the opportunity to get to know the real Crosland over a period of almost 40 years. Alan Watkins had not. Alan Watkins's assessment in *The Spectator* that Crosland's alleged arrogance was better understood as an intellectual's frankness is in the circumstances an insight of especial interest: 'The figure is tall; the expression can be haughty; the eyes always look faintly amused. Moreover, if Crosland believes that someone is talking nonsense he says so. But is it not too simple to call this arrogance? Could it be that other, more estimable qualities are at work? The key to Crosland's character, in so far as any character has a key, is an honesty which he successfully pushes to reckless extremes.'[173] An honesty – and a belief in equality that he actually puts into practice: 'He treats people as if they really were equal. Talk to Crosland and he listens to what you are saying. If he disagrees he will say so. This may be tactlessness: but it is hardly arrogance.'[174] Perhaps it is not; but perception is the ultimate in perversity. There are cogent points that can be put forcefully to a Jenkins or a Gaitskell that would nonetheless be perceived as hectoring intimidation by less-educated, less-articulate members of the community. Those persons, convinced that their views have value but aware at the same time that their expositional skills lack the polish of a finely-honed intellect, are capable of taking Crosland-like frankness to be a superior's-eye view of an inferior's lesser intelligence. The signal received may not be the same as the signal sent, but the outcome is the same. The ego is unstroked and the support is less than enthusiastic.

Crosland was frank; and while this quality obviously endeared him to his friends (Michael Young once answered the charge of brusqueness by saying that 'he was lovable because he did not mind whether he was loved or not'),[175] there is no doubt that his reputed arrogance was the cause of some resentment on the part of his colleagues. A typical reaction is the following entry (dated December 1967) from Crossman's diary: 'I don't suppose there's any man who is more disliked and out of touch with the Parliamentary Party than Denis Healey, unless it's Tony Crosland. Both of them are arrogant and despise their colleagues in the Party.'[176] Crossman, of course, was close to the Prime Minister. Even closer, however, was Marcia Williams – and she is on record as denying that aggressive argumentation was in Crosland's case an indicator of arrogance: 'Tony was a democratic socialist in the best sense of the word.... Tony was a right-wing moderate able to see the other's point of view, strong and firm on unpopular policies which he felt to be right.'[177] Particularly valuable is Lady Falkender's insistence that Crosland may have put his points forcefully but that he never talked down to his listeners: 'His intellectual quality was, of course, his most striking attribute, but it was combined with a gift

possessed by few Labour politicians: the ability to talk to those less intel-
lectually endowed without appearing condescending.'[178] Marcia Falkender
evidently did not find his energy intimidating and did not think that others
ought to find it intimidating either. Yet they did – and not all the accusations of arrogance came from those who had left school at 15. Henry
Kissinger is known to have 'found it difficult at first to understand Tony's
sense of humour, and the somewhat patronising arrogance of his style'.[179]
Closer acquaintance eventually helped Kissinger to understand that no
offence was intended by the irreverence. Not everyone, however, had the
opportunity to discover from personal experience that the bark was seldom
followed by the bite.

A phrase like 'but when one got to know him' recurs with remarkable
regularity in the recollections of those who knew Tony Crosland well. An
example is the following: 'But when one got to know him one realised
that for all his faults he was a genuine radical who instinctively disliked
the society he was living in.'[180] Here again it was closer acquaintance that
made the difference, the same friend initially being in two minds about a
public-school socialist who appeared still to be in the grip of major social
distance: 'My first impression of him was his arrogance, his enormous
insouciance, a classic example of the Hampstead intellectual, a London
sophisticate without any provincial values at all.'[181] Words were not
necessary to communicate the arrogance. Self-presentation and life-style
seemed to say it all.

Others formed the same first impression, that comfortable refinement is
a sensitive indicator of snobbish superiority. Peter Dunn picked up the feel
of their suspicions in a *Sunday Times* profile he wrote when Crosland was
appointed President of the Board of Trade: 'Superficially, Crosland seems
Tory to a degree, the posh voice, the elegant manner; even his egalitarianism appears sometimes to be a provocation.... The new president likes to
eat well and to have a room with a view when he goes away on
Government work and resents the inverted snobbery of people who think
that socialists shouldn't know too much about wine.'[182] Michael Foot wore
a donkey-jacket and Tony Benn went over to Estuary English. Tony
Crosland saw to it that his home telephone was listed in the London
Directory and gave his club in *Who's Who* (Crossman admitted to the
Athenaeum) as 'Grimsby Labour'. Foot and Benn won qualified acceptance from the working-class base and the union-sponsored Members in an
organisation which, after all, is called the *Labour* Party. Crosland was relatively less successful in convincing the rank-and-file that he was a man of
the people. Conspicuously upper-middle-class, suspected of elitism, the
party stalwarts never entirely believed that his socialism was bottom-up

and not the paternalistic arrogance of a missionary raising up the savages. The party stalwarts may have been reading too much into 'the posh voice, the elegant manner'; but the fact remains that the aloof and patrician image cannot have done much to accelerate Crosland's advancement in a party that was explicitly Labour as well as generally socialist. The leadership contest of 1976 is a case in point. Callaghan, in David Marquand's evaluation, was selected in preference to Crosland and Jenkins ('the two most outstanding Radical intellectuals of their time') in no small measure because he was 'the man who could best be relied upon to keep the party close to its proletarian roots'.[183] Callaghan was, in Peter Jenkins's memorable phrase, the 'Keeper of the Cloth Cap';[184] Crosland and Jenkins were occasionally to be observed drinking wine; and thus did class prejudice and cultural stereotyping play its part in impeding Crosland's progress to the very top.

Crosland did not mix in the tea-room, the focal point in the Commons for Labour that is manual. May-Day posturing had no appeal for him: 'He was rumoured to dislike the tea-room', Alan Watkins records, 'and was occasionally to be observed drinking wine. Worst of all, he was an intellectual – the dirtiest word known to Transport House.'[185] Crosland had a deep faith in the power of problem-solving reason: 'If you've got, as I had, an academic background, or have tried serious writing, you tend to believe that problems yield to thought.'[186] He also recognised that a commitment to logic and evidence was by no means a commonplace in the hurly-burly of politics: 'I dare say sustained thinking is a minority occupation amongst Ministers.'[187] Crosland had a deep faith in abstract ideas and programmatic visions: 'The electors deserve – and I believe want – to hear something of the fundamental differences between the philosophies of the Parties, and of the different values which will shape and colour their policies in Government.'[188] He also recognised that the conceptual Left that delights in world-views was hardly the same as the short-terming Left that darts in and takes: 'There is a danger in becoming too pragmatic & empirical in our political thought.'[189]

There is a danger – and there is a great deal of it about. In the 1950s Atlee in his Preface seemed almost to be apologising for the speculative character of the *New Fabian Essays*: 'Only one of the authors has had ministerial experience. I am glad to hear that a second series is planned and hope it will include essays by former members of the Labour Government.'[190] In the 1960s the philosopher Bryan Magee seemed almost to be suggesting that Crosland was a benchmark thinker not least because so few of his contemporaries thought much about thinking at all: 'R.H.S. Crossman has often lamented the booklessness of the post-war

Left in Britain (a condition to which he has contributed).... The sad fact is that Mr. Crosland is the only socialist politician of first-rate intellectual calibre to have written books of importance since the war.'[191] In the 1970s the politician Brian Walden seemed almost to be implying that Crosland bubbling over with ideas was not really a strong argument for theory in a socialist party that was serious about change: 'He has a mania for definitions and labels, believing that he can depict reality from within a formula.'[192] No one actually stated that the structured analysis and the broad sweep were out of place in a political culture that was more comfortable with the piecemeal and the concrete. No one actually put the message in words; but still the perception was clear. Attlee, Magee and Walden seemed almost to be alerting the systemic generaliser to his minority status. The intellectual in politics seemed almost to be replying that it was the blinkered mainstream, too reactive, too factual, that was the real danger.

Irrespective of the real danger to the Party, Crosland's stance was almost certainly a real danger to his own chances of reaching the very top. Reinforcing the reputation for rudeness and arrogance, reinforcing 'the posh voice, the elegant manner', the status of the intellectual in politics made him appear that much more remote from the daily life of ordinary people. The rank-and-file respected Crosland's cleverness. It is unlikely, however, if the median activist or the typical back-bencher ever regarded him with the affection that, say, a Callaghan was able to command.

Self-presentation probably held Crosland back. So, perhaps surprisingly, did performance in office. Crosland held six major portfolios. There were no great disasters and no rumours of incompetence. Still, however, there appears to have been a consensus among Crosland's colleagues that he was, in Roy Jenkins's words, 'not at his best as a minister'.[193] There appears to have been a general feeling that Crosland ought to have been squeezing better results from his undoubted potential. There appears also to have been a strong sense of mystification as to what was going wrong. The bewilderment is well captured by Crossman in diary-entries such as the following: 'Crosland is a strange man. He's extremely able, his contributions in Cabinet are always relevant and usually wise, and yet he's constantly putting up proposals which get defeated and fighting losing battles.... Tony Crosland is fifteen times the man Fred Mulley is but dim little Mulley boring away at his departmental brief gets the Department's way even though he's a bore, whereas despite his brilliance Tony often doesn't even succeed in helping his Department.'[194] Tony Crosland was unquestionably able. His performance, on the other hand, seemed to fall short of his promise.

Impressions influence promotions even where the evidence is anecdotal. Assuming, however, that there was indeed a shortfall in Crosland's case, a significant cause is likely once again to have been the shadow of the Quad. An intellectual in politics rather than a gut-reaction politician, Crosland was unaccustomed to making decisions before he had studied carefully the pros and the cons. The result was a double lag. Crosland, Bill Rodgers recalled, 'relied on painstaking analysis and thorough research, and this sometimes delayed the process of decision-making'.[195] Crosland, Bill Rodgers continued, then delayed the process still further while he reflected and made up his mind: Crosland suffered from 'the lack of a quick political instinct' and the consequence was a 'slowness in reaching firm decisions'.[196] Crosland knew precisely what he was doing, and once reproached Roy Jenkins for not being slow enough: 'What you are pleased to regard as your rational processes seem to me to be just a series of intuitive lurches. You pronounce on things on which I would not pretend to have a sensible view without turning them over in my mind for at least three days.'[197] Roy Jenkins for his own part could fully understand the former academic's 'devotion to lengthy ratiocination'[198] – but he also grasped what Crosland did not, that three days can be too many days in the non-academic world of competitive politics: 'The disadvantage of Crosland's impressively ratiocinative progress towards a view was that when the three days had gone by and he had come out of the dark the issue had often resolved itself. He had not so much taken a more rational decision as lost the opportunity to take one at all.'[199]

The more charitable regarded the delay as the transaction-cost of prudent choice. The more impatient, on the other hand, complained that the intellectuality was being used as an excuse for inaction and the ratiocination as a cloak for indecisiveness. Barbara Castle has put on record her personal exasperation at Crosland's frustrating reluctance to make up his mind: especially telling are her diary-entries on devolution ('Tony C. was all for procrastinating: other options ought to be considered'),[200] on cash limits ('Tony C. made his usual attempt to prevaricate, complaining that he had only received the paper yesterday'),[201] on incomes policy ('As usual, he went on to prevaricate'),[202] on housing ('Tony the indecisive once again').[203] Temporising, postponement and the stop-gap committee were simply no substitute for the definite lead that Tony Crosland, in Barbara Castle's perspective, was unwilling or unable to give.

David Owen reached a similar conclusion on Crosland as a leader: 'I think he has the best mind in the Government, but he just can't come to decisions. That is why he has never got to the very top.'[204] Denis Healey, more tentatively, conveys the same impression of a Crosland unsure:

'Always gay and debonaire, he was the most attractive character in the Labour Cabinet. In intellectual and imaginative power I thought he surpassed his close friend and rival, Roy Jenkins. But he lacked Roy's determination, and ... sometimes used an offhand flippancy as a means of disguising his views or evading responsibility.'[205] Harold Wilson was struck by Crosland's propensity to retreat from the specific into the general: 'In Cabinet he very often contributes an idea but never a policy or a decision.'[206] As the reminiscences mount up, so a collective view appears to emerge of a man who preferred to delay his decisions and sometimes did not decide at all. The cautiousness, ironically, was not always enough. Douglas Jay found Crosland's decision to cancel the plans for a new airport at Maplin in its essentials a gesture wrapped up in a contradiction: 'Crosland's weakness was that he did not seem to be in favour of *any* site, but nonetheless admitted that new airport capacity was essential.'[207] Indecisiveness in such a case would arguably have been preferable to the confusion that was likely to result from the stop-gap decision that was made.

Crosland's performance fell short of his promise because of postponement and ratiocination. The intellectual in him was in that sense a poor ally of the practical politician who wanted to get things done. In that sense – and in another. Crosland as an intellectual was accustomed to trading in reason and appealing to logic. Crosland as a politician had, however, to seek his fortune with quite a different set of skills. The minister got his budget, Crosland was rapidly to discover, not so much through the excellence of his philosophy as through something infinitely tougher, 'by persuading, arguing, cajoling, exploiting his political position, being a bloody nuisance in Cabinet.... It's an endless tactical battle which requires determination, cunning and occasional unscrupulousness.'[208] Allocation by testosterone and not by seminar is haphazard and perhaps even unattractive. On the other hand, 'this is the way it happens in our crude democratic world'.[209] Crosland the politician had no choice but to make his peace with war. He played the game but his heart was never in it: 'In a curious way', Lord Donaldson has said, 'he seemed to be insufficiently calculating.'[210]

Crosland was aware that strategy was not his strongest suit. In a note to himself dating from 1973 he acknowledged the possibility that integrity might be a handicap in politics: 'I've been obsessed by theoretical need for deviousness in pols. for last 2 yrs. as reaction to "men of principle" on Eur.: but in fact must spend less time thinking tactically than any other major politician.'[211] Crosland spent relatively little time thinking tactically because point-scoring and wrong-footing had relatively little appeal to a political idealist for whom socialism and ideology were of considerably

greater interest. Besides that, there is the consideration that to think tactically carries with it the invitation to act tactically – and here Crosland
must have known that he was at something of a disadvantage. Writing to
Philip Williams in 1940, 6474910 Fusilier Crosland informed his friend
that, at least at Marbury Hall, Northwich, Cheshire, the unpleasant fact
was that nice guys were in real danger of finishing last: 'It is an unpleasant
fact for retiring people like you & me, but it is undeniable that as much
pushing as possible is the only sure way of advancement in the Army.'[212]
As with the Army, so with the Cabinet – since, as Angela Brent declares in
Ruling Passions, 'politics being politics, if you want to put someone up,
you need to put someone else down'.[213] Andrew Harwood, trapped by his
culture, was never very good at tripping up his fellow contestants. Ben
Franwell, on the other hand, was taught by his background to scheme and
intrigue. The match is unequal and Franwell knows that it is unequal:
'Harwood is too much of a gent to take the gloves off like those of us
who've pulled ourselves up by our bootstraps.'[214] Susan Crosland's political novel has a happy ending: without giving away too much of the plot, it
can perhaps be hinted that Andrew's wife, a journalist known as Daisy
Brewster, is able to make her own small contribution to the *dénouement*. A
more serious point is, however, this, that not every Andrew gets his just
deserts and often sharp elbows are more effective than intrinsic merit. The
possibility must be recognised that Crosland was too much of a gent to
take the gloves off – and that this worked against his advancement in the
zero-sum arena of political ambitions.

Performance in any case is only of value if it is put on display. Here too
Crosland's character was not on his side. Puritanical at heart, uncomfort-
able about trumpet-blowing, he appears naively to have expected that
virtue would automatically be recognised and be rewarded. Roy Jenkins
was more pro-active: as early as the 1960s he was employing John Harris
to manage his publicity and to secure him the press-coverage that would
establish his image as a future Prime Minister. Crosland long held out
against such flagrant salesmanship: only in the 1970s did he ask his personal and political assistant, David Lipsey, to represent him (and then only
to a limited extent) in his dealings with the media. Crosland was no doubt
on the moral high ground to look askance at politicians who conduct cam-
paigns through photo-opportunities. On the other hand, politics is about
personalities as well as issues; and Crosland's fastidiousness is unlikely to
have done much to advance his career. Roger Berthoud, in the last year of
Crosland's life, stated clearly what many besides himself had long been
thinking: 'It is perhaps surprising that a man with such a strong personality, alternately engaging and prickly, who has consistently been the most

articulate advocate of social democracy in Britain, should have made so little impact on the public imagination.'[215] What is equally surprising, one is compelled to add, is that a man who went into politics to get things done should not have done all that was in his power to secure the offices that pulled the strings.

Self-presentation and performance in office probably kept Crosland from the very top. So most palpably did Harold Wilson. Had Gaitskell lived, Crosland would have stood a good chance of being made Chancellor in the Labour Government which came to power in 1964. The election of the new leader in 1963 meant that Crosland was no longer likely to proceed to the Treasury – or to be groomed for the succession that lay beyond it. Harold Wilson became the Party Leader when Crosland was 44 and remained at the helm until Crosland was 57. In those 13 crucial mid-career years Crosland was repeatedly overlooked for the key offices of State which he needed to establish his credentials.

Crosland among all the Gaitskellites was the closest to the Leader. Lord Donaldson says that 'no one who knew them would deny that Tony was the closest of these'[216] while Lady Falkender expresses the view that 'he, I think, rather than Roy Jenkins, was the true heir of Hugh Gaitskell'.[217] Harold Wilson at one point even believed Tony to be the power behind the throne: 'He was critical of Hugh', Crossman noted in 1958, 'whom he kept talking on about as "Our Leader", and emphasized that he was now too much under the thumb of Tony Crosland'.[218] Gaitskell, Wilson confided, 'takes Crosland's advice regularly'[219] and acts upon it to the discomfort of the Bevanites. Crosland was instrumental in opposing Wilson's bid to replace Gaitskell in 1961. Crosland was believed to have a grudge against Wilson for mounting the challenge and dividing the Party. Crosland was known to have supported not Wilson but first Callaghan and then Brown in the leadership-race of 1963. Crosland, in short, was a Gaitskellite of impeccable pedigree; the Gaitskellites never thought much of Harold Wilson (in Tony Benn's words, 'they really detested him');[220] and Harold Wilson was quite prepared to match the Gaitskellites' contempt with a counterpart loathing that he had never troubled to conceal. Crosland, Rowan implies, never stood a chance once 1963 had repositioned the players: 'He was an attractive man, with the rather dissolute good looks you repeatedly meet in English novels from Sydney Carton onwards; but he was Gaitskell's Jackal, and Harold Wilson suspected him of conspiracies and plots.'[221]

Crosland was a Gaitskellite. So, however, were Patrick Gordon Walker (Wilson's first-choice Foreign Secretary) and Roy Jenkins (Wilson's

Home Secretary from 1965–67 and 1974–76, Wilson's Chancellor of the Exchequer from 1967–69). The Gaitskellite pedigree, it is clear, was not an absolute barrier to the three top ministries. Besides that, Wilson himself was rapidly shifting on to the old Gaitskellite ground. The moderation of his tone as early as the Scarborough Conference of 1963 led Crossman to acclaim him as the greatest revisionist of them all: 'In fact of course Wilson had provided the revision of Socialism and its application to modern times which Gaitskell and Crosland had tried and completely failed to do. Harold had achieved it.'[222] Looking back on the 13 years of the Wilson Leadership, Henry Pelling was able to confirm that the former Bevanite and alleged Leftist had indeed made up his mind to continue the Gaitskellite tradition of radical centrism – 'that he had not only inherited the mantle of Gaitskell but also the party leader's customary tenderness towards moderate opinion in the electorate'.[223] It would have been a matter of the greatest sadness to the Gaitskellites to have seen their leader's work eradicated through a resurgence of extremism. As it was, the leader's work was safe, preserved by the very man who had been its principal adversary only a few years earlier. There is a certain irony in the fact that the principal adversary should subsequently have become the principal beneficiary. An irony, perhaps; but still no grounds for sadness on the part of a Gaitskellite such as Crosland who wanted to get things done.

Some moderates attained high office under Wilson. Anthony Crosland attained only moderate office. Marcia Williams was convinced that his qualities were so outstanding as to have brought him to the very edge of great things: 'These qualities of intellectual brilliance combined with courage would, I believe, have made Tony Crosland a first-rate Chancellor of the Exchequer. Indeed, he was one of the two candidates for that post – the other was Shirley Williams – most in Harold Wilson's mind before his retirement in 1976.'[224] Irrespective of whether or not the glass ceiling *almost* shattered, the historical fact is that it did not. Crosland's Gaitskellism is unlikely to have been the problem. It was almost certainly the personalities and not the policies that caused the tension.

Harold Wilson, two years older than Crosland, has been described by Ben Pimlott as 'a lifelong outsider to Britain's complex Establishment'.[225] Brought up Baptist/Congregationalist rather than Church, educated at the local grammar and not a public school, speaking broad Yorkshire and not Home Counties lah-de-dah, Wilson was a meritocrat who had achieved his Oxford First through ability and application – and who had almost had to drop out of schooling altogether when his father, an industrial chemist, not university-trained, had lost his job in the Great Depression at the advanced age of 48. Even before he became Beveridge's research-assistant, it is clear, Harold Wilson had learned something about the out-of-work and the deprived: 'Unemployment more than anything else', he once said, 'made me politically conscious ... I shall never really know how the family survived.... Our food became more simple.'[226] Wilson was never entirely comfortable with socialists from head-start backgrounds who talked May Day and looked May Ball. Wilson was also in some doubt as to what affluent Southerners actually made of him.

Crosland did nothing to reassure the insecure outsider that he was not being judgemental. Nor did he make any attempt to modulate the exuberance that Wilson appears to have resented as the self-confidence of a Lord reclaiming his Manor. Crosland, not a flatterer, could perhaps have been more sensitive to Wilson's own baggage. Even so, the underlying incompatibility was a fact of life. As Pimlott writes: 'Crosland had the kind of charm that bewitches a certain kind of man or woman, and makes another, chemically different kind, feel insignificant. Wilson was disconcerted, rather than charmed by Crosland's self-assurance; and irritated by the arrogance with which he seemed to take his own future progress in politics for granted. This was distressing to Crosland, a fiercely competitive as well as brilliantly able politician.'[227]

Roy Jenkins fared better than Crosland under Wilson; and an important reason is likely to have been the baggage. Jenkins like Wilson was regional and State-school whereas Crosland was London-based and Highgate. Jenkins like Wilson knew the feel of economic insecurity (Roy's father, Arthur Jenkins, having been in the coal-mines in Wales before he entered the House of Commons for Labour) whereas Crosland's childhood had been Whitehall, Westfield and comfortable. Jenkins like Wilson had a preference for facts (witness the empirical nature of his historical works) whereas Crosland tended to gravitate to philosophical abstractions and theoretical generalisations. Of course the promise of performance will have played its part in the allocation of portfolios – and Jenkins was believed by Wilson to have the superior ability to reach decisions quickly and to control the House of Commons. What must not be forgotten, however, is the extent to which the unspoken and the unseen also had a contribution to make. Tony was an extrovert who made Harold feel dull: 'Implicitly', writes Pimlott, 'Anthony Crosland pointed to the cerebral distinction between progressivism's cavaliers and roundheads in *The Future of Socialism*, published in 1956, when he expressed an aesthete's disdain for socialism based on a good filing system. A good filing system, plus a good slide rule, formed a central part of Wilson's policy approach.'[228] Roy was the Gaitskellite with the common touch who made Harold feel adequate about himself: *The Pirates of Penzance*, *Coronation Street*, meat pies with HP Sauce, the paintings of Lowry – Harold suspected the Hampstead intellectuals of looking down on him but was reasonably confident that Roy at least was prepared to take him on his own terms.

Crosland was blamed where Jenkins was trusted. In the case of disclosures to the press there may have been some grounds for the blame. Thus Crossman records that in July 1969 Wilson's wrath was concentrated on Crosland and Marsh, whom he regarded as the chief sources of the leaks: 'He is probably right, these two do chat maliciously with the press.... The fact remains, however, that we will always have leaks from our Cabinet because Harold is the leakiest of them all.... Harold sees nothing at all improper in doing this, while he bitterly blames Crosland and Marsh for doing the same against him.'[229] With respect to conspiracies and plots, on the other hand, Wilson's political instincts would appear to have let him down. In the winter of unpopularity that followed the 1967 devaluation Wilson seems to have suspected Crosland and Healey of scheming to replace him[230] when in fact the real schemers were Callaghan – and Roy Jenkins. Crosland and Healey exercised if anything a pro-Wilson influence through their indication to conspirators like Rodgers and Marquand that they would not be prepared to serve in a Jenkins Cabinet. It is curious that Wilson, always so afraid of plots, should have appointed as his Chancellor someone who was already popular enough to be spoken of as the natural successor. In the event Jenkins failed to stage his *coup* ('All you do is fucking talk!',[231] an exasperated Crosland once exclaimed) and the opportunity for a leadership challenge gradually receded. An important lesson that emerges from the events of January to March 1968 is that Crosland was suspected where Jenkins was suspicious. Harold Wilson was evidently not infallible. Infallible or not, he imposed a glass ceiling on Crosland's advancement; and that, for 13 years, was that.

Crosland obviously regretted that his ambitions had been frustrated – and frustrated by a man, no Dalton, no Gaitskell, whom he believed to be deficient in a long-run commitment to equality and welfare. The most positive thing he said about Wilson was his observation to Tony Benn that, gimmicky and not good on strategy, at least Wilson kept the various wings of the Party united and was, on balance, 'probably as good a peacetime Prime Minister as this country ever gets.'[232] To his wife Crosland could be more open: 'The trouble with Harold is one hasn't the faintest idea whether the bastard means what he says even at the moment he speaks it.'[233] In the privacy of his notebook Crosland could be more open still. On holiday in the early 1970s he read Harold Wilson's *The Labour Government 1964–70*. He read it 'with horrified fascination: he's learned nothing & forgotten nothing.'[234] Making notes on the book, Crosland almost immediately found himself making notes on the man as well:

'Lunatic rushing about ... mad timetable ... fantasy world of lunatic invi-
tations ... equal fantasy world about ind. restructuring, DEA, computers,
shipbuilding: still imagines it all meant something ... obsession with
b[alance] of p[ayments]: no mention anywhere of r[ate] of g[rowth] ... no
mention of 10/65! ... no candour or honesty or revelations ... self-
deception & dishonesty.'[235] If Wilson had his doubts about Crosland, then
Crosland, clearly enough, also had his doubts about Wilson. The relationship was not made in Heaven: on that point at least the two parties were in
complete agreement.

Jim Callaghan got to Downing Street. Roy Jenkins reached the Home
Office and the Treasury. Anthony Crosland climbed as far as Education,
the Environment and the Foreign Office. As appropriate as his portfolios
generally were for a reformer with an interest in equalisation and regulation, Crosland would have preferred to have been in a stronger position to
shape taxes, resist cuts, alter parities, stimulate growth. Self-presentation,
performance in office and Harold Wilson all held him back. It is very
likely that Crosland in his later years believed that his practical contribution as an intellectual in politics had been somewhat less than he had
intended.

Crosland entered politics, as he later recalled, full of hope: 'I wanted to
go into politics, and specifically Labour politics, ever since I was about
seventeen.... I have always held very strong views about public affairs
and have wanted a chance to influence them. I wanted to be involved in
the actual process of taking decisions and making policies.'[236] Keynes,
Beveridge, Titmuss, Tawney and Kaldor all influenced public affairs from
a base outside the House; and one is tempted to wonder if Crosland would
not have stood a better chance of shaping the future of socialism if he had
stayed an intellectual at Trinity rather than becoming an intellectual at
Westminster in order to bring about change from within. What is striking,
however, is the extent to which Crosland even at Westminster managed to
retain a foothold in the thinkers' camp. His contribution to practical politics may indeed have been somewhat less than he had intended. His contribution to political economy, on the other hand, is likely to prove
somewhat greater than he had envisaged.

3 The World of the Revisionist

It began in 1952 with the *New Fabian Essays*. It continued in 1956 with *The Future of Socialism*. By 1958 it was history: 'The "revisionist" period is over; that is, the business of giving the Labour Party a policy attuned to mid-twentieth-century conditions is more or less complete.'[1] In the darkness that had followed the 1952 defeat there had been socialists who had preached a return to the old faith of class and property. By 1958 they had been routed: the 'pristine semi-Marxist analysis of capitalism has given way to a subtle revisionist theory of the post-capitalist society', Crosland announced in 1958, and the result was, relevance having triumphed over tradition, that 'revisionism ... holds the field'.[2] It is easy with hindsight to accuse Crosland in 1958 of having been too quick to close the book: as Bryan Gould has correctly observed, 'there are never any final battles in politics'.[3] It cannot be denied, however, that major battles were fought in those historic Opposition years that were marked by the electoral defeats of 1951 (Conservative majority 26) and 1955 (Conservative majority 67) that led to the *débâcle* of 1959 (Conservative majority 107) but eventually to the turning of the tide in 1964 (Labour majority 4). Major battles were fought – and the Gaitskellites emerged with the conviction that theirs was a victory that would last.

It is with the period of the struggle that this chapter is concerned. Taking as its text the proposition that *The Future of Socialism* is in no small measure the child of its times, this chapter is divided into four sections. The first section examines the economic and political circumstances of a complacent Britain that had seldom had grounds to be so optimistic. The second section shows that Crosland would have had less of a *Future* if it had not been for the distinguished thinkers of the recent past upon whose shoulders he chose to stand. The third section considers the aims and objectives of the Gaitskellites in the period immediately before and immediately after the election of Hugh Gaitskell as the Party Leader. The final section discusses the intellectual and political similarities between Tony and Hugh in the revisionist years that were the background for Crosland's *Future*.

Fusilier Crosland reading Tawney's *Religion* was prepared to accept that world-views like human beings have only very limited control over their place of birth: 'Religious and ideological movements are to a large extent the reflection of economic changes and conditions.'[4] What the Fusilier could not decide is whether belief-systems, born into circumstances that they never chose to select, might not subsequently grow up to exercise a circumstance-altering power of their own. The Fusilier reading *Religion* raised the question of the extent to which 'ideologies which have a perfectly clear historical origin (e.g. patriotism, liberalism, and certain religious creeds) may develop a power and influence so great as at a subsequent date in history to outweigh the then economic and class factors.'[5] Future generations of fusiliers will no doubt raise the same question in respect of *The Future of Socialism*. This chapter does not say whether consequences have more ideas than ideas have consequences. All that it does is to show that the birth of the *Future* may be situated precisely in time and space.

3.1 THE WORLD OF THE *FUTURE*

The Future of Socialism is a work of hope born into a world of hope. Unemployment in the year it was published stood at 1.2 per cent of the labour force, prices were rising by 3.3 per cent, wages were rising by 7.6 per cent, the balance of payments was comfortably in surplus, the rate of growth was 2 per cent (down from 4 per cent in 1953 and 1954, about to surge again in 1959 and 1960).[1] Socialists in the 1930s had had to address the Depression economics of mass unemployment, capitalist inefficiency, concentrated power. The intellectual climate in the 1950s was not the same. The 1930s had had to come to grips with bitterness, poverty and division against the background of the return to gold at an uncompetitive parity in 1925, the General Strike in protest at wage-cuts for coal-miners in 1926, the Great Crash in 1929, the dictators abroad, the malnutrition at home. The heritage of the 1950s, on the other hand, was the bonfire of controls and the Festival of Britain, mass consumption and proper holidays, clothing without coupons after 1949 and food without ration-books from 1954. Galbraith's *The Affluent Society* in 1958 informed the industrialised countries that absolute deprivation was withering away. So did Crosland's *The Future of Socialism* in 1956. In between there was Harold Macmillan who, speaking at Bedford on 25 July 1957, uttered ten words that were to sum up an era: 'Most of our people have never had it so good.' Progress was in the air and the Conservative Party had only to promise a conservative electorate that it would deliver more of the same. Its slogan in the 1959 election was no more than an appeal to the contented not to rock the boat: 'Life's better with the Conservatives. Don't let

Labour ruin it.' Labour was able to find an audience for nationalisation and control in the turmoil and dissatisfaction of the 1930s. In the 1950s, on the other hand, the electorate was simply not in the market for social-isation and plan. Economically speaking, what the voters wanted was not a radical alternative to a successful system so much as the mobilisation of the tried-and-tested in the service of the fuller trough.

The 1950s built on the achievements of the 1945–51 Labour Governments and largely took for granted 'the impossibility of unscram-bling these scrambled eggs'.[2] The Bank of England had been nationalised in 1946, the National Coal Board had taken over the mines in 1947, the railways and the gas industry had been bought out by the State in 1948. Also in 1948 the free-on-demand National Health Service had been inau-gurated: 5 July 1948 (the date on which the Minister of Health, in Bevan's own submission, accepted responsibility for all the pregnant women in Britain) is a key date in the history of British mutual aid. In 1949 the iron and steel industries had been nationalised. Under Labour the social ser-vices had been extended, New Towns planned, legal aid introduced. Some desultory attempts were made by the Tories to reverse what Labour had done: steel, for example, was denationalised in 1953. By and large, however, there was little interest under Churchill, Eden, Macmillan or Home in putting the clocks back to the world as it had been before Attlee. The mixed economy and the welfare state were effectively to be absorbed and ultimately to be endorsed by a moderate Conservatism that took its cue from Harold Macmillan's pun 'Let sleeping dogmas lie'.[3]

Macroeconomic policy too seemed to be sheltered from ideology beneath the shared umbrella of bipartisanship and consensus. The Beveridge Report of 1942 had called for an attack on the 'five giant evils' of Want, Disease, Ignorance, Squalor – and Idleness, 'which destroys wealth and corrupts men, whether they are well fed or not.'[4] The White Paper on Employment Policy of 1944, taking up the challenge of involun-tary unemployment, had made it a responsibility of the State to manage demand in such a way as to suck the out-of-work back into jobs. By the 1950s it was generally accepted by all political parties that the discre-tionary intervention expounded in Keynes's *General Theory* was the only viable means of steering the economy into full employment without harmful inflation. Keynesian economics appeared also to boost the status of a wise and thinking leadership through its confidence in the capacity of counter-cyclical stabilisation policies to correct a market failure that wage-cuts would only have exacerbated. Keynesian economics seemed to make sense in an era that had experienced the stimulus of the War and was afraid of a slump as a consequence of the peace. By the 1950s even the

Tories were Keynesians. Butler in his 1953 budget (eschewing monetary policy to combat the recession) cut taxes and ran a deficit in order to stimulate consumption and protect employment. Gaitskell, his Labour predecessor, would almost certainly have done the same. The Chancellor, the Shadow Chancellor – so great was the agreement between them that Norman Macrae in *The Economist* coined the name 'Mr Butskell' in order to rubber-stamp the predetermined in an age of convergence.[5]

Public spending was generally acceptable in the 1950s; but it must not be supposed that this concord was necessarily the same as a ring-fenced guarantee for welfare and infrastructure. Defence too was an important consideration. Rearmament had been on the agenda even of the Atlee Government. Gaitskell when Chancellor in 1951 had himself imposed prescription-charges for spectacles and dentures expressly in order to pay for munitions: it was that breach with the free-on-demand principle that had provoked the resignation from the Cabinet of Aneurin Bevan, John Freeman and the younger, more militant Harold Wilson. It had been under Labour that Britain had joined NATO. The Berlin blockade of 1948, the disappearance of one Eastern European country after another behind the Iron Curtain in the late 1940s, the incursion of North Korean and Chinese regular forces south of the 38th parallel in 1950, all gave rise to fears about Russian and/or Chinese aggression – against Iran, against Scandinavia, against Tito's Yugoslavia, against Western Europe itself. Britain in the 1950s was fighting communism East of Suez in Malaya while France was embroiled in a similar mission in Indo-China. The Middle East was a tinderbox of claims and accusations. The Fourth Republic was so unstable before De Gaulle's accession in 1958 that no one could foresee how France would react to a foreign threat. Memories of German militarism left many in two minds as to whether Germany should be allowed to rearm (within NATO) so as yet again to serve as a bulwark against the Soviets. Doubts about the exaggerated anti-communism of the Pentagon and about controversial Cold Warriors such as MacArthur and Dulles undermined faith in the big brother as the defender of the peace. The Americans had used nuclear weapons against Japan in 1945, and not just as a passive deterrent. It was feared that they would use their atomic bomb in 1951 against China. China was believed to be a close ally of Russia. Crosland's socialism was conceived in troubled times. Nearer to the Third World War than it was to the peace-dividend, Crosland's socialism treated as a fact of life the social overhead of high military expenditure. There were many reforms that Crosland would almost certainly have supported that he could not endorse so long as the deadweight of defence remained so regrettable a necessity.

The very year in which *The Future of Socialism* was published bore witness to a sequence of remarkable events which, competing with Crosland's book for the public's attention, showed to what an extent the world remained a troubled place. It was in 1956 that Kruschev denounced Stalin's excesses and the dictator's cult: those revelations about the human costs of Soviet growth must have reinforced the faith of a revisionist like Crosland even if a leftist like Crossman was still able to accuse the mixed-economy moderates of a failure to appreciate the contrast between the dynamism of the Communist countries and the descent into inaction of the West.[6] It was in 1956 that Khrushchev travelled (with Bulganin) to London: there he was so provoked by the anti-totalitarian constitutionalism of Gaitskell (who once presented Malenkov with a copy of *The Politics of Democratic Socialism*) and Bevan (Khrushchev had expected better treatment from a former miner) that he exclaimed, no doubt unaware of the irony, that 'I have not met people like you for thirty or forty years'.[7] In 1956 Gomulka was released from prison in Poland (as early as 1948 the hard Left had been hounding him for 'mistakes and false concepts') and was made First Secretary of the Polish Communist Party: Soviet troops in Western Russia were moved towards the Polish border, Kruschev himself flew to Warsaw to size up the situation, and an invasion seemed a real possibility.

Poland was spared. Hungary was not. In 1956 Soviet tanks thundered through Budapest. The deposition and subsequent execution of Imre Nagy had the unexpected consequence of driving wavering British Communists out of Mr Gollan's Party and into that of Mr Gaitskell. The powerlessness of the West in the face of over-aggressive absolutists no doubt struck a familiar chord in a generation still able to remember the 'peace in our times' of Munich. Not that the Great Powers with an electoral mandate acquitted themselves that much more honourably in 1956: incensed by Nasser's nationalisation of the Suez Canal, an Anglo-French expeditionary force was dispatched to Egypt without waiting for the authorisation of the United Nations. This last burst of gunboat diplomacy occurred in October 1956. So did the Hungarian uprising and the Polish Eighth Plenum. Crosland's *The Future of Socialism* was published in October 1956.

The world remained a troubled place; and that is why the debate about public spending in the 1950s always had to incorporate the cost of military preparedness. Gaitskell denied that international communism was a monolithic threat; and he also accepted that neutrality in the Third World need not be regarded as a hostile rejection of the democratic West. Domestically, however, he was in favour of National Service (only ended in 1960), modern weaponry and an independent British nuclear deterrent. The cost was high; and multilateral disarmament (combined with a strengthened NATO for collective security) was regarded by the Labour moderates as being the optimal solution. In the last analysis, however, it was agreed that the cost would have to be borne. Some money at any rate was saved in 1960 when the Conservatives cancelled the land-based Blue Streak rocket.

Unilateralism was strong within the Labour Party; and much anxiety was expressed about the testing of the British H-Bomb on Christmas Island in 1957. The first Aldermaston March took place in 1956. The Campaign for Nuclear Disarmament was launched in 1958. In 1960 Bertrand Russell formed the Committee of 100 within CND to take non-violent direct action. Aneurin Bevan surprised the advocates of 'Ban the Bomb', of 'Better Red than Dead', by siding with the Gaitskellites on the issue of multilateral disarmament. Britain could not, he said at Brighton in 1957, go 'naked into the conference chamber'.[8] Bevan was, however, the exception on the Labour Left. Revisionists like Crosland were repeatedly challenged to defend their position – and to justify the cost.

NATO, of course, would have continued to provide an umbrella even if Britain had abandoned her deterrent. Yet NATO too was a cause of friction as between the various factions of a divided Labour. Flatly against the alliance were the extremists who, pro-Marx, pro-Russia, said it was wrong to depress the living standards of the working classes in order to assist the Americans in their crusade against communism. Then there were the nationalists who, anticipating De Gaulle's later withdrawal from the organisation, felt it was an infringement of Britain's sovereignty to host American bases (not least those accommodating the deadly Polaris missile such as the submarine base at Holy Loch). Inevitably too there were the sceptics who believed it was a danger to depend too much on the American partner who might force Britain into policies she did not want or even retreat into isolationism rather than risk annihilation to save a distant ally. Overriding all was the unthinking anti-Americanism of so much of British society in the 1950s. America was the country that had sent over the GIs and the chewing-gum in the War. America had offered aid for reconstruction on the Lend-Lease basis and had done little to dismantle her protective tariffs. America to the Left was the land of monopoly capital, Wall Street, Big Business and (up to 1954) Joe McCarthy. America to the Right was the home of childlike informality and bad spelling where mass consumption and show-business democracy had led to a fall in standards. Confronted by the fellow travellers on the one side and the Little Englanders on the other, the revisionists' attachment not just to NATO in general but to the United States in particular becomes all the more striking.

The attraction was a cultural as well as a political one. Thus Roy Jenkins has written as follows about Gaitskell and his attitudes: 'He believed deeply in the Western Alliance and in friendship with the United States. He was naturally a mid-Atlantic man, almost as much at home in New York as in London.'[9] And Stephen Haseler, probing more deeply, has said of the Crosland of the '50s that he 'saw virtues in American society ... that he readily admitted were in keeping with certain of his revisionist socialist principles (equality, social justice and freedom)'.[10] The Americans were committed to comprehensive education through the community-based high school; to social location that was a function of equality of opportunity and advancement by merit; to human interaction that was spontaneous, cordial, unconnected with birth. Besides that, the Americans were strong individualists with anarchistic tendencies, whose hot jazz was a brilliant contrast to British drabness. The revisionists did not equate the future of socialism with the actualisation of the American Dream. Nor were they naive enough to assume that the open society necessarily encompassed the whole of the American reality. What they did find, however, was that British socialism had a certain amount to learn from the leading capitalist nation. The fact that Gaitskell and Crosland felt comfortable on a personal level with Stevenson and, later, Kennedy must have contributed as well to the North Atlantic community of ideas.

The American Dream had bestowed upon the hopeful politics of equitable meritocracy the capacity to take the individual or the region as the primary focus for political allegiance. Class-structure and property-ownership had traditionally played a much smaller part in the American political culture than they had done in the Britain of parentage and blood. Crosland accepted that the British past had been one of political polarisation centred upon economic class. Crosland anticipated, however, that the British future would be characterised by a political convergence that would emanate from a convergence in social status. In the past there had been the fallacious Marxian prediction of bifurcation and confrontation: 'Society as a whole is more and more splitting up into two great hostile camps, into two great classes directly facing each other: bourgeoisie and proletariat.'[11] In the present there was the idealised American model of mobility and consensus, moving up and coming together. In the future there would be a socialist Britain – but only if Britain's socialists, tired of losing elections, moved with the times on to the middle ground: 'Universal suffrage forces both Left and Right towards the centre, since neither can win elections without the support of centre opinion.... The marked change in the social climate has the same effect.'[12] Harold Macmillan had long been stressing to the Conservative Party that the core of British politics could only be 'the struggle to occupy No-Man's-Land – to seize the middle ground'.[13] Britain's Prime Minister from January 1957 until October 1963, Macmillan showed in office what it meant to be Centre-Right. An early casualty of his politics of compromise was the resignation of his first Chancellor of the Exchequer, Peter Thorneycroft, in protest of Macmillan's categorical refusal to countenance spending cuts. Anthony Crosland in the 1950s was arguing that Labour should meet the Conservatives on the same middle ground and should demonstrate to the electorate the absolute supremacy of the Centre-Left position. Labour, he believed, had no alternative but to settle where the consensus dwelt. Status groups were converging. Political parties had no option but to follow suit.

Status groups were converging in the Britain of the 1950s. The process was one of felt levelling up rather than of perceived levelling down – and the rate of *embourgeoisement* was so rapid as to pose a threat to a Labour Party that had not updated its image. As Crosland wrote in the Fabian Tract *Can Labour Win*? that was his personal *post mortem* on the 1959 defeat: 'If Labour continues to be thought of as an essentially proletarian and one-class party, it faces the certainty of steady decline.'[14] Left-Left or Centre-Left, the problem of the class-identity was an embarrassment in its own right in an affluent Britain that was seeing less and less of the old-style cloth cap. The old-style cloth-cap was moving on to the endangered-species list. The reason was the success and not the failure of the capitalist mode of production.

Consumption *per capita* increased dramatically in the 1950s. Living standards rose more between 1951 and 1959 than they had done in the whole of the period from 1913 to 1939. Living standards had not risen at all from 1945 to 1951: that stagnation had tainted the socialists with austerity and stringency that was made that much more stigmatising by the knowledge that the puritanical Left had no real sympathy with affluence and prosperity. Full employment and economic growth in the 1950s gave the working-classes a stake in the consumer durables boom. Mass production and hire-purchase retailing made a further contribution to the narrowing in *visible* social distance that the revisionists regarded as so attractive a by-product of the economic dynamic.

The process of *embourgeoisement* was accelerated by the decline of the older basic industries such as coal that had in the past been the seed-bed of the class-conscious Labour vote; by the expansion of the service sector in which middle-class cultural attitudes tended to predominate; by the increasing proportion of white-collar to blue-collar workers in the labour-force that Crosland called the 'continuing move away from a proletariat towards a salariat'.[15] The mass media eulogised car-ownership and even home-ownership far more than they praised the mutual aid and the instinctive solidarity of the Northern unskilled manual male who remained the Identikit archtype of the Labour voter. The perception that upward mobility was in the air (not least as a consequence of the educational opportunities that had been offered under Atlee's Labour) tended to undermine the fundaments of traditional loyalty: young people, ambitious to leave the class of their birth, had a diminished stake in party of their parents. Resettlement from the long-established communities of the inner city to the melting-pot freshness of the New Towns further undermined the cultural identity of the traditional proletariat. Accelerating the evolution from class-based confrontation to perceived behavioural assimilation, the geographical move reinforced the social move in making a politics of *Labour* appear something of an anachronism in the altered circumstances of High Street homogeneity and issues-orientated citizenship.

Crosland as a revisionist reached the conclusion that economic transformation was making it increasingly difficult to sell an outdated model: 'The steady upgrading of the working class, both occupationally and still more in terms of social aspirations, renders Labour's one-class image increasingly inappropriate.'[16] Electoral capital was obviously a serious consideration when Crosland in the 1950s called cloth-cap Labour 'a party of the past':[17] a practical politician, he recognised that without an appeal to the present-day his party would find it very difficult to return to power. Importantly, however, he also maintained that it would be more socialist as well as more expedient for the party to abandon its traditional association with a single class: 'To be so identified is not only imprudent, it also betrays a fundamental socialist principle; for a "classless" society will never be achieved through a wholly class-orientated instrument. The object is to create a broadly-based, national, people's party.'[18] Such a people's party would not be the front-line representative of the labouring class, narrowly defined. Rather, it would be a rallying point for a Centre-Left of conviction that made no distinction between blue-collar and white.

A non-class party deserved a non-class name – if only, as Douglas Jay so trenchantly observed, because as Labour now stands 'we are in danger of fighting under the label of a class that no longer exists'.[19] Crosland's friend, Michael Young, was especially sensitive to the linguistic cleft that was emerging between the old name (with its overtones of the Marxian two-class conflict) and the new reality of a progressivism that could no longer be based on ownership and shares: 'Class based on production is slowly giving way to status based on consumption as the centre of social gravity.... Politics will become less and less the politics of production and more and more the politics of consumption.'[20] Looking to the future,

Michael Young said, the cutting edge would not be the capital–labour
nexus but instead the life-style concerns that have the higher income-
elasticity – entering the EEC and ending resale price maintenance, liberalising licensing-laws and legalising homosexuality, improving State
education and democratising council housing. The agenda is broad and it
is classless. A name like the Labour Party hardly does it justice. A name
like the Consumer's Party would be a better choice. After all, 'it is as consumers that we look out on a much larger and more varied scene than
when we are at work'.[21]

Young, writing in 1960, came up with quite an original new name for a
Centre-Left party that had in his view effectively outgrown the old name
of Labour. Crosland, writing in the same year, expressed a preference for a
radical departure that was also a familiar friend: 'I myself for twenty years
for various reasons have wished in Britain we were called not the Labour
Party but the Social Democratic Party, and moreover it can be argued
that the name Labour has certain disadvantages in an increasingly non-
proletarian society.'[22] Crosland in *The Future of Socialism* had in 1956
used the term social-democratic to denote precisely the kind of life-style
socialism that Young had identified as appropriate in the new-style politics
of consumption: 'As our traditional objectives are gradually fulfilled, and
society becomes more social-democratic with the passing of the old injustices, we shall turn our attention increasingly to other, and in the long run
more important, spheres – of personal freedom, happiness, and cultural
endeavour.'[23] As late as his Fabian Pamphlet of 1971 on *A Social-
Democratic Britain*, Crosland was continuing to use the term social-
democratic in essentially the same sense, to mean superstructure socialism
that at the margin depends unashamedly on the economic success of
profit-seeking capitalism.

Crosland was attracted by the term. He was less attracted by the idea of
actually doing anything with it. Perhaps because of indecision, perhaps
because he feared a collision with the Left, Crosland seems not to have
pressed strongly for a radical departure that was also a familiar friend.
Labour was to reform itself but Labour was to retain the name of Labour.
So reconciled was Crosland to the survival of the second-best that at one
point he snapped at an interviewer who had used the good-bad term in his
presence that a Social Democrat was properly to be defined as 'somebody
about to join the Tory Party.'[24] As the revisionist period drew to a close, it
would appear, there remained much in Labour that even the busy Crosland
had not quite managed to revise.

The cloth-cap image was buttressed by the link with the unions. That
special relationship was a further feature of economic and political life in

the Britain of the 1950s that the Labour revisionists had willy-nilly to acknowledge and to address.

The unions had attracted a considerable amount of adverse publicity. Justly or unjustly, they were widely associated with the demarcation dispute and the closed shop, the intransigence of the shop-steward and the disruptiveness of the national strike. The unions were blamed for the collective bargaining of pay in excess of productivity that had led to cost-push inflation. They had been the focus for unwelcome attention in the media due to the influence of powerful Communists in unions like Amalgamated Engineering. The unions, justly or unjustly, were not universally perceived to be serving the national as opposed to the sectional interest – and Labour was known to be close to the unions. The unions sponsored individual Members of Parliament; they subscribed to Labour funds through the political levy; and they controlled a block vote so massive that a small number of union leaders were in a position to exercise a *de facto* dominance over the annual Party Conference. The decisions of Conference have never been more than guidelines to the Parliamentary Labour Party. Periodically the unions tried to amend the Party Constitution in order to make the Conference resolutions properly binding.

The unions were not universally trusted. Some of the unpopularity was bound to rub off on the political party which insisted, in its Clause III, that every Party member had also to be a member of a union. It was widely believed in the country that the acknowledged symbiosis between Labour and labour made it highly unlikely that the Party would have the strength to stand up to the State within the State even on an issue of national importance. Postal balloting to protect the rank-and-file from an undemocratic union leadership is an example of the kind of reform which many in the country suspected that the Labour Party because of its special relationship would never have the courage to introduce. Labour was able, of course, to contend that it was precisely this special relationship that put it in a unique position to preach self-control in industrial relations or to secure voluntary adherence to a prices and incomes policy. On balance, however, these arguments could never be very persuasive in view of the extent to which Labour was known to be dependent upon the unions. The revisionists had no choice but to accept that the unions were something of an electoral albatross to a socialist party that wanted to be thought of as even-handed, impartial and classless.

Aware of the problem, Crosland was never able to find a convincing solution. His unwillingness to grasp the nettle is well-illustrated by the duality of the perspective that he was still endorsing as late as 1973. On the one hand the Labour Party must nurture its relationship with the corporatised proletariat: 'Labour's special link is, and must be, with the organized working class, and its solid base is in the trade union movement.'[25] On the other hand the Labour Party must speak for the organism and not for the cell: 'The Labour Party should not automatically agree with everything that union leaders say, still less be dictated to by them. For all our special links with the unions, we are a national party, responsible to the people as a whole.'[26] Crosland recognised that union leaders might not faithfully represent the views of the ordinary members ('Indeed, in the case of Mr Hugh Scanlon and a minority of extreme left-wing leaders they clearly do not')[27] – but he was silent on the nature of the mechanism that would make the officials more accountable to the constituents. Crosland recommended the greater devolution of collective bargaining to the level of the individual plant ('The extension of local bargaining is a key element in industrial democracy')[28] – but he did not explain how to prevent the occurrence of unofficial walk-outs in pursuit of trivialities. Crosland accepted that restrictive practices were a brake on the growth that financed the socialism – but he never called for a concerted socialist attack on the overmanning and the resistance to change that were damping down productivity and retarding the process of innovation. Aware that organised labour was a problem, Crosland was remarkably reticent on the need for a radical solution.

Organised labour, ironically enough, was not always prepared to repay the moderation with cooperation. Two years and four months after Crosland's death it was to be the unions' aggressiveness that, making its own contribution to the relative attractiveness of the monetarist New Right, was to cost Labour the 1979 election that followed the much-resented dislocation of the 'winter of discontent'. Almost twenty years before that it had been the block vote of four of the six major trade unions affiliated to Labour that, in 1960, had put an end to the Gaitskellites' hopes for a Party Constitution purified of the Clause IV Commandments. The Party Conference (passing resolutions without recourse to the democratic principle of 'one member, one vote') was so frequently at odds with the Parliamentary Labour Party (selected by the electorate and directly accountable to the people) that Crosland in one place was driven to describe a defeat at Conference as all but a victory for a responsible leadership. Even if the vote went against the leadership, Crosland wrote, still 'an important object would be achieved: the Labour party would be seen by the country to be dominated neither by the bloc votes of the trade unions nor by an unrepresentative minority of left-wing activists'.[29] Perhaps this was so; but a far more obvious recommendation would have been for the Labour Party to revise its own Constitution as a first step towards the reform of the society as a whole. Aware of the problem, Crosland refused to grasp the nettle. The revisionists were able to incorporate into their world-view the good times and the Butskellism, the Cold War and the cloth cap, the *embourgeoisement* and the convergence that were such prominent features of the changing Britain that was the material backdrop to the new initiatives of the 1950s. In respect of organised labour, however, Crosland, like the other revisionists, was obviously of the opinion that the *status quo* was a second-best that had not yet reached the end of its productive life.

3.2 THE MIXED ECONOMY

The Future of Socialism was the work of one inspired author and many sources of inspiration. The whole was greater than the sum of the parts. It rather adds to than detracts from the importance of Crosland's contribution to say that Pigou passed him his paper and Hugh Dalton blended his ink when he was engaged in the task of synthesising the past in order to influence the future.

An economics graduate and a former don, a voracious reader and an intellectual in politics, Crosland was in a strong position to appreciate just how multifaceted had been the continuing debate in the nation of compromise and pragmatism on the proper balance between mix and market, private-sector freedom and public-sector intervention. The great Adam Smith had himself provided the model. On the one hand, Smith had said, each self-seeking unit in the larger economic whole is in effect 'led by an invisible hand to promote an end which was no part of his intention':[1] 'The study of his own advantage naturally, or rather necessarily leads him to prefer that employment which is most advantageous to the society.'[2] On the other hand, Smith had argued, the butcher, the brewer and the baker leave the nation conspicuously under-provided with roads, canals and the regulation of banking: felt demand here calls forth inadequate supply, the consensus here suffers from frustrated hopes, and the State must in the circumstances serve as the residual of last resort that assumes on behalf of all 'the duty of erecting and maintaining certain public works and certain public institutions, which it can never be for the interest of any individual, or small number of individuals, to erect and maintain'.[3] On the one hand enterprise, on the other hand authority – *The Wealth of Nations* in 1776 issued a warning to the ideologues of all parties that wisdom consists not in absolutism but in matching the means to the end that is sought.

Eclecticism and justification were at the heart of Adam Smith's message. The heritage was a British tradition of *political* economy that, accepting that two hands wash cleaner than one, took mix for granted and travelled extensively along the shifting frontiers. Smith attacked the Settlement Laws but defended the Post Office. Bentham was opposed to a ceiling on the rate of interest but in favour of a ceiling on the price of grain. Nassau Senior objected to the imposition by statute of the 10-hour day but supported free public education, the regulation of child labour and the parish provision of a workhouse for the poor. Foxwell believed in private property but also in public health, public housing and a 'national economy' of managed capitalism. Each author began with individual choice and had a lexicographic preference for the decentralisation of exchange. In Alfred Marshall's words: 'We believe that a private company which stands to gain something by vigorous and efficient management, by promptness in inventing, as well as in adapting and perfecting improvements in processes and organization, will do more for progress than a public department.'[4] Each author was nonetheless prepared to welcome in the State where the alternative to intervention would have to be a market that failed. In Alfred Marshall's words: 'So I cry "*Laissez-faire* – let the State be up and doing"…. Let everyone work with all his might; and most of all let the Government arouse itself to do that work which is vital, and which none but Government can do efficiently.'[5] Alfred Marshall's words are the influential words of an instinctive Hegelian who had graduated from Mill on socialism to Mill on liberty without ever losing sight of the need for a division of labour.

Marshall's *Principles of Economics* will have been one of Crosland's principal texts when he was an undergraduate at Oxford. Absorbing from it the meat-and-potatoes of marginal cost and marginal revenue, the downward-sloping demand curve and the forward-falling supply curve, he cannot have failed to notice that the standard reference was clearly the work of a missionary as well as of a mathematician – of a concerned moralist, in short, who set down the following as one of 'the chief questions to which the economist addresses himself':[6] 'Taking it for granted that a more equal distribution of wealth is to be desired, how far would this justify changes in the institutions of property, or limitations of free enterprise even when they would be likely to diminish the aggregate of wealth?'[7] Marshall's emphasis on maximal felt utility led him to endorse the progressive income tax on the basis of the inter-personal comparison that 'a shilling is the measure of less pleasure, or satisfaction of any kind, to a rich man than to a poor one'.[8] Marshall's commitment to minimal economic waste led him to advocate the hypothecated taxation of 'goods which obey the law of diminishing return', the devotion of the revenues raised to 'a bounty on the production of those goods with regard to which the law of increasing return acts sharply'.[9] Marshall was a supporter neither of the isolated market nor of the leaderly State but rather of the two together in a balanced package. The *political* economy of his far-ranging *Principles* cannot have escaped the attention of a politically sensitive student like Anthony Crosland. Reading the 1920 edition of the 1890 classic in the new dawn of Attlee's first year, Crosland must have seen that the ambitious systematiser was in effect a fellow believer in the valuable partnership of the mixed economy.

It may have made a difference that Crosland was writing his Oxford essays on supply and demand for a Trinity tutor who, coincidentally, was himself a Labour Party man and a strong supporter of the symbiotic solution. Robert Hall began with the ethical supremacy of choice ('In the last resort everyone who is neither feeble-minded nor inexperienced must be the judge of his own good')[10] and employed it to legitimise the allocative expediency of exchange ('In the economic world, all values come from the estimation of others through the market, and we are worth only what we can induce others to pay for our services').[11] Sir Robert was nonetheless prepared to invoke the aid of the visible hand where the alternative to conscious regulation would have been a free market that was performing less well: 'It is possible to argue that a controlled system working to a central plan is better than a competitive one which is working badly.'[12] In his major work on *The Economic System in a Socialist State* (1937), Robert Hall had demonstrated that a productive economy remained a theoretical possibility even where the ownership of capital had been comprehensively socialised by the State. Sir Robert had specified, however, that this result presupposed the willingness of the socialist planners to make extensive use of flexible pricing in order to generate a monetary measure of final satisfactions: 'There is no theoretical difficulty in the way of calculating costs, whatever the form of control over production, so long as there is a market in consumer's goods.'[13] Lord Roberthall, Chief Economic Adviser to eight Chancellors of the Exchequer, was a lifelong believer in a government that, not necessarily nationalising, still was unafraid, in Alfred Marshall's submission, to act on the maxim of '*Laissez-faire* – let the State be up and doing'. There cannot have been many Oxford tutors with whom Crosland could have had better discussions on the *political* economy of Marshall's *Principles* than with the practical, no-nonsense Australian who had no *a priori* objection to the economic involvement ('Today it has a finger in every pie, and often both hands')[14] of the modern State. In 1981 Lord Roberthall took the Social Democratic Whip in the House of Lords.

Crosland's tutor published on socialism in 1937. So did Marshall's student. Pigou had succeeded Marshall to the Cambridge Chair in 1908 and (retiring in 1943) had sought to perpetuate the Marshallian approach to theory and policy. The proper mix for the modern mixed economy being so significant a part of the Marshallian tradition, it is no surprise that the market versus the State should have figured so prominently in the four editions (between 1920 and 1932) of *The Economics of Welfare*, Pigou's most influential contribution. Building on Marshall's diminishing utility from marginal income, Pigou in *The Economics of Welfare* put forward a theory of redistribution in which growth alone would seem to impose a limit to equalisation: 'Any cause which increases the absolute share of real income in the hands of the poor, provided that it does not lead to a contraction in the size of the national dividend from any point of view, will, in general, increase economic welfare.'[15] Impressed as well by Marshall's reliance on taxes and subsidies to shepherd resources into social optimality, Pigou in the same book fell back on the same weapons to bring the marginal *private* net cost into line with the marginal *social* net cost. A tax on pollution would discourage the unwanted externality of one person's smoking chimney, another person's laundry bill. A subsidy to research would encourage the productive spillover of one person's silent contemplation, another person's improved yield. The net result would be a more satisfying allocation of resources than the free market left to itself would have been able to promote. Equalisation of sacrifice and opportunity, regulation of production and consumption – it is easy to see why philosophical socialists as well as economic theoreticians should have been so attracted by the force of the Pigovian deductions.

British interventionism owes much to the redistribution and the justice that may be pyramided upon Pigou's non-party-political calculus of subjectivity and satisfaction. Hugh Dalton, one of Pigou's earliest tutees at King's College, Cambridge, has written as follows about the impact on his development of his former tutor's *Wealth and Welfare* of 1912: 'It was a book that helped me, more than any other, to formulate my own approach from ethics, through politics, to economics. He was splendidly free from party or class prejudice, but he believed, as Marshall did before him, that great inequalities of wealth and opportunity are both unjust and wasteful of welfare.'[16] Anthony Crosland, similarly, read Pigou at an impressionable age – and not least the *Socialism versus Capitalism* of 1937 in which the pious disciple who loved to say that 'it's all in Marshall' appeared to be brushing aside the reservations of the master with respect to the State ownership of a natural monopoly. Marshall, Pigou said, had anticipated that nationalisation would be followed by a bureaucratisation of initiative that would stifle novelty and retard advance.

Marshall's model had been the governmental department like the Post Office, dependent and directed. It had not been the semi-autonomous public corporation like the London Passenger Transport Board, set up in 1933 by Herbert Morrison with a view to boosting efficiency by means of devolution to management.

   Marshall, Pigou said, had not foreseen that the new model of short-run operational independence, overall public accountability, would allow the advantages of market alertness to be matched up with the attractions of democratic supervision in such a way as to ensure that the community as a whole secured the maximum of welfare from the exploitation of its economies of size. Had Marshall lived on into the '30s, Pigou inferred, he would have been less willing to settle for State regulation when public ownership had become so viable an option. Pigou's own set of targets extended to armaments and the Bank of England certainly, coal and the railways probably, water, gas, electricity possibly – 'If all went well, further steps towards nationalisation of important industries would be taken by degrees.'[17] The path was to be the path of gradualness; but still the destination was more and more likely to be an economy that was mixed.

Pigou was a pragmatist on the middle ground. So was John Maynard Keynes, whose Sidney Ball Lecture of 1925 on 'The End of Laissez-Faire' contained the following warning to dogmatic libertarians not to expect the impossible from the invisible hand: 'The world is *not* so governed from above that private and social interest always coincide. It is *not* so managed here below that in practice they coincide. It is *not* a correct deduction from the principles of economics that enlightened self-interest always operates in the public interest. Nor is it true that self-interest generally *is* enlightened.... Experience does *not* show that individuals, when they make up a social unit, are always less clear-sighted than when they act separately.'[18] Sometimes the part is more clear-sighted than the whole. Sometimes the structure is more clear-sighted than the atom. Trapped in an eternal discussion-group that recognises no permanent frontiers between market and State, it was the essence of the Keynesian message that the political economist must have the courage not to parrot but instead to think.

   Keynes himself cannot be described as an admirer of indiscriminate *dirigisme*: State socialism, he wrote in 1926, 'is, in fact, little better than a dusty survival of a plan to meet the problems of fifty years ago'.[19] Keynes himself welcomed the exchange mechanism at the very least because it was a psychological safety-valve through which 'dangerous human proclivities can be canalised into comparatively harmless channels': 'It is better that a man should tyrannise over his bank balance than over his fellow – citizens.'[20] Yet Keynes was a Cambridge realist who acknowledged that free markets sometimes fail; and that, when they do, there must be a strong case for a prudent leadership that leans as effectively against the forces of nature as does a skilled dentist when he squares up to a decaying tooth. Keynes's *General Theory* of 1936 was a macroeconomist's account of markets that let the side down and of governments that save the day.

Automaticity had demonstrably failed to reduce the level of unemployment below 10 per cent for more than a decade. The coordinated reduction of absolute wages (relative wages remaining unaffected) is a theoretical impossibility in a decentralised economy. Thriftiness (pushed by the fear of idleness and not pulled by the rate of interest) cuts total demand even if inflexible wages do not cut households' incomes. Under-consumption (long anticipated by the critics of Say's Law from Malthus and Marx to Hobson and Mummery) generates no self-correcting alternative to gluts and surpluses. The market, Keynes concluded, had condemned the economy to an under-employment equilibrium – and the State was needed to move the capitalists and the workers alike into a less wasteful, less stagnant utilisation of productive capacity. Thus it was that Keynes came down in favour of public spending and public works, the budget deficit and demand-management. His reasoning can be debated, his tacit assumption of omniscience and beneficence rejected as an illegitimate extension of Bloomsbury elitism, but at least there can be no doubt as to his underlying model: the dentist corrects the teeth, the State corrects the market, and the invisible hand is sometimes not visible for the simple reason that it is simply not there.

Keynes was not a socialist. Speaking of Marxism, he dismissed it as 'a creed which, preferring the mud to the fish, exalts the boorish proletariat above the bourgeois and the intelligentsia who, with whatever faults, are the quality in life': 'How can I accept a doctrine which sets up as its bible, above and beyond criticism, an obsolete economic textbook which I know to be not only scientifically erroneous but without interest or application for the modern world?'[21] Speaking of Labour, he scorned it as 'a class party, and the class is not my class': 'The *class* war will find me on the side of the educated *bourgeoisie*.'[22] Unfriendly to the boorish workers and their equally boorish unions, opposed to wholesale nationalisation and in favour of managed capitalism, Keynes never secured a personal foothold in the Labour Party even when the National Government following the 1931 election made the Party appear a wiser and a tamer beast. Personalities as well as viewpoints clashed. Keynes made little effort to conceal his contempt for the less-educated socialists. The socialists made little effort to conceal what they thought of Keynes's fabled arrogance.

Keynesian economics was, of course, a different matter. Widely discussed by Party economists like Jay, Dalton, Durbin, Gaitskell and Clark in the New Fabian Research Bureau (established in 1931) and the XYZ Club (set up in 1932), in Labour day-schools and university seminars, Keynes's ideas seemed to coincide almost by accident with much that socialists had come to regard as the hard core of their mission. Keynes had shown that unemployment need not be a work-shy shirker's self-inflicted default and could be the natural consequence of a collective failing. Keynes had provided a theoretical justification for the public projects that the results-minded governments of Roosevelt and Hitler were already funding in an attempt, priming the pump, to get the involuntarily idle back into wealth-creation. Keynes had been so offended by the unpatriotic acquisitiveness of a parasitical plutocracy that he had spoken of 'the euthanasia of the rentier'[23] in order to release for productive investment the savings that had been so conservatively squirrelled away. Keynes had indicated that economic growth was steadily reducing the relative urgency of vulgar materialism: 'Assuming no important wars and no important increase in population, the *economic problem* may be solved, or at least within sight of a solution, within a hundred years. This means that the economic problem is not – if we look into the future – *the permanent problem of the human race.*'[24] Keynes, it is clear, had said much with which the Labour interventionists and the Labour moralists could readily identify themselves despite the fact that Keynes was on balance an advocate of the private-enterprise market whereas the British Left had a long-standing interest in socialisation and control.

Particularly important was the overlap of opinion in respect of the Pigovian pollutant of unequal incomes. Roy Jenkins has written as follows about the coincidental similarities that unexpectedly linked the prophets of the new order to the technocrats of the *status quo*: 'Keynes was not interested in socialism, and was never a supporter of the Labour Party. But the impact of his teaching was greatly to strengthen the socialist hand. The Labour Party had always favoured more equality, because it believed that great inequalities of wealth and income were wrong in themselves and were distributively inefficient, since they reduced the total welfare which could be obtained from a given national income. Keynes pronounced no judgement on this issue, but he set alongside it the equally important point that, in the circumstances of the time, such inequalities were also productively inefficient, since they led to a low propensity to consume and the consequent restriction of investment opportunities.'[25] A good case should not, of course, be pressed too far. Counter-cyclical Keynesianism only legitimates downward redistribution in a slump or recession: In a period of inflation it shifts its loyalties to the rich with a surplus to save. Also, Hobson and the Labour under-consumptionists (without, however, the support of a Labour leadership determined to nationalise capitalism and not to rationalise it) had sought in documents like *The Living Wage* (1926) to protect demand by means of protected pay; whereas Keynes, opposed to a minimum wage, agreeable to real wage cuts through rising price-levels, wanted expansion wherever possible to be investment-led rather than the short-sighted consequence of savings extinguished in order to pay for consumer demand. More interventionist than Keynes, moreover, some of the Keynesians of the Left wanted not only investment-led stabilisation but also government-led investment: proposals for a National Investment Board and for nationalisation of industry in order to produce a degree of microeconomic control without which the macroeconomic fine-tuning would peter out into nothing demonstrate just how much the socialists altered Keynes even as they incorporated him. Differences there obviously were as well as the similarities. Even so, it is striking that Keynes on market failure should have had so much in common with the non-Marxian socialism of the Labour Party which Anthony Crosland joined two years before the appearance of the *General Theory*.

Keynes could talk to Labour but was happy to be a Liberal: 'Great changes will not be carried out except with the active aid of Labour. But they will not be sound or enduring unless they have first satisfied the criticism and precaution of Liberals.'[26] Keynes's assertion that the Liberals were the true vanguard of reform is a salutary reminder that Labour was not the only party that was committed to correcting the inefficiencies and injustices of the market order. Under Gladstone the Whigs had invested heavily in freedom of trade and the minimal State, the inexorability of natural law and the ineluctability of personal responsibility: while a mix of paternalism and spillovers will account for apparent exceptions such as the Education Act of 1870, still the liberal faith tended to the norm of the man *versus* the State and to a Spencerian Darwinism that proclaimed the 'stern truth' that 'all socialism involves slavery'.[27] Later the Liberals were to experience a crisis of conscience as to what, precisely, it meant to be a party of individual emancipation and personal unfolding. An intellectual catalyst for the new Liberalism of assisted take-off and empowered development was the Balliol Hegelian T.H. Green, who pointed to the hungry without money, the cold without work, in support of his contention that 'the mere removal of compulsion, the mere enabling a man to do as he likes, is in itself no contribution to true freedom'.[28] By the time of Asquith the new Liberals were investing heavily in civic duty and the integrated community, the collective hand up and the reform of the social whole that had let down the individual part: thence the old age pensions (1908), the surtax on higher incomes (1909), the national health insurance (1911), the sickness, unemployment and maternity benefits (1912). Fiscal intervention (as opposed to socialist appropriation) had an especial appeal to Lloyd George and other Liberals who shared his quasi-Fabian indictment of 'functionless' wealth and the 'unearned' surplus: 'In this respect', Peter Clarke observes, 'the new Liberalism was not proto-socialist but revisionist.'[29] Not Bevanite but Gaitskellite, what is clear is that the engineered equalisation of opportunities and of outcomes was a conspicuous part of the new Liberalism even before the First World War.

Hobhouse, the Hammonds and Graham Wallas continued to refine the perspectives of a reforming Liberalism that saw the value of *freedom to*. So, importantly, did William Beveridge, whose famous report on *Social Insurance and Allied Services* (1942) was a veritable blueprint for an active State, 'up and doing'. Laski from Labour wrote to Beveridge that his comprehensive proposals, published a few days after Monty's victory over Rommel at El Alamein which many saw as the turning point of the war, were indeed the route from 'the cradle to the grave' that would properly be adopted in the peacetime collectivism of a managed reconstruction: 'Your Report is the test of whether we can make democracy viable.... Do fight for your principles; their enemies are the enemies of light.'[30] An anonymous Nazi, familiar no doubt with the statism of the German Historical School and the welfarism of Bismarck's social insurance, was evidently not convinced that Beveridge's principles offered little or nothing to the enemies of light. Writing to Hitler (the documents were discovered in 1945 in the Führer's final bunker), the anonymous Fascist was generous in his praise for a plan which he identified as 'an especially obvious proof that our enemies are taking over national-socialistic ideas'.[31] History does not record if the anonymous Nazi had access to *The Road to Serfdom* of 1944 in which Hayek, expounding the thesis that interventionism and freedom could not be combined, had insisted that the slippery slope ran straight from well-intentioned reform to 'something so utterly different that few of those who now wish it would be prepared to accept the consequences': 'By the time Hitler came to power, liberalism was to all intents and purposes dead in Germany. And it was socialism that had killed it.'[32] The anonymous Nazi may or may not have had access to *The Road to Serfdom*, but Beveridge certainly did. The Director of the London School of Economics who in 1931 had tempted the Director of the Institute for Economic Research to take the road from Vienna, Beveridge was second to none in his admiration for the distinguished theoretician who was using the Reform Club to work on the *Road* at the same time that Beveridge was using it to work on the Report. Yet there was a difference between the fellow enemies of the enemies of light, and it hinged on the meaning of freedom. The Briton born in Austria was an old liberal in the Gladstone sense of *freedom from*. The Briton born in Bengal, on the other hand, was a new liberal in the Lloyd George sense of *freedom to*.

Social Insurance and Allied Services is a veritable blueprint for *freedom to*. The giant of Want is to be challenged through social insurance, family allowances, old age pensions and the statutory minimum wage; the giant of Disease through better housing, better sanitation, improved nutrition and a free medical service; the giant of Ignorance through raising the school-leaving age, extending access to the universities, expanding the network of adult education; the giant of Squalor through State planning to restrict the location of industry, to stimulate more pleasant surroundings, to develop a good infrastructure of public transport. As for the giant of Idleness, Beveridge, like Keynes, looked to fiscal policy for full employment – and, unlike Keynes, to direct controls where the price mechanism was unable to contain the Pigovian pollutant of macroeconomic instability. So concerned was Beveridge about price inflation in a sellers' market, so impressed was he by the effectiveness of wartime planning, that in his 1944 book on *Full Employment in a Free Society* he seemed to be predicting that an incomes policy would be necessary to remedy a market failure: 'There is no inherent mechanism in our present system, which can with certainty prevent competitive sectional bargaining for wages from setting up a vicious spiral of rising prices under full employment.'[33]

Beveridge's inference that the power of the unions would have to be curbed was unlikely to have been shared by the Labour mainstream. Nor was his relative neglect of economic regulation nor, needless to say, his insistence on 'socializing demand rather than production'[34] which was taken to be a rejection of all but the minimum of nationalisation. Beveridge's emphasis on State-sector welfare (as opposed to voluntary bodies and private charities) and his acceptance of bureaucratic inflexibilities (as opposed to market-sector negotiations) were, of course, unlikely to have made him very popular with the Hayek-type libertarians who believed so strongly in classical *laissez-faire*. Beveridge, caught between Left and Right, entertained no unrealistic hopes for the middle ground in its struggle to vanquish the five giants: 'Their defeat could not be secured without on the one hand state planning and on the other relaxation of Trades Union restrictions; two things which together would forfeit all the votes in the country.'[35] Practical politics might let him down – every Liberal by 1942 had heard that a thousand times before. Pragmatism and priorities, on the other hand, reassured him that he was right – since his new Liberalism, mouthing few dogmas, was targeted specifically on the blighted exchanges and the under-developed lives that a defaulting spontaneity had passed for redress to a reforming State that believed in *freedom to*.

Liberalism at the time of Cobden and Bright stood for what Adam Smith once encapsulated as 'peace, easy taxes, and a tolerable administration of justice'.[36] Liberalism by the time of Mark Bonham Carter and Jo Grimond had moved on to the middle ground of opportunity, redistribution, moderate regulation and relief as-of-right. One wonders in retrospect why Anthony Crosland believed he was a Labour man when he had personal reservations about further nationalisation and about the power of the unions; or why he chose to entitle his major work *The Future of Socialism* when its true subject was so transparently *The Future of the Centre-Left*. One suspects with hindsight that Anthony Crosland might have felt more comfortable championing equality and welfare with the Liberals than he ever did arguing capital versus labour with the hard-liners; and that his search for a new name for the Labour Party would have been unnecessary if he had simply joined the Liberal Party instead. The possibility must at any rate be acknowledged that Anthony Crosland was, regarded impartially, a Liberal amongst the Labourites, and that his impeded advancement may have owed something to the perception that he was a fish that had somehow mistaken its pool.

Ambitious to succeed, Crosland will have recognised that it made better sense to join a large party with a track-record in power than it did to join a small party that stood little chance of propelling him to high office. The fact that the Liberals in the election of 1959 secured only 5.9 per cent of the votes cast – and only six seats – will have demonstrated to Crosland, re-entering Parliament for Grimsby, that Labour was the better choice for a politician who wanted to get things done. Opportunism must have entered into his calculus; but so, most probably, will ideology and belief. Negatively speaking, Crosland is likely to have thought that much good could be done for the cause of equality and welfare simply by stopping the advocates of Clause IV and Ban the Bomb from destroying the credibility of the democratic Left. Positively speaking, moreover, Crosland is likely to have felt that Liberalism was not radical enough for the social upheaval that Labourism alone was in a position to bring about. The wealth tax, the comprehensive schools, the public ownership of development land – policies such as these are likely to have convinced Crosland that he was a genuine socialist and not a would-be Liberal in a mistaken pool. Critics will say that Crosland had a tendency to inflate the socialistness of his socialism (consider his hands-off tolerance towards the public schools) and to play down the reformism of the other parties (it was the Conservatives, after all, who were responsible for the capital gains tax and the pay-policy of a 'guiding light'). Critics will suggest that Crosland's insistence that he was a true socialist shows signs of a distorted self-image. They may even speculate that his indifference to a Lib–Lab pact with the Liberal Party might mean that he remained a young man rebelling against his roots.

Crosland may have chosen to race with an unexpected team, but at least he was not alone in so doing. The Conservative Prime Minister at the time of revisionism's triumph was himself a moderate on the middle ground who would have been a credit to a Liberal or even a Gaitskellite Cabinet. Harold Macmillan had been the Member for Stockton-on-Tees throughout the 1920s and 1930s when up to half of his male constituents were out of work and child poverty was the rule rather than the exception. Macmillan, appalled by what he had seen, had early come down in favour of social policies to assist the absolutely deprived. Able to contrast the comfort of Birch Grove and Chatsworth with the lice and malnutrition that preceded the Welfare State, the privileged Etonian reacted to the Five Giants of the Depression with a mixture of compassion and guilt that, described by the young Shinwell as 'sort of Fabian stuff', led him, in the words of the young Butler, to be 'suspected of being pink'.[37] Macmillan, like Keynes, was convinced that 'the era of strict *laissez-faire* has passed into history',[38] like Beveridge that squalor is a collective responsibility which no Good Samaritan has the moral right to shirk: 'Housing is not a question of Conservatism or Socialism. It is a question of humanity.'[39]

Macmillan in the 1930s had hoped to deal with macroeconomic instability by means of fiscal fine-tuning – and with microeconomic inefficiency through a 'planned economy, operated by the co-ordination of industry, finance and Government'.[40] Macmillan in the 1930s called for the nationalisation of the coal-mines and the railways. He also proposed the institution of a National Investment Board, operated with trade-union participation and briefed to favour the enhancement of productivity over paper speculations that generate no lasting wealth. Macmillan in 1938 set out his proposals for mix and equity – neither the 'intolerable restriction' of the totalitarian State nor the 'unfettered abuse of freedom' of the libertarian market[41] – in his deeply-felt treatise on *The Middle Way*. Twenty years on, a Centre-Right Prime Minister implementing a Centre-Right policy, Macmillan reaffirmed his faith in the typically British constructs of judgement and compromise: 'I believe today, as surely as I believed twenty years ago, that the only position in politics that we Conservatives can occupy with honour is the middle ground.'[42] Twenty years after that, a Centre-Right survivor about to criticise the monetarists and the privatisers for 'selling the family silver', he was rightly regarded by David Marquand as a middle-of-the-roader who had chosen to fight with an unexpected alliance: 'There is at least a case for saying that the most impressive social-democratic politician of the last 30 years was the author of *The Middle Way*, Harold Macmillan.'[43] Crosland may have been perceived by many to be a social democrat amongst the socialists; but at least he was not the only social democrat to have been suspected by his contemporaries of being a fish that had somehow mistaken its pool.

Both Crosland and Macmillan campaigned actively to keep their respective parties on the middle ground. Unlike Crosland, however, Macmillan was open to new coalitions even as he sought to moderate the extremes and the discordances that inhered in the *status quo*. Recognising how unsatisfactory it was for centrist democrats to be divided between the three major parties, Macmillan never excluded the possibility of realignment through the breaking of the mould. In 1931 he was attracted by Mosley's New Party because of its commitment to planning and to protection. In the mid-1930s he was active, with Archbishop Temple, Lord Cecil and centrists of all parties, in the Next Five Years Group that pressed for State intervention in support of employment and expansion: he is believed at the same time to have been contemplating a new Centre Party, presumably with Lloyd George and Herbert Morrison in prominent positions. In 1938, alarmed by the *Anschluss* and by Munich, he broached with Dalton the idea of a revived National Government to meet the foreign threat. In the late 1940s, a front bench spokesman for the party of property, he was privately in great sympathy with Morrison and the Labour Centre-Left on issues such as the nationalisation of coal ('This is an industry that has long passed out of the phase in which social purposes can best be served by the private profit incentive')[44] and the integration of education ('In so far as snobbery and class alienation exists in this country, it is largely a product of class differences in education'):[45] 'Our views were not very far apart',[46] he was able years later to reveal.

Also in the late 1940s Macmillan was exploring the possibility of a Lib–Con alliance with the Liberals (presumably in exchange for proportional representation) and was flirting with new names (the New Democratic Party was the front-runner) for a party that he was embarrassed to call Conservative. By the late 1950s, pleased in one sense that Labour under Gaitskell was moving on to the middle ground, he appears to have expressed a new concern about the threat to his own Government of the Centre-Right from the convergent moderation of the revisionist Centre-Left. The return to polarisation in the late 1970s reawakened his hopes for a new party of the *via media*. Refusing to join the Social Democrats in 1981 (he believed, correctly, that the refugees from Militant would far outnumber the emigrés from Thatcherism in the idiosyncratic mix), he delayed his entry into the House of Lords until his 90th birthday in 1984 in case a new coalition should have need of his services. Macmillan, it is clear, never believed that what he once described as 'a party dominated by second-class brewers and company promoters'[47] was the ideal home for his amalgam of statism, capitalism and compassion. In contrast to Crosland, however, Macmillan took the view that an existing party could not be infinitely reformed. He therefore campaigned actively for new alliances that would perhaps be able to make him appear that much less of a fish that had somehow mistaken its pool.

Crosland's revisionism stands on the shoulders of Pigou and Keynes on market failure, of Beveridge and Macmillan on social reform. It is also in a tradition of Labour Party thinking that rejected the Marxian hypotheses but insisted nonetheless on radical change.

The Labour Representation Committee had been set up in 1900 to speak for the working classes and the trades unions but not specifically for socialism. The *raison d'être* for the new party had been expressed by Keir Hardie in the following words: 'I aim at a party which, on labour questions, shall lead Liberalism and the nation, and which shall not be content to play the part of a political Lazarus sitting at the gate of a rich man's party humbly begging crumbs from his table.'[48] The new Liberals were the party of welfare and redistribution (to such an extent, indeed, that influential members of the Fabian Society, founded in 1884, were initially hoping to collaborate with them) but they were also the party of the employing class. Thence the argument for a new party that would provide political representation for the blue collar on a wage.

Labour entered Parliament in 1906: Ramsay MacDonald (widely perceived even then as a Liberal in all but name) had been responsible for a secret pact whereby only five of the 29 Members returned had had to stand against a Liberal candidate. In 1918 the party became socialist as well as labourist when its new Constitution (drafted in the wake of wartime collectivism and the Russian Revolution) committed it to the nationalisation of industry. Labour became the official Opposition in 1923 and fielded its first Prime Minister (MacDonald) in 1924. In 1931 MacDonald was forced into a National Government with the Liberals and the Conservatives by the refusal of international bankers to lend to a Britain governed by

Labour: MacDonald was subsequently accused of betraying his class and was expelled from the Party. In the 1930s Strachey and Laski openly questioned the possibility of a peaceful transition to socialism; while Cripps and Brockway defended unity and collaboration with the Communist Party. Attlee became the Leader of the Labour Party in 1935 (he was the successor to George Lansbury, Christian, pacifist and moderate). In 1945 he became the Prime Minister. In 1950 Anthony Crosland began his career in the House as the Labour Member for South Gloucestershire.

Crosland was the heir to half a century of names and dates. He was also the heir to the authors and the books that had given the moderate Left a distinctive identity all its own. Crosland's revisionism would appear to owe an especial debt to the work of five Labour thinkers who had speculated on the future of democratic socialism in the inter-war period of Depression and poverty. Those five thinkers were Cole, Tawney, Dalton, Jay and Durbin.

G.D.H. Cole expressed his support for national economic coordination in his *Principles of Economic Planning* (1935). He also argued strongly in favour of extensive public ownership. Nationalisation would assist the planners to avoid economic crises and to accelerate economic growth. It would also confer a non-material social benefit: in so far as socialisation reduced the differences between equal citizens, it would be likely to improve the integration and the sense of community of a nation that, as a whole, has a different feel from the sum of its parts. The warmth of cohesiveness is a social impossibility, Cole maintained, so long as there is a social divide between the class that supplies the labour and the class that hires the hands: 'A Society that rests upon a class basis can attain to unity only by the destruction of its basis and the substitution of democracy for capitalism.'[49]

Cole denied that the problem of low pay and widespread destitution could adequately be addressed through the redistribution of income without the nationalisation of capital. He further advised the nationalisers that equitable consumption could not be the essence of socialism so long as power too remains a difference that divides: 'Higher wages will not make less dreary or automatic the life of the worker who is subjected to bureaucratic expert control and divorced from all freedom and responsibility.'[50] Opposed to slavery as well as to poverty, Cole had put forward a guild socialist's vision of participation and involvement in his aptly-titled early work *Self-Government in Industry* (1917). There his commitment to self-determination through personal activity led him to make the following recommendation: 'The control of industry should be democratised.... The workers themselves should have an ever-increasing measure of power and responsibility in control.'[51]

What this would mean in practice would not be worker-ownership on the syndicalist model and not (lest exploitative pricing seize the place intended for good citizenship) the workplace distribution of the economic surplus. The State would hold the property-rights and would cream off the profits to enterprise – in that sense the term *national*isation was to mean precisely what it said. On the other hand, the shop-floor was to influence and to participate – to that extent the cooperative ethos was to live on through a more consultative and less authoritarian system of management. The unions were to be the channel through which the preferences of the rank-and-file were to be communicated upwards and compromises negotiated. Within the unions, moreover, it was the shop stewards who were the most likely to be in touch with grassroots opinion: 'The only way of securing real democracy in the national Trade Union movement is by building it up on a basis of real democracy locally.'[52] Shop stewards in nationalised undertakings were in Cole's opinion the proper channel for power-sharing. Worker-directors in capitalist corporations were not: such an exercise in tokenism would be worse than no consultation at all since, lending a spurious legitimacy to the never-legitimate, it 'varnishes the class-structure of industry instead of destroying it'.[53]

R.H. Tawney, like G.D.H. Cole, was a Labour thinker who wanted to restructure the economic order and not simply to redecorate it. Tawney was opposed to the 'functionless perversion'[54] of private property whereby the passive and the absent enjoy a license to garner 'income irrespective of any personal service rendered'[55] in the form of mineral royalties, ground rents, monopoly profits, *rentier* dividends and other rights that come without duties attached. Tawney was shocked by the economic wastes of competitive duplication and anarchic under-provision ('Pits are drowned out by water, because companies cannot agree to apportion between them the costs of a common drainage system');[56] by the overhead extravagance of 'the whole apparatus of adulteration, advertisement and quackery which seems inseparable from the pursuit of profit as the main standard of industrial success';[57] by the market dominance of manipulative cartels and the entry barrier of scale economies ('No one can argue that a monopolist is impelled by "an invisible hand" to serve the public interest').[58] Tawney was saddened that remuneration without personal service in combination with the slippages of gain-seeking private enterprise should have produced a labour-side disequilibrium in which the worker-craftsman, unconsulted, demoralised and uninvolved, was alienated from the work to which his professionalism could otherwise have contributed so much: 'It is idle to expect that men will give their best to any system which they do not trust, or that they will trust any system in the control of which they do not share.'[59] Dissatisfied with the ethics and the economics of capitalism, Tawney, like Cole, sought to bend back the bent rod through an ambitious programme of nationalisation (beginning with the commanding heights occupied by stranglehold industries: 'The mopping up of the remainder will follow in good time')[60] and of consultation (thereby releasing the latent resource of 'active and constructive cooperation on the part of the rank and file').[61] Tawney, like Macmillan, could see much scope for legislative regulation as well: witness his proposals for a National Investment Board and a statutory minimum wage. In contrast to the Liberals and the Liberal-Conservatives, however, Tawney could envisage no tolerable future that did not involve extensive socialisation and extensive participation as the economic precondition for a just and integrated community.

Tawney, like Macmillan, was attracted by the ideal of citizenship, solidarity, and One Nation not torn apart by culture: 'What a community requires, as the word itself suggests, is a common culture, because, without it, it is not a community at all.'[62] Nationalisation and participation would help to reduce the perceived gap between the arrogant and the servile, the privileged and the luckless; but so too would equalisation of condition through fiscal socialism (death duties, progressive taxes, income support) and welfare services (housing, health, education). Schooling, central to culture and to opportunity alike, was of crucial significance in Tawney's socialism: 'The English educational system will never be one worthy of a civilized society until the children of all classes in the nation attend the same schools.'[63] Tawney, like Crosland, was nonetheless unprepared to recommend the outright abolition of the private sector, isolated and expensive. Arguing as he did that the public school system had done 'more than any other single cause, except capitalism itself, to perpetuate the division of the nation into classes',[64] his tolerant individualism is a reminder that the inevitability of gradualness even to the Tawney of the inter-war years could inevitably be very gradual indeed.

Tawney was at his most militant in the classic manifestos of *The Acquisitive Society* (1920) and *Equality* (1931) that were to be so much of an inspiration to Attlee's reformers. Later on, mix and welfare in place, he could afford to be more pragmatic about the next step. The following statement, from 'Social Democracy in Britain', shows that Tawney in 1949 was able to anticipate by seven years Crosland's look-and-see approach to the future of nationalisation: 'Whether in any particular instance, it is desirable or not is a question to be decided in the light, not of resounding affirmations of the virtues either of free enterprise or of socialization, but of the facts of the case.'[65] Apparently more Gaitskellite than Bevanite in his post-Attlee years, it was probably with complete sincerity that Tawney wrote to the new Labour Leader in 1955 to compliment the Party on the wisdom of its choice: 'It was a great pleasure to know that one whose courage, in addition to other qualities, I admire is to be in command.'[66] In 1960 (so did Attlee and Dalton) Tawney lent his support to the Campaign for Democratic Socialism that had been formed to endorse Gaitskell's resistance to the leftist pressures of the Clause IV traditionalists.[67] Certain questions remain unanswered – one is why Tawney is reported to have put down *The Future of Socialism* 'with some anxiety';[68] another is what Tawney was able to make of secular rationalists who could not share the Christian socialist's Christian conviction that capitalism was 'not so much un-Christian as anti-Christian'.[69] Overall, however, it is clear that Tawney, never formally a revisionist himself, had much in common with the moderates and the modernisers of the 1950s. And, of course, they with him: 'I always think of him as *the* Democratic Socialist *par excellence*',[70] Hugh Gaitskell said at the Memorial Service for R.H. Tawney in 1962.

Crosland's revisionism owed much to the work of Cole and Tawney. It was also much influenced by Hugh Dalton and his *Practical Socialism for Britain* (1935). On the one hand there was the divisiveness of MacDonald and the aggressiveness of the dictators. On the other hand there was the stagnation of unemployment and the pessimism of the Marxists. Dalton's programmatic synthesis, more than just a tract for the times, had sought to demonstrate, as Crosland's *Future* was itself later to do, that democracy and expenditure both pointed clearly to the middle way of the Centre-Left.

Dalton's socialism was a socialism that attacked the deprivation and the distance that, wasting talent, restricting initiative, choking off comradeship, retarded growth and devalued citizenship: 'Socialists seek, by the abolition of poverty and the establishment of social equality, to build a prosperous and classless society.'[71] Dalton's socialism was a socialism of liberation *from* want and of freedom *to* develop: 'Intellectuals are apt to put too much stress on freedom of opinion and its expression. Even more fundamental is freedom to eat sufficient food, to occupy sufficient house room, to possess sufficient clothes, to enjoy sufficient comforts and amenities, to be able to live like a human being.'[72] Dalton's socialism was also a socialism of performance that had little time for the duplication of capacity, the absence of coordination, the arrogance of authority that had so discredited the supply of electricity, the coal mines, the manufacture of armaments and other key areas of the Depression-years capitalist economy. Those areas were, he said, in no small measure 'a story of wasteful inefficiency, of lack of enterprise, and of high profits based on high charges drawn from lazy local monopolists.'[73] Just as equalisation of outcome and empowerment through opportunity were central objectives in Dalton's socialism, so too, it is clear, was the correction of a market failure about which the LSE Reader in Economics had read so much in the economics of Marshall and Pigou.

The ends selected, the next step was to identify the means. Equalisation of outcomes was to be entrusted to higher and steeply-graduated death duties (levied on inheritances received rather than estates left behind and payable where appropriate in land and securities); a gifts tax to discourage passive acquisition and a capital levy to break up agglomerated wealth; a progressive income tax that knew when incentives imposed ceilings and made it necessary for the confiscation to stop; a reliable system of unemployment benefits and poverty relief that, no substitute for the eradication of the causes, would be able at least to alleviate the symptoms. Empowerment through opportunity was to be the responsibility of a school-leaving age raised to 15 and then to 16 and of better school-buildings with smaller classes, maintenance grants for older schoolchildren and university grants for tertiary students, town planning for slum clearance and re-housing schemes to re-settle and upgrade. Then there was the economy; and here even the middle way led directly to more public ownership and more State control.

Nationalisation with fair compensation makes no direct contribution to the equality of wealth. What it does is to facilitate the creation of self-financing public corporations in under-performing areas of industry. Transferring their economic surplus to the Exchequer, collaborating with the unions through works councils and pit committees, improving their service to the community above all, the 'cold antiquated waiting-rooms with prehistoric furniture'[74] of private-sector corporations give way to the improved facilities and lower prices of the State-sector successor that is so convincing an argument for the transfer of title: 'With plain men', Dalton writes, 'only inefficiency can discredit Socialism in action'.[75] Public ownership can be efficient. Public ownership can also be just. Dalton's example of justice involves not the Marxian deduction of surplus value (in British socialism, Dalton observes, 'Marxian influence has been small')[76] but rather the toil-free increment of the demand-led reward: 'The land, which no man has created, but which forms the physical basis of our life, should belong to the community, not to a few favoured members of it.'[77] Dalton regards the separation of remuneration from function as morally unacceptable. His logic is the work-ethic and not the exploitation of labour. His argument is that it is unseemly for a gentleman to reap where he never troubled first of all to sow.

Nationalisation can contribute to regulation: witness the way in which the public ownership of land can influence the location of new towns and industries, the way in which the socialisation of the Bank of England can improve the sensitivity of monetary policy. Nationalisation can contribute but it is not the *sine qua non*. A National Investment Board can license and channel new issues without itself needing to supply the resources. Regional planners can insist on factories before dog-tracks without having themselves to provide the plant. Nationalisation can support control, but still control will often be sufficient by itself to protect the public interest. The student of Pigou and the colleague of Robbins, Dalton knew that laws could be drafted to preserve an open space or to compel the use of smoke-less fuel, that subsidised loans could encourage industrial reequipment and that discriminatory taxation could ration away the luxury trades. Laws can steer and direction can direct. The nationalisation of private property-rights, always a means and never an end, must not therefore be confused with the equalisation, the empowerment and the efficiency that are the true essence of the socialist's message.

Advocating regulation, supporting control, Dalton was *de facto* a planner in the very obvious sense that he ranked conscious choice above automaticity and accident: 'Planning or drifting, looking ahead or living from hand to mouth, are two different styles of conduct. I should define Economic Planning, in its widest sense, as the deliberate direction, by persons in control of large resources, of economic activities towards chosen ends.... A good plan, well executed, is always better than no plan at all.'[78] Dalton had visited the Soviet Union in 1932 with the New Fabian Research Bureau. There he had seen for himself how capital could be mobilised and resources targeted at a time when free enterprise in Britain was so frequently at variance with what he believed to be the public's interest: 'Advances are often made to mere speculators, and to assist busi-nesses which have no social utility, but are often withheld from socially valuable and financially sound undertakings.'[79] Dalton had, moreover, returning to academia from politics after the temporary loss of his seat in 1931, been in a position to draw the quasi-Marxian, pre-Galbraithian infer-ence from scholarly works like Berle and Means's *The Modern Corporation and Private Property* in 1932, Joan Robinson's *The Economics of Imperfect Competition* in 1933, that private planning in cor-porate capitalism was elevating power in economics to the throne occu-pied (in 'a short and peculiar phase in our history') by individualism and rivalry: 'Free enterprise.... is not a phrase which accurately describes modern industry. In a large measure, free enterprise has vanished. But private enterprise, by no means the same thing, remains the dominant type of economic organisation.'[80] Dominant, predominant – and lacking in the mandate and the accountability that alone would make the private plan morally acceptable in a democratic society. Recent trends in capitalism,

Dalton wrote, 'have strengthened the case for Socialism, by concentrating real power in the hands of a small number of men, who have come to exercise a dangerously dictatorial influence over our economic and financial life'.[81] Advocating regulation, supporting control, Dalton wanted to politicise and to democratise the power to plan that could be 'dangerously dictatorial' when exercised by cliques and oligarchs.

Crosland's 'The Transition from Capitalism', Crosland's *The Future of Socialism*, are in the tradition of Cole and Tawney, of Hugh Dalton and his *Practical Socialism for Britain*. They are also in the tradition of *The Socialist Case* by Douglas Jay, published in 1937 and clearly the work of a man who had passed through the brook of fire of *The General Theory* in the previous year.

Douglas Jay presented his socialism as a declaration of war on the deprivation and the distance of *laissez-faire* capitalism. Deprivation – because 'acute economic privation is an immeasurable evil',[82] chronic absolute impoverishment 'the cause of almost all other evils' and 'an almost impassable barrier to the things that give value to human life':[83] 'The fundamental case for socialism rests on the necessity to alleviate economic privation.'[84] Distance – because inequality of outcome is an evil in itself and 'because it is a cause of poverty': 'One of the chief reasons why the poor are very poor is that the rich are very rich. Only when there is more than enough for all can unlimited inequality be possible without poverty.... At present, there is not more than enough for all. At present, therefore, poverty and inequality imply one another, and poverty cannot be removed without some mitigation of inequality.'[85] Jay's *Case* is an attack on poverty and inequality. Crosland's *Socialism* is a defence of welfare and equality. The *Socialism* was in the tradition of the *Case*. Jay was understandably satisfied with Crosland's *Future*. In his *Socialism and the New Society* (the sequel of 1962 in which Jay informs the reader that 'Social-Democracy in this book is used as synonymous with Socialism')[86] Jay puts on record his appreciation for Crosland's 'pioneering and highly persuasive book'.[87]

Jay recalls Marshall in his belief that the redistribution of purchasing-power (a contrast to the scepticism of Robbins and Hayek in respect of the comparison of subjective intensities) is likely to raise the sum total of happiness in society: 'We have no doubt that a community in which everyone is enabled to be reasonably prosperous is better than one in which the majority are destitute and a few are luxuriously affluent. We have no doubt that it is justifiable to increase the happiness of a large number of comparatively ill-provided people at the expense of a sacrifice by a few of

the best-provided ones.... To deny these propositions would be absurd.'[88]
Jay recalls Pigou in his insistence that incentives and growth must to all
levellers impose a ceiling to the Robin Hood transfer that will by some
levellers be taken to indicate a floor and a target as well: 'There is a
certain point beyond which greater equality will mean greater poverty for
all, individually as well as collectively; and beyond that point it would
clearly be foolish to go. But it would also be foolish to stop short of it.'[89]
Jay recalls Tawney in his condemnation of the uncommon culture ('a false
servility and sycophancy on the one hand, ... a false complacence on the
other')[90] and in his stigmatisation of reward without service: 'The traditional socialist belief that unearned incomes are the main removable cause
of poverty and inequality is true and of dominating importance.'[91] Jay also
recalls Keynes – since it was the brook of fire of 1936 that allowed him to
couple the over-saving of the rich with the unemployment and insecurity
of the poor in his proposals for a war on poverty that would be a campaign
against inequality as well.

   The proposals themselves bear the unmistakeable stamp of the pedigree
and the tradition. Jay envisaged only a limited rise in the rate of personal
income-tax ('No very great increase in the tax on earned incomes, except
the highest, is desirable beyond the point already reached, at any rate in
Great Britain')[92] but a considerable reliance on the confiscatory bite of
stricter inheritance-duties ('Inheritance, and its consequence, inherited
income, ought as far as possible to be abolished').[93] Jay was in favour of
family allowances, improved educational opportunities, tax-remissions for
commodities consumed disproportionately by the poor. Jay could also see
a role for public ownership – but not on the Marxian grounds that the divisions between the haves and the have-nots were a function of capital and
the power that it conferred: 'Socialists have been mistaken in making
ownership of the means of production instead of ownership of inherited
property the test of socialization.'[94]

   Jay did not argue for public ownership in the language of class and
command (since it was to him the transmission of title rather than its
detention that was the real problem) or seek to justify it with reference to
poverty and inequality (since the compensation paid would ensure that
'practically no redistribution'[95] would result from a process that was
essentially only the swap of one asset for an equivalent in value). Instead,
he tended to argue for nationalisation on the basis either of an unearned
increment (the logic behind the contention that 'there is no form of socialism more desirable than the ownership of land and houses, and therefore
of rent, by the State')[96] or of a market failure (as where the Bank of
England in the private sector would lack the incentive to control the

money-supply and private gas or private rail would be strongly tempted to squeeze from the consumer the profit surplus of the natural monopoly). Sometimes unethical, sometimes inefficient, Jay argued, case-by-case assessment would sometimes mean that private enterprise would have to be bought out by the State.

Sometimes it would. More frequently it would not – so long as the Watchful State were prepared to regulate and to legislate, to prescribe decent working conditions and to protect the security of employment. So long as the Watchful State were prepared to intervene, it could normally be excused the burden of ownership. Jay like Dalton criticised past social-ists for exaggerating the importance of property: 'Control seems simply to have been confused with ownership',[97] he said sadly of the knee-jerk nationalisers. Jay like Dalton stressed that very frequently a good law was all that was needed.

Even control, however, had to be kept within limits: 'Partial interfer-ence with the price system is possible but wholesale destruction of it is not desirable.'[98] Jay believed that the supply-and-demand mechanism could legitimately be modified in places but that it had nonetheless to be retained overall as the most reliable guide to the *what* and the *how much* of produc-tion. The price system was attractive to the socialist because it was effect-ive in the allocation of outputs. No less was the market attractive to the socialist because it was tolerant of the individual's choices: 'Those who wish to "plan" everybody's consumption should recall what their feelings are in a restaurant when they order green peas and the waitress brings them onions.'[99] Of course the distribution of purchasing power had first to be made socially acceptable through taxes and subsidies, lest economic automaticity put the rich man's cigar before the impoverished child's milk. The redistribution accomplished, however, freedom *from* had then to take over from freedom *to* in order to ensure that even the less well-off were treated with respect: 'Just as in fact liberty is worthless to a starving man, but of incalculable value to one with just enough to eat; so con-sumers' choice is worthless to a penniless man, but of incalculable value to one with just enough to live on.'[100] *The Socialist Case* was evidently a case for markets and choices at the same time as it was a case for equalisa-tion and empowerment. Crosland was in the circumstances probably underestimating the thrust of the authors' contribution when he described Jay's book and that of Dalton as deficient in evolutionary economics: 'These and similar books dealt essentially with short-term problems, and contained no long-run analysis of the future of capitalism.'[101] The truth in respect of the British mixed economy is almost certainly somewhat differ-ent – that Jay like Dalton had seen the future and had seen that it was essentially the same as the present minus the occasional wrinkles that it would be the task of the socialists effectively to iron out.

Crosland's revisionism stood on the shoulders of Jay and Dalton, of Tawney and Cole. It also stood on the shoulders of a fifth Labour thinker, Evan Durbin, whose widely-read *The Politics of Democratic Socialism* was published in 1940. The *Politics* was read in manuscript by Tawney and Gaitskell: the latter had also read and commented on the draft of Jay's *Socialist Case*. Had Gaitskell returned to university life after the war, he might well have wanted to complete Durbin's *The Economics of Democratic Socialism*, left unfinished when the LSE economist turned Labour Member for Edmonton was drowned in a swimming accident in 1948, aged only 42.

Durbin, like Gaitskell, had been tutored by Lionel Robbins at New College, Oxford. Robbins was content to take the individual as the unit of analysis. Durbin was not: the son of a Baptist Minister in Devon, brought up on strict ethics (alcohol and theatre-going were forbidden), taught the value of community service (which in the case of his parents extended to the State-sponsored safety-net of Lloyd George's interventionist Liberalism), Durbin believed that 'we are not only parts of a society, but society is part of us'.[102] Durbin was convinced that the social cake could not meaningfully be factored down to the individual ingredients: 'A pile of bricks is not a building. In the same way a mere aggregate of human beings is not a society.'[103] Durbin regarded the social matrix as at once a cause of and an emanation from the individual's will. Methodologically speaking, his two-way model made him want to explain the complex of patterned relationships in terms of institutional life as well as of individual choice. Morally speaking, his sensitivity to organic interdependencies, to integration and belonging, reinforced his childhood communion of duty and made him a socialist with a commitment to care: 'The social services are, for all their deficiencies, a primitive recognition of human solidarity, a crude realization of the splendid idea of corporate responsibility for individual disaster, of the profound social truth that we are members one of another.'[104] I am I but I am also We – Durbin's socialism is closely linked to his perception of the individual as a part of a structure and not as an atom alone.

Durbin wanted to reconcile the best of individualism with the best of belonging. His search for the whole of the duality rather than for the either/or part led him to the mixed economy. Durbin wanted to reconcile the best of free enterprise with the best of collective control – since the private sector, dynamic and progressive, was in his view indifferent to the cost of its unacceptable externalities: 'Expansion is', Durbin wrote, 'the great virtue of capitalism; inequality and insecurity are its greatest vices.'[105] Durbin wanted to reconcile the sustained material improvement of the capitalist market economy with the narrowing of intolerable relativities and the modulation of avoidable anxieties that were at the root of the engineered socialist complement.

The State, Durbin believed, had to supplement the market's shortfall in areas such as education and healthcare, unemployment benefits and old-age pensions. The State, he maintained, should implement counter-cyclical policies to ensure full employment and should even risk a budget deficit to pay for pump-priming investment in a severe recession. The State should also make imaginative use of regulatory legislation in order to secure, as may be illustrated with reference to Adam Smith's own example of the banking industry, a transfer of power without the need for a transfer of title: 'It is obvious that adequate control over the lending policy of the joint stock banks could be obtained in this country by measures far short of full social ownership.'[106] In some cases, of course, regulation by itself will not be enough; and then the State should not hesitate to take, say, a natural monopoly into the public sector. Durbin was in favour of the nationalisation of a 'considerable, but limited, section of the industrial system'[107] and of the establishment of a Supreme Economic Authority to plan the prices and coordinate the outputs of the public corporations. In special circumstances Durbin could see the advantages of State ownership and a national plan. In normal circumstances, however, it was his belief that the market sector, appropriately regulated, could be safely entrusted with the responsibility for growth.

Durbin welcomed rising living standard as an end in their own right. He also regarded growth as a means and an input, a cause of social progress and not simply a consequence of economic efficiency. Growth meant integration through *embourgeoisement* and a more common culture: 'The general increase in production, and the consequent rise in the standard of living, has attenuated to a marked degree the proletarian character of the proletariat.'[108] Growth was favourable to political democracy whereas bad times, at least in Germany, had 'swept away the faith of the people in the democratic method': 'Democracy was tolerable to the German people while things were going well.'[109] Growth was likely to foster moderate altruism and in that way to boost the popularity of the socialist party: 'Prosperity often moves the English electorate towards the left. The British people appear to feel more optimistic about reform, and less fearful of change, when they are doing well.'[110] To Durbin as to Crosland, it is clear, sustained growth was an intrinsic part of the socialist's enterprise.

Thus it was that Durbin repeatedly warned the British Left not to stifle the golden goose that had been so successful in delivering the goods.

Higher death duties safely attack a functionless privilege but higher income taxes represent a 'serious danger' to the accumulation of capital: 'If it goes much further the increase of taxation will wipe out social saving altogether, and leave us with a relatively stagnant economy.'[111] Moderate State intervention is a defence against exploiters and externalities but excessive State intervention means the *de facto* destruction of capitalism's main supports: 'Freedom of enterprise is dying.... In its place is appearing an ever-thickening jungle of uncoordinated government control, whose main purpose is restriction, and whose chief fruit is the substitution of monopoly for competition.'[112] The absentee shareholder is nowadays a functionless parasite ('He does nothing, he says nothing, he knows nothing. He is just paid an income')[113] but still the managerial revolution in itself is insufficient reason for the across-the-board socialisation of the joint-stock sector. In instance after instance, in short, Durbin left the reader in no doubt that his ideal was the middle way that reconciled the best of the market with the best of the State.

Some in the Labour Party did not think very highly of the middle way. Aneurin Bevan, speaking of *The Middle Way* and of its author, Harold Macmillan, made clear that he had little time for a Solomon who could content himself with half a child: 'He still doesn't know where he is. He and all his middle-of-the-roaders are the parasites of politics.'[114] Emmanuel Shinwell, complaining that the middle-of-the-roader was by nature an indecisive 'mugwump' ('a person who sat on the fence with his mug on one side and his wump on the other'), changed his metaphor as if to issue a threat: 'If you stand in the middle of the road, it is well known that you stand to get run over.'[115] Not everyone in the Labour Party was in the look-and-see tradition of Marshall and Pigou, Keynes and Cole, Tawney and Durbin. Some, however, were. Gaitskell and Crosland were. One consequence was *The Future of Socialism* that was able so successfully to climb on to the shoulders of the past in order to proclaim to the world its message of mix.

3.3 GAITSKELLITE ECONOMICS

In the late 1940s, full employment achieved, core industries nationalised, the Health Service in place, the Labour Party began to recognise that it was time to look beyond the objectives set out in *Let Us Face The Future*, its 1945 manifesto. The Fabian Society in particular was keen for there to be a major intellectual reappraisal of the tasks still facing the socialists in the wake of the changes that had been brought about. The result was a series of three conferences on 'Problems ahead'. The first two conferences (in July 1949 and January 1950) were held at Buscot Park, the stately home in Oxfordshire of Lord Faringdon, an active Fabian and the Chairman of the Fabian Colonial Bureau. The third conference (in June 1950) was held at University College, Oxford: Crosland, reading a paper on 'Happiness in the Welfare State' at the second Buscot conference, had accidentally broken a priceless vase belonging to Lord Faringdon and his family.

The general election of February 1950 introduced a worrying new dimension to the specification of Labour's 'Problems ahead'. Labour in the election was returned with an overall majority of only 5. By the time of the University College conference it was clear that the Government was unlikely to survive a full five-year Parliament and that the Conservatives might even be the victors in the election that had to come soon. G.D.H. Cole was the Chairman of the Fabian Society from 1948–50, as he had been from 1939–46: Laski had been the Chairman from 1946–48. (Crosland was to be the Chairman for 1961–62). Cole decided that it was urgent to produce a volume of essays that, building on the conferences of 1949 and 1950, would stimulate discussion in the run-up to the next election. Crosland and Crossman drew up the synopsis and Crossman took on the editorship. The title, *New Fabian Essays*, was intended to refer back to the original *Fabian Essays* that had been edited by Shaw in 1889. The anticipated election in the event overtook the publication of the book. When the book finally appeared in Spring 1952, Labour had moved into Opposition and the *New Fabian Essays* was read as a *post mortem* on unpopular policies no less than it was debated as a reappraisal of socialist beliefs.

The *New Fabian Essays* was the first step in the direction of re-thinking socialism in the light of the post-war accomplishments and the subsequent electoral defeats. Crossman wrote in support of philosophical speculation in place of short-termism and hunch: 'The Labour Party has lost its way not only because it lacks a map of the new country it is crossing, but because it thinks maps unnecessary for experienced travellers'.[1] Crossman, more forcefully than he was later to do, also drew attention to 'the threat of the managerial society': 'The planned economy and the centralisation of power are no longer socialist objectives.... The main task of socialism to-day is to prevent the concentration of power in the hands of *either* industrial management *or* the state bureaucracy – in brief, to distribute responsibility and so to enlarge freedom of choice.'[2] Crossman's interest in consultation and involvement was shared by Austen Albu, who (noting that the Morrisonian public corporation did little to involve the workers in decision-making), called in his paper for democratic participation at the level of the firm. Ian Mikardo wrote optimistically about trade union power in a fully-employed economy, Margaret Cole about educational opportunity and social equalisation, Denis Healey about socialist foreign policy in a world of blocs and alliances. John Strachey contributed a paper in which he acknowledged the influence of Keynes and Jay in bringing to an end his involvement with Marx. Roy Jenkins contributed a paper in which he explored the possibilities for the fiscal levelling both of incomes and of wealth. The longest paper was by Anthony Crosland. Writing on 'The Transition from Capitalism', he said that capitalism was expanding instead of collapsing, that public ownership and plan were not the answers to all of the socialist's questions. Crosland in his paper associated the future of socialism with perceived equality and the empowerment of the deprived – with 'the new society of which socialists have always dreamed, a society which is not bedevilled by the consciousness of class'.[3] It was not the last time that he was to associate the future of socialism more with cultural inter-action than with economic productivity.

The *New Fabian Essays* was the first step in the direction of revising socialism to take account of the post-war developments. It was, in the words of Patricia Pugh, 'a considerable achievement', but for all that an undertaking that was inevitably held back by an unadventurous climate of opinion: 'In 1952 the climate of opinion was such that no dynamic philosophy of socialism could emerge to galvanize a Labour movement exhausted by what it had already done to regenerate society, in an unfavourable international context. The essayists were hobbled by the need to furnish their theories on socialism with practical solutions immediately applicable to the evils of the day.'[4] *The Times* recognised the sense of a vacuum in the theories of authors desperate to say something new: 'Nothing, the Socialists appear to agree, threatens the Labour Party more than the possibility that it will soon hold office again and be as lacking in a sense of direction as it was during the last years of Mr Atlee's administration.'[5] The *Tribune* recognised that anxiety and desperation were not in themselves enough to revitalise a demoralised party or to give it a new social purpose: the *Essays*, 'an obvious failure', the *Tribune* said, had regrettably not taken the opportunity 'to contribute new thought or new spirit to the flagging cause of social democracy.'[6] The *Manchester Guardian* treated the new socialism of managed capitalism as something of a joke: 'The ribald may be tempted to chaff the Labour movement, inspired by the earlier Fabians, with having jumped from the capitalist fire into, or at least on to the rim of, the managerial frying-pan. There is a grain of truth in the chaff.'[7] J.K. Galbraith (whose *American Capitalism* appeared in the same year as the *Essays*) treated it as a cross between a misnomer and a disappointment: 'One is left with the unshakable conclusion that very little socialism is left in socialism, and nothing much else is available to take its place.'[8]

Galbraith's assessment was part of a twelve-page symposium on the *New Fabian Essays* that was published in the *Review of Economics and Statistics*: someone had evidently decided that the book was important enough to justify the scrutiny of a battery of independent experts. Not one of the Americans, all of them academics with a personal interest in the Centre-Left, was able to say that he found the *Essays* at all satisfying. Galbraith complained that the discussion tended to concentrate on the marginal, the non-confrontational and even the trivial: 'We need debate on social alternatives – nothing, surely, could be more necessary for a vital society. But the debate must be on alternatives that are important.'[9] Arthur Schlesinger, Jr, objected that the authors had not spelled out the case for a radical departure in a society in which the masses were increasingly affluent, contented and conservative: 'Is it a just or a sensible criticism of a society that it meets the needs of most of its members?... What, indeed, are we to push on to?'[10] Samuel Beer observed that the authors had adopted a negative rather than a positive posture in that they had treated socialism as little more than capitalism reversed: '"Parity of esteem" is not simply lack of class feeling: it is a positive feeling of respect for all engaged in a common purpose.'[11] David McCord Wright inferred that the socialists' future was not very different from American capitalism augmented by a State-sponsored freedom *to*: 'It seems to me that the ethical norms of these admittedly high-minded and conscientious authors ought to call for a fluid American kind of competitive capitalism with much income inequality modified by welfare services: "equality of opportunity" in other words.'[12] David McCord Wright concluded that the *New Fabian Essays* was not especially socialist and not especially persuasive: 'Intended as a rallying point, it seems to me much more a confession of intellectual bankruptcy.'[13] A confession of intellectual bankruptcy or an implicit acknowledgement that little socialism still belonged in socialism, what is interesting is how much the American reformers who reviewed the *New Fabian Essays* in 1952 were effectively anticipating by four years the kind of comments that other reformers would soon be making when, in 1956, they wrote their reviews of *The Future of Socialism*.

The *New Fabian Essays* was published in 1952. So was *In Place of Fear*. While Crossman and Mikardo were soon to move to the Left, the *Essays* in its time was consensually an expression of the middle-ground's perspective. *In Place of Fear* was not. Aneurin Bevan's book looked forward to a less-accommodating future, to a socialism in which less of a compromise would be struck with the historic enemies of the working class. Bevan having resigned from the Labour Government over Gaitskell's introduction of healthcare-charges, he believed himself to be in a strong position to speak for moral values and to criticise the moderates for tolerating the intolerable.

Bevan's ideal was altruism in place of acquisitiveness, generosity in place of greed: 'A free health service is pure Socialism',[14] he said in his book. His grand vision was one of a caring community in which each, in core areas such as the protection of health, should enjoy the collectivity's reassurance that all had been freed from the tyranny of fear: 'Society becomes more wholesome, more serene, and spiritually healthier, if it knows that its citizens have at the back of their consciousness the knowledge that not only themselves, but all their fellows, have access, when ill, to the best that medical skill can provide.'[15] He also believed that the socialist community could simply not put down the roots that it would require so long as competitive capitalism, hedonistic and individualistic, remained the predominant mode of economic organisation: 'The issue therefore in a capitalist democracy resolves itself into this: either poverty will use democracy to win the struggle against property, or property, in fear of poverty, will destroy democracy.'[16]

Bevan expected that it would be the working classes who would take the lead in the defence of the exposed and the campaign against the wealthy. Less than imaginative in his assumption that the traditional proletariat was likely to retain its separate identity, he insisted that Labour could not compromise on its links with the mines and the shop-floor. Stating as he did that 'a political party which begins to pick its personnel from unrepresentative types is in for trouble',[17] Bevan was curiously insensitive to the contribution that middle-class intellectuals like Foot and Wilson could make to the success of his campaign. Bevan's socialism presupposed the extensive nationalisation of the economic base. Clause IV was indispensable since it would socialise the power of property, end the wastefulness of unbridled profit-seeking, and make easier the control and direction of investment: 'The facilities given to national planning when industries are publicly owned are obvious.'[18] Bevan's socialism also incorporated the scientific revolution and the white heat of rationality: the capitalistic market was anarchic, centralised coordination was economic, and thus could democratic leadership promote productive efficiency by means of the same measures that provided an outlet for compassion and comradeship.

Bevan wanted to nationalise the shipbuilding industry, sugar and cement; to politicise the flow of credit; to level the disparities of wealth and status. Most of all, however, he wanted to improve the moral nexus through the suppression of short-sighted selfishness and the diminution of ambitious materialism. An ex-miner from Tredegar, brought up a Welsh Baptist with a sense of right and wrong, Bevan was offended by the immorality of much that he saw around him. Bevan found it 'evil' that pensions were low, 'abominable' that health was under-funded, 'disgraceful' that speculators made windfalls:[19] If expediency argued for a mixed economy then so, in his view, *a fortiori* did the ethical constraint. In the words of Michael Foot: 'Bevan detested the expressions of the casino society of the Macmillan age more than most other politicians; he hated all forms of gambling (particularly in steel shares on the Stock Exchange) – it was the one remnant of his Welsh puritanism; he felt that the rickety edifice of hire-purchase and the "never-never" made the worker conservative in instinct, afraid of change, unready for the communal restraints without which the move towards a Socialist society would be impossible.'[20] Gaitskell and the revisionists, it would be fair to say, had no such reservations about the rightness and the wrongness of supply and demand. For them the self-seeking orientation of the market mechanism represented no serious threat to community service or to the social-democratic compromise of welfare and mix.

In Place of Fear could have been the great philosophical statement of the Labour Left. In the event it was not: 'disappointingly woolly', in the estimation of John Campbell, 'pervaded by a dismaying sense of muddle and irrelevance',[21] Bevan's short book was quite clearly the work of a self-taught enthusiast who had no real grounding in the great theories and no formal training in the presentation of evidence. Unacademic and anecdotal, stronger on passion than it was on proof, *In Place of Fear* in the intellectual vacuum of 1952 is probably deserving of Campbell's description of it as 'the manifesto that wasn't': 'The opportunity to stake out the agenda for the next Labour Government had been missed: the initiative had been handed back to the right. In due course Tony Crosland, for the Gaitskellites, filled the gap which Bevan had left. *The Future of Socialism* was everything that *In Place of Fear* was not. It became the bible of the revisionists, and captured the mind of the party for the next twenty years.'[22] *In Place of Fear* lost the debate at least as much as *The Future of Socialism* may be said to have won it. John Strachey's *Contemporary Capitalism*, also published in 1956, reinforced the revisionist message of Crosland's high-profile book. It is tempting to speculate on what it might have meant for the future of British socialism if an author of Strachey's persuasive articulacy had decided to throw in his lot not with the Centre-Left which was in possession of a *Future* of its own but rather with the non-Soviet, non-Marxian Left-Left that was in need of an intellectual legitimation more rigorous than *In Place of Fear*.

The ex-miner lacked the expositional skills of the ex-don. Yet there was a further reason why the *Future* succeeded while the *Fear* failed to persuade. That reason has to do with the time-warp that was widely believed to separate the washing machines and the televisions of 'You've never had it so good' from the hunger and the hostility of the world of the past in which Bevan appeared still to be dwelling. Writing of the time-warp that had shut out the rise in living-standards, Foote has arrived at the conclusion that Bevan's socialism was seen to be the socialism of 'an earlier age': 'There was something peculiarly inappropriate about Aneurin Bevan's ideas on the struggle between poverty and wealth in the boom conditions of the fifties. The existence of class divisions remained fundamental to British society, but the impression given by Bevan was one of a society frozen in the political and social attitudes of twenty years before. The revisionists seemed to have the edge in theoretical terms as well as in terms of political power during the decade.'[23] The average real earnings of British industrial labour rose by more than 20 per cent in the 1950s. Faced with the affluence and the optimism, as Howell says, the older theories of deprivation and conflict were seen to be strikingly out of touch: 'The old gods had failed the left – the intellectual poverty of Bevanism reflected in part this barren heritage.... Whatever its deficiencies, revisionism had little positive challenge within the party.... No real challenge came from the Labour left except a defence of traditional values.'[24] Bevan failed, Curran has said, because it was in the nature of the cars and the telephones that they should render obsolete the intellectual challenge of 'the last of the demagogues': 'In the coalfield from which he came, Marx and Engels have been supplanted by Marks and Spencer; and the sound of class war is drowned by the hum of the spin dryer.... There will be no more Aneurin Bevans.'[25] Others, more charitably, would say that the *Future* succeeded while the *Fear* failed to persuade at least in part because Bevan in his philosophy of socialism was unprepared to cut loose his theory of social justice from his economics of bad times that the capitalism of good times was increasingly calling into question.

Following the electoral defeat of 1955, Clement Attlee was persuaded to step down as Leader of the Labour Party. He was 72 and had been Party Leader since 1935. Even if the Labour vote had not fallen by a further 1.5 million since the previous defeat in 1951, it would probably have been time to consider the succession.

In December 1955 the Parliamentary Labour Party met to select its new Leader. Herbert Morrison, Attlee's deputy, received only 40 votes: only five years younger than Atlee, unpopular with the left of the party, more an administrator than an entrepreneur, Morrison was believed unlikely to hold together the fragile coalition or to attract in the floating voter. The real contenders for the post were the working-class champion Aneurin Bevan and the moderate intellectual Hugh Gaitskell. The revisionists carried the day: Gaitskell received 157 votes to Bevan's 70. The Labour Party was in that sense captained by revisionism at the time of the publication not just of *The Future of Socialism* but of *The Conservative Enemy* as well. It was also surprisingly united: when Gaitskell as Leader made his first appearance at Conference in 1956 his Shadow Foreign Secretary was Bevan and his Shadow Chancellor was Wilson. No one could have known that Bevan, then 57, was to die in 1960; that Gaitskell, 49, would be dead at 56 in 1963; and that it would be left for Harold Wilson to reap the electoral harvest that had been sown by both of his political fathers.

The Leadership contest in 1955 was influenced in no small measure by the personalities of the candidates. Dalton compared Gaitskell to 'a high snow peak', Bevan to 'a steaming tropical swamp'.[26] Callaghan is known to have called Bevan 'a temperamental Celt'.[27] Bevan is reputed to have called Gaitskell 'a desiccated calculating machine'.[28] Bevan complained of 'the pure economist's mind' surrounded by 'the clique of statisticians': Gaitskell, he said, was 'sincere enough in his own beliefs – but no Socialist'.[29] Gaitskell complained of the emotive theatricality and the unstatesmanlike confrontationalism – something which unmistakeably differentiated Bevan's personal style from Gaitskell's more polished, more measured mode of self-presentation. Gaitskell looked middle-class and fitted in: 'High-minded, clubbable and cliquish', Pimlott observes, 'Gaitskell was more liked and admired by Tory reformers and progressive mandarins than any other leading Labour politician before or since.'[30] Bevan, on the other hand, was conspicuously not Establishment and notoriously not diplomatic. He did, of course, boast other qualities, including the 'amazing command of language', the 'strong personal attraction', the 'quickness of wit in debate', the 'essentially constructive outlook', the 'breadth of vision' that had led the undergraduate Anthony Crosland to give voice to the opinion 'that Aneurin Bevan not only will be, but ought to be, the next Labour Premier.... If only Aneurin could lose his imbecile wife, he would have Crosland solidly behind him.'[31] By 1955 Crosland had clearly changed his mind. Perhaps he had had second thoughts about his earlier assessment of Bevan as a man of 'moderation', a leader of potential who gave 'the appearance of a sane & very practical administrator'.[32] The leadership contest in 1955 was at any rate influenced by the very different personalities of the two principal contenders; and here, it must be suggested, Gaitskell had a certain advantage over Bevan when the party came to vote.

Gaitskell had a further advantage with respect to policies and programmes. Following the electoral defeats of the 1950s the British Left was not able to side-step the basic question ('as old as the Labour Party itself') of whether, in the words of Ralph Miliband, 'the Labour Party is to be concerned with attempts at a more efficient and more humane administration of a capitalist society; or whether it is to adapt itself to the task of creating a socialist one'.[33] Bevan and his supporters (true Bevanites like John Freeman, Jennie Lee, Tom Driberg, Barbara Castle, Michael Foot, Richard Crossman, Ian Mikardo, Harold Wilson; '57 varieties' of more extreme left-wingers like Sydney Silverman and Konni Zilliacus) were known to be suspicious of what Miliband has described as 'that grand reconciliation between the Labour movement and contemporary capitalism which is the essence of revisionism'.[34] For the Labour Left there could be no compromise with capitalism so long as the wage-earners and their employers remained divided by a systemic conflict of interest that no amount of *embourgeoisement* would be able to eradicate. Gaitskell and his followers (the inner-circle 'Hampstead set' of Crosland, Jenkins, Douglas Jay, Frank Soskice, Patrick Gordon Walker that was so frequently made welcome at 18, Frognal Gardens, NW3, Gaitskell's home; the outer-circle modernising reformers like Healey, Strachey, Christopher Mayhew, Alfred Robens who shared Crosland's vision of 'a progressive, national, social-democratic party')[35] were, on the other hand, known to be favourable to the challenge that, in the words of Foote, 'culminated in the technocratic, class-neutral ideology of the Wilson era'.[36] For the Labour Centre there could be no excuse for a socialism that made a fetish of property ownership when the real enemies had been exposed as inequality and distress. The Labour Centre believed that across-the-board nationalisation had become an irrelevance (as Howell puts it: 'The maxim was "Business as Usual – only more Efficient"')[37] and that social levelling no longer required a major restructuring of economic power. Given that common ownership and cloth-cap aggressiveness were electoral liabilities as well in the '50s Britain of 'Conservative freedom works', it is only logical that the party should have opted for the leadership of the candidate who seemed the more likely to appeal to the median voter.

The next general election cast the great bulk of the votes in the leadership contest of December 1955. Roy Jenkins in 1953 had stated clearly that without a decisive change of image there was unlikely to be an early return to power: 'The electorate is extremely Conservative-minded and we can never win except with the kind of attitude represented by the right-wing leadership.'[38] Hugh Gaitskell, discussing pension schemes with Crossman and Crosland, said openly that even the conviction politician had to recognise the narrowing focus of the public's tastes and preferences: 'I shouldn't worry about morals if I were you. What people want to hear is how little they will pay and how much they will get from our scheme.'[39] Crossman's view was that to compromise on socialism in order to satisfy the selfish would be in effect to alienate the electorate from a Party that had damned itself with unprincipled opportunism: 'The voters would learn to despise it and its members would lose their last shred of self-respect. What makes Revisionism a vote-loser is its obsession with winning votes.'[40] Crosland, on the other hand, saw the process of adaptation and alteration in the more positive light not of a sell-out but rather of a new beginning.

Crosland in that sense welcomed Gaitskell in December 1955 not only as the leader who would win the support of the median voter but also as the leader who would release the latent dynamism of the socialist Centre-Left. Many others shared his view of Gaitskell as a politician of potential who was also an ideologue of vision. Roy Jenkins, almost 40 years on from that historic December, has written as follows of Gaitskell and the 'inspirational quality of leadership' which he appeared to promise: 'Gaitskell offered a change of generation. He also opened the prospect of a modernised social democratic Labour Party of conscience and reform. In some of us he aroused an enthusiasm which was positively Wordsworthian. "In that dawn it was joy to be alive ...".'[41] Obviously the Party had to return to power – and Gaitskell was perceived to be the man who would bring in the votes. Equally, however, the Party had to re-think its role – and Jenkins was not alone in believing, in 1955, that Gaitskell had the intellect and the determination to lead his followers out of the vacuum that the conservative enemy had made up its collective mind to cherish and to defend.

3.4 CROSLAND AND GAITSKELL

Gaitskell at an early stage recognised in Crosland a kindred spirit. Susan Crosland (who first met Tony in the *annus mirabilis* of 1956) has recalled their political friendship in the following words: 'The two men admired, loved, maddened one another.... They shared what might be called an egalitarian attitude to people, their manner unaffected by someone's position.... Both men threw themselves into their work. Both had a large capacity for enjoyment. Both viewed power as a vehicle for putting principles into practice, not as an end in itself. Both believed in political team-work.'[1] Like attracts like. Crosland and Gaitskell had much in common.

Thus Gaitskell, twelve years Crosland's senior, was, like Crosland, the product of a privileged background. Like Crosland, his father had been in the civil service (in his case, in the Indian Civil Service); his family had had servants and a nanny (in his case, a Burmese amah); he had been edu-cated at an old-established English public school (in his case, like Cripps and Crossman, at Winchester); and he had obtained a First in PPE at Oxford (in his case, like Evan Durbin, at New College, in 1927). Like Crosland, he had been a university teacher of economics (in his case, at University College, London, where he lectured for 11 years in contrast to Crosland's Trinity, Oxford, period of three) before he had opted for a full-time career as a Labour politician (in his case, as the Member for South Leeds, which he represented for 18 years–the same number of years as Crosland for Grimsby – from 1945). Like Crosland, he was more com-fortable with socio-political and historically-orientated lecture-courses (in his case, with Comparative Social Institutions and with Political and Social Theory) than he was with the pyrotechnics of abstract economic analysis: the inference easily drawn from his *Chartism* (1929) or his *Money and Everyday Life* (1939) is that W.A. Robson was not too wide of the mark when he described Gaitskell the academic as 'a nice ordinary competent economist, we all meet dozens of them'.[2] This is not to say that Gaitskell the scholar would not have made a serious contribution had he, returning to University College from his wartime attachments at the Ministry of Economic Warfare and the Board of Trade, completed the PhD thesis on the Austrian theory of capital which took him for a year to Vienna in the 1930s: the two sections that were published in the *Zeitschrift für Nationalökonomie* in 1936 and 1938 are all the more impressive when one recalls that they were originally presented as seminar-papers in German. Like Crosland, it was Hugh Dalton who caused him to choose politics instead.

Gaitskell, like Crosland, had been a witness to the mass unemployment of the inter-war years. Both were confident that Keynesian economics pro-vided a reliable guarantee of jobs and did so without simultaneously unleashing the destructiveness of inflation. Both survived the 1930s without any significant flirtation with Marxism, revolution and class-conflict. Both were middle-class in their culture but regarded their origins as presenting no particular obstacle to the leadership of a Labour Party that was evolving into classlessness from its earlier posture of proletarian protest. Both had in any case learned about the working-classes at first hand, Crosland (like Tawney on the Somme) through the cameraderie of the war, Gaitskell (like Tawney in Edwardian Manchester) through his Workers' Educational Association lectures to Nottinghamshire miners, many of them out of work, in the years following the General Strike (in which Gaitskell had himself participated by driving an ambulance). Gaitskell at the start of his political career told the House of Commons that he was there because the miners had taught him how it felt to be dependent upon the State for the guarantee of freedom *to*: 'They taught me what economic feudalism was. They taught me what the naked exercise of arbitrary power meant. They taught me what it was to be victimised.'[3] The workers taught and the reformers learned. Neither Gaitskell nor Crosland had gone hungry like Wilson or had, like Bevan, watched a parent shrivel up from an occupational disease. Both, on the other hand, had transcended the narrowness of birth and had made it their business to find out how the other half lives.

Sympathetic to the deprivation of the have-nots, neither Gaitskell nor Crosland showed any real interest in the preservation of the distinctive and traditional features of the working-class way of life. Richard Hoggart eulogised in the working-class culture a variety of positive attributes – cheerful debunking, constructive make-do, neighbourly cooperation, the shared pleasure that comes from the knowledge that 'every wireless in the street is linking the neighbours in a sort of communion'.[4] Hoggart expressed the fear that economic improvement and life-style homogenisation might erode to a dangerous degree 'the still considerable moral resources of working-class people.... The question, of course, is how long this stock of moral capital will last, and whether it is being sufficiently renewed. But we have to be careful not to underrate its effect at present.'[5] Both Gaitskell and Crosland, on the other hand, had this in common, that they were more sensitive to the inconvenience of the outside lavatories than they were to the communalism of the supportive peers. One is reminded of the verdict of the Yorkshire rough diamond in Susan Crosland's *Ruling Passions* on public-school sentimentalists bent on capturing the Westminster commanding heights: 'That's where all those Whig nobs believe they have a natural right to be. They rabbit on about equality of opportunity and One Nation, but they start from the premise that everybody wants the opportunity to be *just like them*. They have not a doubt in their little heads that they're innately superior.'[6] It cannot be denied that there is a certain amount of 'raising up the poor' in the duty-bound service ethos of Gaitskell and Crosland. The following observation by Hugh Gaitskell (speaking privately to Richard Crossman in 1959 on the subject of Roy Jenkins) gives the feel of the top-down paternalism tinged with Christ-like dedication that was by no means absent from the revisionists' world-view: 'He is very much in the social swim these days and I am sometimes anxious about him and young Tony. We, as middle-class Socialists, have got to have a profound humility. Though it's a funny way of putting it, we've got to know that we lead them because they can't do without us, with our abilities, and yet we must feel humble to working people. Now that's all right for us in the upper middle class, but Tony and Roy are not upper and I sometimes feel they don't have a proper humility to ordinary working people.'[7] Gaitskell need not have worried. Tony's attitude with respect to the relatively deprived was in all essentials the same as that of Hugh – that the lower classes did not glory in their lowishness and that politics, like growth, is the art of moving up.

Temperamentally, too, Crosland and Gaitskell had much in common. Both men, as Philip Williams points out, had a capacity for exceptional industriousness but also for exceptional hedonism: 'Anthony Crosland practised astringent intellectual puritanism and preached unabashed libertarianism and private enjoyment – a combination particularly attractive to Gaitskell as it recalled his own youth.'[8] Both men tended in politics to put evidence above emotion and to adopt a cautious, logical, scientific approach to problem-solving of which David Wood, referring specifically to Gaitskell, has written as follows: 'He did not like leaping instinctively to an answer, and when he did he could reach the politically inexpedient answer. He carried into politics his economist's need first to know the facts and then to move on from there along a purely rational plane.'[9] Both men, grounded though they were in real-world proof, recognised a need for general principles and intellectual systems in preference to the purposelessness of muddle through and the step-by-step short-termism of Herbert Morrison's 'We'll see how we go'. Both men, it is clear, were at one with Crossman when he criticised the 'actions, not words' orientation of so many British socialists, determined to reject abstract theories as 'dangerous Teutonic verbiage', convinced that visions and speculations were best 'left to the exponents of American free enterprise and Russian communism.'[10] Wood notes that Gaitskell 'never ceased to be an academic, a dealer in ideas'.[11] He also asks with reference to Gaitskell 'whether his view of politics and party leadership was not more rigidly intellectual than was good either for his own comfort or perhaps for the unity of his party.'[12] If Gaitskell's studious agenda-setting and structured course-charting may be said to have restricted his popularity, then even more must this be said of Crosland, his ideologue. Like attracts like. Gaitskell and Crosland had much in common.

So, of course, did Gaitskell and the other Gaitskellites – and Gaitskell and Roy Jenkins, arguably, most of all. Looking back on Hugh and Tony, Jenkins has revealed that in many ways he was probably the Leader's *second* choice: 'In my retrospective view, with both of them long dead, Gaitskell was more excited by the idea of Crosland than he was by the idea of me, but found me rather easier to be with.'[13] Tony and Roy were at any rate the Leader's close collaborators and, later, his literary executors. They, together with the other moderates, sought to ensure that the middle ground was effectively secured and that the continuing threat from Labour's Left was successfully beaten off.

The continuing threat was a very real one. The Victory for Socialism Group, the red-blooded Bevanites, the *Tribune*, the *New Statesman*, the CND unilateralists, all were undermining the Leader's authority by complaining that Gaitskell was offering neo-Liberalism when what the Left really required was a confrontation with capital. The electoral defeat of 1959 (when the Conservatives increased their majority to 100 seats and Labour's showing was its worst in almost 25 years) seemed to confirm the suspicion that the voters would not reward the socialists for concluding a peace of convenience with the profit-seeking classes and the grasping invisible hand. Harold Wilson spoke for the whole of the Labour Left when he blamed the low standing of the Party on Gaitskell's reluctance to put idealism before expediency: 'We are an ethical movement and one based on socialist principles – and we shall neither win nor deserve to win elections if we merely stand forth as a technocratic alternative to the Conservatives.'[14] Then (pushed on by Castle, Cousins and Crossman) he challenged Gaitskell for the Party Leadership. Anthony Greenwood was already standing when Wilson entered the contest at a relatively late stage. Greenwood had little chance of turning Gaitskell's vulnerability to his own advantage. Wilson was in a stronger position to bring about the dumping of a king who had not done enough.

Wilson knew that Bevan was no longer a credible alternative and that Foot, Castle or Crossman lacked the political charisma that was needed. Wilson's own appeal was not in question. Within the Parliamentary Labour Party he topped the poll for the Shadow Cabinet in 1959; while in the same year he came second (in 1962 first) in the union-dominated vote for membership of the National Executive Committee (a Party Committee, interestingly enough, to which Anthony Crosland was not once elected). Wilson in the House was the Chairman of the Public Accounts Committee and was Shadow Chancellor: had Labour won the election of 1959, he would have been Britain's youngest Chancellor since 1903. Wilson was in the forefront of the struggle to prevent the Gaitskellites from blaming Clause IV for the 1959 defeat: his success in persuading the Party not to dine out on its sacred cows no doubt strengthened his conviction that the rank-and-file wanted a return to the pre-Gaitskellite red shirt. Wilson in any case had a feel for the ethical and emotional underpinnings of British socialism to which he believed that the rational Gaitskell was on balance insensitive: 'What Hugh never recognized was that, from the Party's earliest days, a great number of converts had joined Labour because they believed that socialism was a way of making a reality of Christian principles in everyday life.'[15] Gaitskell probably did under-rate the political significance of popular passions. The emotive solidarity of feeling of old-style trades unionists, the anti-capitalist resentments that sustained the calls for public ownership, the fears and anxieties that led to the foundation of the CND, the patriotism shown at the time of Suez, the anti-German xenophobia that pervaded the rearmament debate – Gaitskell, detached and reserved, must have been surprised at the extent to which the heart took over from the brain even when the issues at stake were properly to be decided on their merits alone. Wilson, in contrast, could not be accused of neglecting the sense in which Labour was a party of faith. Having observed the charismatic Bevan at first hand, Wilson knew that there was more to popular appeal than the careful tabulation of costs and benefits.

The Gaitskellites recognised that the ambitious Wilson was a problem that would not go away: 'One of the basic tenets of Gaitskellism', Roy Jenkins has written, 'was that Wilson was a tricky fellow.'[16] Jenkins regarded him as secretive, devious, opportunistic and uncongenial: 'The fact is that Harold is a person no one can like, a person without friends.'[17] Rodgers saw him as autocratic, shifty, and totally unprepared to think beyond tactics: 'He was dull, insubstantial and did not take a positive stand.'[18] Gaitskell and Wilson were, as Anthony Howard has recorded, 'very different figures – Gaitskell social and gregarious, Wilson wary and almost, by instinct, a lone wolf'.[19] The Gaitskellites recognised, as Peter Shore has explained, that the revisionist's moderation would never be safe so long as the ambitious Wilson represented a continuing threat: 'They really detested him. They had a loathing of Harold. They felt he understood the problems, but deliberately used his first-class mind not to face them.'[20]

The Gaitskellites had a loathing of Harold. The Wilsonians in return had a loathing of Hugh. Thus Konni Zilliacus (later to be suspended by the Party for publishing in the Prague-based *World Marxist Review*) objected in 1960 that Gaitskell was 'indistinguishable from a Liberal in home affairs and from a Conservative in foreign affairs'.[21] The *New Statesman* in the same year brought in Crosland, Jay and Jenkins as well: Kingsley Martin (later to be removed as editor for having caused a drop in circulation, not least through the virulence of his anti-revisionist rhetoric) declared his displeasure that the leader had fallen into the hands of 'a small and much disliked group of anti-Socialist zealots'.[22] Ian Mikardo, invoking the name of a moderate school of Tory middle-grounders, sneered at the 'Crosland-Jay branch of the Bow Group'.[23] Wilsonians said that Frognalites were exclusive, self-satisfied and self-righteous. Wilsonians were hurt by jokes implying that Harold was lacking in refinement and taste. Wilsonians found it inappropriate that the Hampstead Leader, while admittedly keeping in touch with prominent union moderates (Arthur Deakin of the Transport Workers, Will Lawther of the Miners, Tom Williamson of the General and Municipal), should nonetheless be socialising so intensively with the Belgravia upper classes. The Wilsonians in short did not think much of the Gaitskellites. Not happy with Hugh, they looked to Harold to take his place at the helm.

The electoral defeat of 1959 was the catalyst. In 1961 Wilson challenged Gaitskell for the Leadership. In the ensuring ballot 166 members of the Parliamentary Labour Party voted for Hugh but 81 – almost a third of the 258 potential electors – voted for Harold. Harold was never forgiven by the Gaitskellites, but at least his treachery had meant that he had most decisively put down his marker. Disliked as he was, Wilson remained in the Shadow Cabinet (he polled no more than ninth place in 1960 but bounced back to first in 1961) and retained a top portfolio (Shadow Foreign Secretary if not Shadow Chancellor). In 1962 he decided once again to try for high office: standing against George Brown for the Deputy Leadership, he lost but not by an impossible margin (103 votes to Brown's 133). It was only a matter of time until he would be ready for a return match at the very top.

Concerned about Wilson and anxious about the Left, the middle ground fought back. In 1960 the Campaign for Democratic Socialism was set up in order to encourage the propagation of revisionist ideas at constituency, trade union and Parliamentary Party level. The idea for the CDS came from Bill Rodgers (then General Secretary of the Fabian Society and not yet a Member of Parliament) and Anthony Crosland (who with Philip Williams was the principal author of its manifesto). Patrick Gordon Walker, Dick Taverne, Douglas Jay, Desmond Donnelly, George Brown, Denis Healey, all had links with the Campaign, as did elder statesmen of the standing of Attlee and Dalton (the latter making his last public appearance at a CDS rally in 1961). The CDS published its own broadsheet (*Campaign*) and also enjoyed the support of the social-democratic *Socialist Commentary* that, in Roy Jenkins's words, 'provided a beacon of light within the Labour Party from 1941 to 1978'.[24] Anti-Communist and anti-Marxist (unsympathetic to Jagan and Nkrumah in the colonies, the far left of Labour at home), opposed to the extremes both of Soviet State planning and of American free enterprise, the *Socialist Commentary* (officially the journal of the right-of-centre Socialist Vanguard Group) provided a counter-weight to, say, the *Tribune* by arguing for a mixed economy, a classless Labour Party and a loosened link with the unions. The editor of the *Socialist Commentary* from 1955 until her death in 1971 was Rita Hinden. A friend of Gaitskell and a supporter of revisionism, she was happy to use her influence to advance the cause of the CDS.

The CDS was a Centre-Right coalition within the Labour Party that supported Gaitskell on public ownership, on social equality, on prudent multilateralism – on all issues, in fact, save one. Gaitskell could see no case for Britain to become a member of the European Communities unless rigorous guarantees could first be negotiated in respect of Commonwealth interests, home agriculture, the autonomy of British economic planning and the independence of British foreign policy. The members of the CDS, in contrast to Gaitskell, tended to be in favour of entry. Not denying the complications, they were able to overcome their uncertainties (about the dynamic effect of competition on innovation, efficiency and growth) and to swallow their reservations (about the regressive effect of higher food prices and the new indirect tax).

Possibly Gaitskell saw some electoral advantage in 1962 in opposing the EC application. Possibly, as Haseler suggests, 'it was simply a question of the generation gap. While his younger revisionist followers were impressed and excited by the modernisation and technological advance involved in European cooperation, Gaitskell, who had lived through two world wars, was intensely patriotic.'[25] Whatever the reasons, Gaitskell in 1962 was obliged to ally himself with the Labour Left and to act in opposition to the Gaitskellite intellectuals. Potentially the breach between the Leader and the CDS could have been a damaging one. In practice it was not: De Gaulle blocked the British application, the issue of entry was shelved, and the CDS survived united until it was wound up in the aftermath of Labour's 1964 electoral success.

By then the unexpected had happened and Wilson had become Gaitskell's successor. The Gaitskellites regarded Wilson as a former Bevanite who could again turn left-wing, a disloyal opportunist who had done wrong to challenge the Leader in 1961. Wilson's victory could possibly have been prevented had the Labour moderates been able to rally behind a single candidate with the acknowledged capacity to be a future Prime Minister. As it was, some in the first ballot (like Roy Jenkins) supported George Brown while others (like Crosland) were in favour of James Callaghan. By the second ballot there remained no moderate but

George Brown to stop Harold Wilson: 'Are we going to be led by a neurotic drunk?',[26] exclaimed Anthony Crosland. Crosland characterised the
contest as a choice between 'a crook and a drunk'.[27] In the second ballot
he himself voted for the crook.[28] The race was close – Wilson secured 144
votes, Brown 103 – and there can be little doubt that Crosland was not
alone in voting *against* far more than in voting *for*. A middle-grounder, a
unionist, a graduate of the university of life, George Brown would have
been an attractive choice for the Gaitskellite revisionist had it not been for
the fact that his difficult personality and idiosyncratic image would have
been electoral liabilities for a party that was tired of Opposition. Wilson
was arguably the more likely to win elections than was the appealing but
unpredictable Member for Belper who became the Deputy Leader instead.
No nationaliser and no unilateralist in 1964, Wilson was able to convey an
impression of reliability and stewardship, technocracy and economy,
which won back the middle ground for the divided coalition. In that sense
he had the effect of ensuring that the heritage of Gaitskell lived on despite
the fact that he himself to the revisionists had been a conservative enemy
who was among the most to be feared.

Gaitskell once said of Durbin's *Politics* that, 'though it is the work of one
man, it illustrates the attitude of a wider group'.[29] Precisely the same must
be said of Crosland's *Future*. Crosland set out to codify a socialist programme that would at once re-unite the faithful and attract in the unde-
cided. Crosland wanted 'to let the country know precisely where we
stand', to combat the 'impression of ambiguity and schizophrenia'[30] that
had been so damaging to the Party in the recent past. Crosland's *Socialism*
was his work alone; but it was also the reasoned restatement of a world-
view that was a common possession. Crosland's publications defended
positions that were the shared doctrines of the Gaitskellite group. Not least
did they defend positions that had already been defended by Hugh
Gaitskell himself. Too busy with practical politics to be able to write
extensively on socialist theory, still it is the testimony of Gaitskell's
speeches, his articles, above all his Fabian pamphlet on *Socialism and
Nationalisation* (published in the year of *The Future of Socialism* but
apparently completed three years before) that the older intellectual in politics had long been in sympathy with a range of ideas and policies that it
was left to the younger intellectual in politics to develop and legitimate.

   Thus Gaitskell had long defined socialism as the pursuit of the classless
society, the attack on distance through birth: 'An underlying hatred of
inequality and the Class Structure', he declared in 1935, is 'the *germ* of all
Socialist feeling.'[31] Speaking to the Margate Conference in 1955, the

would-be Leader made clear to his Party that socialism to him continued to mean the moralist's challenge to poverty and squalor at the bottom of the ladder, contempt and privilege at the top: 'I am a Socialist and have been for some 30 years. I became a Socialist quite candidly not so much because I was a passionate advocate of public ownership but because at a very early age I came to hate and loathe social injustice, because I disliked the class structure of our society, because I could not tolerate the indefensible differences of status and income which disfigure our society.'[32] Gaitskell in Margate made clear that socialism to him meant the engineering of a united and a team-spirited community: 'I am a Socialist because I want to see fellowship, or if you prefer it, fraternity.... [while preserving] the liberties we cherish.'[33] Gaitskell in Margate also made clear that socialism to him meant a levelling State, unafraid of taxes and subsidies. He had said much the same in the 1930s when he had told a Labour League of Youth school in Godalming that equalisation presupposed intervention and was unlikely to proceed satisfactorily without it: 'Budgetary policy must take steps as soon as possible to reduce social and economic inequality. That, I take it, is the major aim of Socialism.'[34]

The 'major aim' of socialism, to Gaitskell as to Crosland, was the promotion of social and economic equality: 'In the goal of equality, the determination to uproot the conditions of economic injustice, lies the true characteristic of a Socialist. All Socialist activity must ultimately be judged by its successes in achieving this end.'[35] All socialist activity must ultimately be evaluated in terms of more equal outcomes and more equal opportunities. These key socialist objectives must not be confused with capital-ownership *per se* ('Nationalisation.... is a vital means, but it is only one of the means by which we can attain these objects')[36] or with economic planning *per se* ('Economic planning, the institutional machinery of [the] Socialist State, is not a monopoly of Socialism and can exist without Socialism'):[37] 'A Socialist party is different from other parties not because it offers a different mechanism for the same object, but because the object itself is different.'[38] The major aim itself is different – and more directly focused on the minimisation of those inequalities that the nation rejects as unjust.

Progressive income-tax, functional differentials respected, is a step in the right direction: 'While we do not say that all should receive the same income, we hold that the differences should be related to generally-accepted criteria of merit – such as the nature of the work – more being paid for dirty, harder, more skilled, better performed, more responsible jobs. We say too that these differences should not be greater than are necessary to provide adequate incentives in the interest of economic progress.'[39] To Gaitskell as to Crosland, productivity would appear to legitimate a gap even if social distance is the unwelcome result. To Gaitskell as to Crosland, in any case, it is not the income from work that constitutes the primary target for the socialist leveller: 'The existence of unearned income is wrong in itself no matter how it is distributed.'[40] Gaitskell when he was Chancellor of the Exchequer is known to have been contemplating the taxation of wealth (either the capital gains from disposals or the underlying stock of assets itself). In Opposition in the early 1950s, Gaitskell had said that equality of opportunity was 'only possible if privately-owned wealth is fairly evenly distributed' ('if therefore a strict limit is placed on the extent to which it can be inherited'):[41] he had also proposed that death duties become payable through the transfer of shares to the State. Crosland in 1956 might not have needed to call for measures such as these had the defeat of 1951 not deprived Gaitskell of the chance to introduce further reforms in his subsequent budgets.

In favour of subsidised services as well as taxes on the comfortable, Gaitskell, like Crosland, looked to the empowering State for an infrastructure of access in areas such as health and education. Like Crosland, Gaitskell believed that politicians could not forever turn a blind eye to the snobbery of the ancient independents: 'In the end they must abolish the public schools',[42] Gaitskell in 1961 said frankly to the editor of The *Guardian*. Again like Crosland, however, Gaitskell had serious doubts about doing in the here-and-now that which would probably have to be done much later, 'in the end'. Mill on liberty would seem to have been his mentor when he wrote to his daughter at Oxford that he saw 'real practical difficulties' in the abolition of the fee-paying head start: 'I'm afraid I do take the view that to forbid parents under any circumstances to pay for the education of their children is to go too far in interfering with people's liberty.'[43] Abolition with democratic support would have been Gaitskell's ideal: in that sense he would have been prepared to see the schools of a minority closed down to fit in with the consensus of the majority. Abolition without consensual support was, however, simply not to be contemplated. Morality aside, abolition would be a political liability: 'We should lose literally millions of votes – from catholics and other denominations as well as some good solid Labour ones too. The truth, I'm afraid, is that even the working class is *not* against the public schools: they're mostly not interested in the problem. But they *are* interested in better State education.'[44] The levelling-up of the State schools, not the levelling-down of the private ones, was to Gaitskell the short-term solution to the present-day inequalities in educational standards and opportunities. He proposed that it should be complemented by the provision of free places in the public schools for able children who would otherwise have attended their local grammars. Gaitskell intended that the subsidised mixing of the less affluent with the wealthy and the well-connected should serve as a workable compromise between abolition and inaction until such a time as *festina lente* had altered popular perceptions and gradualness had evolved into the endorsement of the inevitable.

Gaitskell's tolerance towards the fee-paying head start, so similar in its essentials to Crosland's reluctant acceptance, is a special case of a broader perspective – that enablement and empowerment are almost always to be ranked above prescription and constraint: 'To me the pursuit of happiness has always seemed such an individual and personal matter that it is in the main best left to people themselves to decide.... If the State were to direct ordinary people on how to pursue happiness, it would be intervening far too much with individual freedom.... What the State should do is to provide a framework, the opportunities through which people have the best chance of finding happiness for themselves.'[45] It will generally be in keeping with this perspective for the State to subsidise concerts and art-galleries in order that doors should be opened and new choice-sets revealed. It will occasionally be in keeping with this perspective for the State to legislate on gambling and alcohol in order that negative spillovers be prevented and moderate guidance provided. It will never be in keeping with this perspective, however, for the State to assume that it normally knows best what its citizens need: that way lies tyranny and tyranny is bad.

Thus it was that Gaitskell adopted a populist's stance in his legitimation of economic growth: 'People do want a higher standard of living, and I do not see why we should not accept this. Certainly if we fail to accept it there is precious little chance of getting ourselves accepted by the electorate.'[46] Unlike the austere and the abstinent in his party, it was Gaitskell's position that more money was very likely to mean more happiness and was most unlikely to mean less: 'I just cannot share this Gandhi outlook.... If people have more money to spend they may, it is true, gamble or smoke or drink it away. But a lot of them will also enjoy nicer holidays, which is a very good thing for them. We really must keep under control, and pretty strict control, the area within which "the man in Whitehall knows best".'[47] It was by means of precisely such an appeal to the common sense of the ordinary citizen that Gaitskell was able to argue against the more extreme proposals for participation and involvement. People, he said, very often want merely to be left alone: 'I get impatient with those who think that everybody must continually be taking an active part in politics or community affairs! The vast majority find their happiness in their family or personal relations, and why on earth shouldn't they!'[48]

Gaitskell's bias in favour of individual choice is further revealed in the libertarian position he adopted on issues of personal morality. He wanted to see a reform of the licensing laws, for example, and he supported the introduction of commercial television as a consumer-driven alternative to the State's BBC. A practical politician who sensed the reservations of some of Labour's staunchest supporters – the chapel, the working men's clubs, the paternalists, the organicists – he knew that it would be unwise to campaign too actively for causes of conscience (the abolition of death penalty, say) which he himself found attractive but on which his party was acknowledged to be split. Wherever possible, however, Gaitskell's bias was in favour of those policies that were most in line with the individual's own revealed preferences. One consequence of this bias in favour of sovereignty and pluralism was a guarded approbation extended to the decentralised market that more and more socialists were coming to share. As he wrote in 1955, marking the end of the ration-books and the wartime controls: 'To-day the party attitude in the main is that free choice must be continued and unfairness corrected rather through redistribution of income and wealth than through direct controls.'[49]

Redistribution of purchasing power, rationing through market price, can do much to correct excessive inequalities while protecting individual rights. Public ownership is more problematic: to be treated exclusively 'as a *means*', never to be grouped 'with the ultimate ends',[50] nationalisation, as compared with discriminatory taxation and social services, full employment and union power, was regarded by Gaitskell as an instrument of only tangential relevance to the cause of social justice. Nor could Gaitskell accept that the economic gains (in terms of economies of scale, structural change, concentration of plant) would necessarily be enough to compensate for the efficiency-loss that could so easily be the consequence of a lessening of rivalry and a bureaucratisation of initiative: 'While competition is wasteful it is also stimulating',[51] Gaitskell wrote. Uncertain *a priori* about the implications for performance, Gaitskell therefore proposed that the policy-maker should proceed pragmatically, 'as circumstances require'.[52] Circumstances in the past had required State ownership in order to ensure the productivity of the railways and the coal-mines. Circumstances in the future would no doubt reveal further instances where selective nationalisation would be entirely in the public's economic interest.

Uncertain *a priori* about the implications for efficiency, Gaitskell nonetheless hazarded the guess that the wholesale transfer of title to

capital was unlikely to be required by any circumstances that could reasonably be foreseen. Gaitskell attempted (unsuccessfully) to amend the
Clause IV commitment: he would not have done this had he believed that
the future of socialism was likely to require a major reconsideration of
property-rights. Gaitskell was also of the opinion that nationalisation was
no longer a vote-winner, that the electorate was more interested in social
questions like pensions and housing. Believing as he did that public ownership had evolved into marginality, he chose, not unexpectedly, to concentrate on the cutting edge while putting aside minor matters such as the
shopping-list until after the return of Labour to power.

   That having been said, it would be a mistake to think of Gaitskell as a
right-wing strategist who secretly hoped that the whole issue of capital
ownership would quietly be forgotten. The fact is that Gaitskell throughout the post-1955 period continued to argue forcefully for the nationalisation of an ambitious sub-set of British industry – steel, road-haulage,
aircraft, chemicals, machine-tools[53] – and was also in favour of the public
ownership of urban and development land. As he said in the House of
Commons in 1960: 'I have always regarded the case for the public ownership of urban land, or land about to be built upon, as exceptionally
strong.'[54] Like Crosland, Gaitskell did not anticipate any threat to
efficiency from the buying out of the anonymous, the powerless and the
irrelevant: 'Shareholders nowadays are purely passive and virtually
without function.'[55] Like Crosland, Gaitskell did not view productivity
as the sole maximand of professional managers made subject to
Parliamentary accountability: 'Nobody can be sure that the decisions must
always be better, but at least they are far more likely to be made after
taking into account all foreseeable consequences for the nation.'[56] Like
Crosland, Gaitskell did not imagine that the case for nationalisation might
ever extend to de-nationalisation as well: circumstances dictate and politics obeys, but still the process is irreversible and privatisation is not the
future of socialism. Sceptical as he was about the wholesale transfer of
title, what emerges nonetheless is that Gaitskell, like Crosland, was an
advocate of selective nationalisation – and of the mixed economy to which
it continued to have a useful contribution to make.

Crosland was influenced by Gaitskell and his fellow Gaitskellites. In that
sense his socialism was a shared socialism, the intellectual property of a
wider group. Yet Crosland was also an independent thinker, determined to
extend the revisionists' world-view even as he sought to systematise it.
Rightly or wrongly, Crosland was persuaded that his own socialism was
more ambitious than that of Gaitskell – and that Gaitskell lacked the

determination to bring about the fundamental changes that were required. The title of *The Conservative Enemy* is indicative of Crosland's frame of mind in the late Gaitskell years.

In *The Conservative Enemy*, working downwards from the macrocosm, Crosland expressed his regret that the British character had become imbued with deep traditionalism: 'Generally, the national mood is one of conservatism, antipathy to innovation, an absence of audacity, and an unwarranted complacency with things as they are.'[57] Britain, Crosland wrote in *Encounter* at the time of the 1959 defeat, was simply not enthusiastic about anything new: 'A dogged resistance to change now blankets every segment of our national life. A middle-aged conservatism, parochial and complacent, has settled over the country.'[58]

As with the country, Crosland continued, so with the Party. The Labour Right 'still lacks a truly radical appeal and often seems insular, class-oriented, conservative and middle-aged'.[59] The Labour Left 'is conservative in a different and more pernicious way, clinging to an outdated semi-Marxist analysis of society in terms of ownership'.[60] Both wings of the Party were locked into stale ideas and past attitudes. Neither wing had the freshness to overcome the national mood of stagnation – or even to re-think the problems that were keeping the Party in opposition: 'The Party seems blanketed under an oppressive weight of conservatism and inertia. Few people are even alive to the need for change.'[61]

As with the Party, so with the Party's leadership: 'Certainly the leadership gives no hint of having a constructive programme of reform, or indeed a plan of any kind.'[62] The conservatism of the country's culture can hardly be challenged by the Labour Party, Crosland argued, so long as the Party's leadership shows no real determination to bring about a significant change of direction. A letter to Gaitskell dated 7 November 1960 is indicative of his reservations: 'We must face the fact that the impression has got around – and, also, I myself largely share it – that the middle class leadership of the party (yourself, Gordon Walker, Soskice, etc.) is leading from an extreme and rather rigid Right-wing position, and has no emotional desire to change any major aspect of the society in which we are living. The element of radicalism and discontent, which even the most moderate Left-wing party must possess, seems lacking; even Kennedy sounds more radical than we do.'[63] By the early 1970s Roy Jenkins too had joined the list of well-intentioned reformers who were far too conciliatory to go far enough: 'Roy has come actually to dislike socialism.... It is Roy's misfortune that because of his father, he's in the wrong Party. As a Liberal or Conservative, he might make a very good Leader.'[64] The judgement was prophetic in view of what was to come. Crosland for his own part always distanced himself (in contrast, say, to Woodrow

Wyatt) from proposals for a merger, an alliance or a 'Lib–Lab pact'. In the militant '70s as in the Gaitskellite '50s, Dick Leonard recalls, Crosland had no time for a reassignment of the boundaries: 'He did take seriously the threat of the party being split in two – and the prospect of the more right wing half being realigned with the Liberals had absolutely no appeal to him.'[65] Nor, however, did the prospect of a Labour leadership that, resolutely independent of the Liberals, still refused to commit itself to the radicalism and the discontent that alone could distinguish it from the conservative enemy. Crosland even in the years of high Gaitskellism was by no means convinced that the Labour leadership was committed enough.

As with the leadership, finally, so with the Leader. Crosland respected Gaitskell's personal integrity and intellectual distinction: there can be no doubting the 'extremely close ties of friendship, loyalty and admiration'[66] that bound together these two distinguished moderates. Yet it is true as well that Crosland, in deploring 'the absence of really effective reforming leadership',[67] was also deploring the reluctance of Gaitskell the Leader to move decisively in the direction of far-reaching change. Praising Gaitskell's statesmanship in a *Socialist Commentary* tribute to mark the tenth anniversary of Gaitskell's death, Crosland qualified the appreciation with the reminder that there was more to socialism than statesmanship alone: 'Whether he was a sufficiently radical leader for a left-wing party is another question.'[68] Hugh Gaitskell, as Stephen Haseler has found, was economical even in the use of the emotive term itself: 'Not once during his seven years as Leader did Gaitskell, when referring to Labour, use the term "Socialist Party" in a public performance.'[69] Seen in that context, the identity of *The Conservative Enemy* is likely to have been somewhat less specific than Mr Macmillan, Sir Moneybags and Lord Shirefox on their own.

In what sense Crosland believed himself to be more radical than Gaitskell is not, as it happens, all that easy to establish. A case in point is his plea to his party in the run-up to the election that was, ending the short-lived Heath Government, to restore Harold Wilson to the Premiership. Then, writing in *The Observer* in 1973, Crosland stipulated that Labour needed 'detailed egalitarian policies' and the will to act on them – but that, still more, it had to be unafraid to take from the rich if it was to be successful in giving to the poor: 'Still more it needs a determination to "bash the rich", by a wealth tax, a gifts tax, the public ownership of land, and to communicate to the country a clear vision of a fairer and more equal Britain.'[70] Crosland stipulated that Labour had to be a party of active redistribution and not simply a coalition of complacent economists confident that growth and social services would do all that was needed. What he says is of real interest in itself – but the essence of his message had already been endorsed by Little Hugh and Big Hugh alike. It is difficult in fact to think of a single major proposal advanced by Crosland with which Gaitskell would have wanted to take issue. If Hugh was insufficiently radical for a post-conservative future, then so, logically speaking, must Tony have been.

Crosland believed that some members of the Labour Party were *excessively* radical and therefore a threat. Writing to Gaitskell in 1960, he issued an explicit warning about a potential lurch in the wrong direction: 'Every party must have its extremist wing.... But our Left is clearly too numerous; it constantly pulls us towards the Left when the electorate is moving Right, it forces us into constant, damaging paper compromises, and generally it makes the Party virtually ungovernable.'[71] Crosland's proposal in 1960 was to expel altogether the 20 hard-left Members of Parliament and to seek an accommodation with left-of-centrists such as Wilson and even Benn ('Of course he's a hopeless neurotic; but he could be won back').[72] The extremist wing was convinced that private capital was a source of social privilege and political influence. The extremist wing took the view that the economy formed the basis for the culture, that the workers could not be freed from alienation and depredation so long as the wealthy continued to collect the surplus from exploitation. The extremist wing was persuaded that the personal social services were at the cutting edge – and Crosland, as Benn remembers from the Cabinet in 1976, was not so sure: 'Crosland then launched into a great attack on how many long-haired social workers there were. It was disgusting.'[73] Not every Tony Benn would have agreed with Tony Crosland that the extremist wing was in the event *excessively* radical: some would have wished no doubt to describe it as *just radical enough*. In the case of the 'loony lefties', the 'beardy-weirdies', the militant Trotskyists, the residual Marxists, however, at least Crosland came forward to give the reasons for his assessment. In the case of Hugh Gaitskell, *insufficiently* radical despite having so much in common with the Plato to whom he so frequently took the part of the Socrates, Crosland did not. Whatever the differences may have been, the most that can be said with any confidence is that they are unlikely to have been very great. All things considered, *The Future of Socialism* may reasonably be called the single clearest statement of the economic and social thought of the broader Gaitskellite faction – and of Hugh Gaitskell, the Leader, himself.

The Future of Socialism was published on 1 October 1956. Its appearance coincided with the first day of the Blackpool Conference – the first Labour Conference under the new Party Leader. The symbolism was not lost on *The Times* which, devoting a leader of its own to the events, had this to

say about Crosland and the relevance of his book: 'Mr Gaitskell will find
here an ally for the policy of equality and the classless society into which
he himself has been trying to steer the party.'[74] At 42 shillings, the book
was not cheap. At 540 pages, it was not short. Relishing its subordinate
clauses, bristling with footnotes and statistics, inadequately indexed, the
book was not easy to read. On the other hand, *The Future of Socialism*
seemed to be saying what a number of others were already sensing and
thinking – including Hugh Gaitskell, the Leader, himself.

Lord Altrincham, writing in the *National and English Review*, hinted
that Crosland's book might be regarded as an indicator of a future
Government's socialist reforms: 'His book is important, not only on
account of its intrinsic merits, but also because he is generally reputed to
be one of Mr Gaitskell's kindergarten. In other words, there is some
reason to suppose that he has given us views about the future of Socialism
which, though very definitely his own, may also in a sense be treated as
the quintessence of Gaitskellism.'[75] P. Elliott, writing in the *New Epoch*,
confirmed the impression that one intellectual's work might also be the
quintessence of a group: 'The book does expound in detail many of the
views on future policy recently voiced by Mr Gaitskell.... Frankly, I do
believe that *Future of Socialism* is the blue-print of policy which can be
expected while the present leadership and majority forces are dominant in
the Labour Party. In other words, the right wing cards are on the table.'[76]
The right wing cards were on the table. People who wanted to know what
the right wing thought were directed to the detailed exposition in
Crosland's book.

Crosland's book was a synthesis but it was also a reappraisal. Its double
contribution was early recognised as such by the LSE lecturer William
Pickles in a broadcast talk for the European Service of the BBC: 'Mr
Crosland's book is in my view the most important on its subject since
Eduard Bernstein published his famous *Voraussetzungen des Sozialismus*
[in 1899]. It is the first thoroughgoing attempt in any language since that
date to re-examine the whole of the arguments for socialism, prune away
the irrelevant parts, and re-state what is left in terms of modern facts and
needs.'[77] Hugh Dalton, himself responsible for so many of the right-wing
cards that had been dealt, was able to go along with the view that
Crosland's *Future* ('By far the most considerable book on Socialism since
the war')[78] had enriched the tradition that it had so conspicuously inherited: 'This is a most important book, brilliant, original and brave. It has
already had much clarifying influence on current thought, both inside and
outside the Party. And its influence will grow.'[79] Reviewing the *New
Fabian Essays* in 1952, Dalton had singled out the author of 'The

Transition from Capitalism' for his highest praise: 'Crosland is outstanding among our younger socialist economists. He has a direct and bracing approach to economics and shrewdness in political judgement.'[80] Reading *The Future of Socialism* in 1956, Dalton must have recognised in Crosland's economics of mix much of the non-Marxian eclecticism that he had himself worked so hard to make acceptable: 'I was never much of a Marxist.... My Socialist watchwords – from Cambridge, the Webbs and William Morris – were Equality, Efficiency and Exhilaration. They serve me still.'[81] Equally, however, Dalton was clear in his own mind that Crosland, standing on the shoulders of giants, had succeeded in reappraising the moderate's case, re-thinking social democracy in a manner that was new and fresh. Dalton would have seen no need to dissent from Frank Packenham's verdict, that Crosland's book on balance was likely to be an influence for good: 'If any outsider wanted to know what University dons mean by "an alpha mind" they will find it here.... I see no limit to its possible influence and almost all of it for good'.[82]

Crosland's contemporary, Roy Jenkins, had no doubt in 1956 that Crosland's *Future*, admittedly weak on 'the world scene', was nonetheless an important book, 'thorough' and 'original': 'This is the most important book on socialist theory to appear in this country since Evan Durbin published *The Politics of Democratic Socialism* in 1940.'[83] Looking back on the excitement of 1956 with the perspective of age, Roy Jenkins was later to say that the *Future* had indeed achieved the eminence that he at the very beginning had predicted for it: '*The Future of Socialism* was well received at the time, but only gradually, over the next decade or so, achieved its position as the most important theoretical treatise to be written from the moderate left of British politics in the 25 post-war years.... It was at once libertarian and strongly egalitarian. It saw no conflict which could not be resolved by the flowing tide of continuing economic growth. It was in the mainstream of the optimism, many would now say the complacency, of the English liberal tradition. It influenced a generation.'[84]

One young socialist who was influenced by Crosland's *Future* was William Rodgers. At Oxford in the 1950s, Rodgers was deeply impressed by the logic and the range of Crosland's modern classic: 'Initially, our main texts were Aneurin Bevan's credo *In Place of Fear* and the eclectic *New Fabian Essays*. Others shared my own preference for Evan Durbin's *The Politics of Democratic Socialism*. But from the public arguments of that time – and the exchanges between the Bevanites and the Gaitskellites had an uncompromising bitterness now often forgotten – emerged Anthony Crosland, glamorous, arrogant and above all clever. *The Future of Socialism* soon became the book we kept at our elbow.'[85]

So did the young David Marquand. Marquand admired the brilliance of Crosland's mind and the suitability of his mix: 'Mr Crosland is, by any reckoning, the most impressive Socialist thinker produced by the British Labour movement since the days of Tawney and the Webbs.'[86] Marquand also recognised that there were many on the British Left who refused to share his enthusiasm for Crosland and for the *Future*: 'By one of the cruellest paradoxes of contemporary British politics, he is widely regarded by the militants of his own party as an arch-opportunist, willing to jettison every inconvenient principle for the sake of electoral victory, or at best as a crypto-Liberal with no real Socialist convictions.'[87] Graham Hutton, reviewing Crosland's book for The *Spectator*, put his finger on the nature of the gulf between the ownership-orientated socialists and the equality-and-welfare socialists that Rodgers and Marquand had done right not to under-estimate: 'As one puts his big book down, one recalls *The True Intellectual System of the Universe* by delightful Dr Cudworth in 1678, who tried to confute "all the reason and philosophy of atheism" and demonstrate its impossibility, but set it out so fully and fairly that it converted more Christians to atheism than atheists to Christianity.... His book is damaging to many dogmas held dear by British Socialists. Will it convert him, or they him? And if it converts them, can it possibly be to anything like Socialism?'[88] It is not known how many socialists Crosland converted to social democracy, how many social democrats he repelled into socialism. Nor can it be established if social democracy is essentially a variant of socialism (as Crosland appears to have believed that it was) or if to adhere to the former is fundamentally to renounce an allegiance to the latter (as was implied by the *Tribune* when it reviewed Crosland's *Future* under the banner 'Socialism? How Dare He Use the Word!').[89] What is known, on the other hand, is what happened later in life to William Rodgers and David Marquand. Both left Labour to become founder-members of the new Social Democratic Party.

Crosland and his *Future* represented the views of one vocal faction within the broader Labour movement. As the *Daily Mail* put it at the time of Crosland's death: 'He was not the voice of his party. He was the keeper of its social democratic conscience.... He took things as he found them – parliamentary democracy, the mixed economy, a diverse and unrevolutionary people – and tried to explore ways of shaping from this very English clay a fairer society.'[90] Crosland was the spokesman for socialism as social democracy and for slow inevitability as the conservative *friend*. Others in the Labour movement were less prepared to stop short at a *Future of Socialism* that was so remarkably close to the capitalist present-day.

Thus it was that Norman Birnbaum, obviously persuaded that upgrading, meritocracy and welfare were little more than capitalism without the threat, argued that even in Crosland's ideal future it would remain business as usual for the Pall Mall clubs and the public school contacts, for nepotism and intermarriage, for background and accent, for profits and power: 'He is an enemy of snobbism, of Establishmentarian humbug, but he proposes to do very little which could eradicate the real bases of these attitudes.'[91] Richard Crossman, again, complained that the revisionists' future was dull and routine, the triumph of technocracy over imagination, of means over ends: 'The Labour Party was founded as a movement of moral protest, which denounced the capitalist *status quo* and preached the need for a Socialist transformation of society. To tell our party workers that the need for a Socialist transformation has been eliminated, and that the leadership must now show it can manage a mixed economy as well as the Tories, will destroy the morale of the rank-and-file without regaining the confidence of the electorate.'[92] Rita Hinden herself, reviewing *The Future of Socialism* in the revisionists' own *Socialist Commentary*, expressed the opinion that, nationalisation, planning and fraternity downgraded, liberty, equality and the United States enthroned, Crosland appeared to be predicting the evolution of a property-owning democracy rather than the transcendence of the gain-seeking society by something qualitatively different: 'What Crosland really seems to be arguing, is that there is no future for socialism at all; we are outgrowing it.'[93] Rita Hinden believed that Crosland had stopped short at a *Future of Socialism* that was insufficiently differentiated from the capitalist present-day. She was clearly not alone in asserting that Crosland in his *Future* had not gone far enough.

It is never easy to say precisely how far a theorist of the mixed economy ought ideally to go. What is clear, at any rate, is that Crosland's vision of the future as welfare capitalism seems to have found a responsive readership in the Britain of the 1950s. It found its audience – and, as Maurice Kogan has implied, it catalysed their attitudes: his argument 'was strategic in converting the Labour Party away from the flat-cap adherence to Clause Four of its Constitution and reinforcing Gaitskell's, and the party's, acceptance of a mixed, but controlled, economy.'[94] Crosland stood on the shoulders of Marshall and Pigou, Keynes and Beveridge, Dalton and Jay in order to proclaim to an era that had never had it so good that socialism had to move with the times but that it was hardly the time for socialism to wither away. An advocate neither of extensive nationalisation nor of across-the-board plan, Crosland was a pragmatist who favoured intervention where intervention was needed, free enterprise where the market was better able to do the job. Chapter 4 on Ownership and Chapter 5 on Control demonstrate the way in which the intellectual in politics sought to resolve economic issues on the basis of performance and of consequences alone.

4 Ownership

The Constitution of the Labour Party committed the Party to public ownership. The relevant undertaking may be found in Clause IV (Section 4). Drafted by Sidney Webb in 1918, the passage is uncompromisingly collectivist in its endorsement of the following objective: 'To secure for the workers by hand or by brain the full fruits of their industry and the most equitable distribution thereof that may be possible upon the basis of the common ownership of the means of production, distribution, and exchange.' The Gaitskellites failed in their attempts (most notably in 1959–60) to secure a reworking of a Clause that they regarded as redundant, doctrinaire and dated: 'Changing a sacred text', Roy Jenkins recalls, 'proved more trouble than it was worth. Crosland and I thought Gaitskell ought to have cut his losses earlier.'[1] The moderates failed and the Clause remained. Crosland throughout his political life was the representative of a Party, however undogmatic its leadership in practice, that had committed itself on paper to the complete and total nationalisation of the whole capitalistic enterprise. Clause IV (Section 4) was still being printed on the Labour Party membership-card at the time of Crosland's death in 1977. The commitment had become a tradition and an article of faith.

Crosland was never opposed on principle to the idea of public ownership: a strong advocate of nationalisation where nationalisation was needed, it was Crosland's position that 'a mixed economy is essential to social democracy'[2] and that no government can afford to treat property as inviolable. Simply, Crosland asserted, each case must be considered on its own merits: 'I've got no objection to nationalisation as long as I know exactly why it's being used. My objection only is to the notion that if you do that enough you somehow achieve the socialist utopia.'[3] Crosland's position, in other words, was that all argument must wait upon evidence and that the circumstances must always be made the subject of impartial assessment: 'Until the study has been made, it is best to keep an open mind.'[4]

This chapter is concerned with Crosland's pragmatism when that cautious intellectual on the middle ground turned his attention to the ownership of capital. The discussion is divided into three parts. The first, Looking Backward, considers Crosland's view that the benefits from nationalisation had all-too-frequently been over-estimated by past enthusiasts. The second, Looking Forward, reminds the reader that Crosland despite his reservations remained a selective nationaliser with a list of his own. The third, Performance and Politics, shows that Crosland's quest for social efficiency did not cease at the moment when business equity crossed the border from the private sector to the State.

4.1 LOOKING BACKWARD

The Labour Party in the inter-war years answered the challenge of under-employed capacity and inefficient utilisation with a call for rationalisation and modernisation that it believed must go unheeded so long as property-rights remained in private hands. It called for public ownership as a means to the end of economic recovery that it believed must remain elusive so long as wasteful duplication, unexploited scale and uncoordinated planning stood in the way of full employment and sustained growth. It expressed particular concern about concentrated power and blinkered profit-seeking in the commanding heights that are at the apex of activity: 'The first requirement', Tawney wrote in 1931, 'is, clearly, to master the key positions of the economic world, whence the tune is piped to which the nation dances. Banking, evidently, is one, for it determines the economic weather more directly than any other; transport a second, and power a third; while the coal industry, in England the sole source of power, is a fourth, land and agriculture a fifth, and armaments a sixth.'[1]

Tawney's shopping-list was long but by no means exceptional in the age of uncertainty that bore silent witness to continuing depression and continental dictatorship. Nor should it be forgotten that Labour's roots extend back to the neo-Ricardian socialism of the early Fabians, able to be as tough on unearned remuneration as any Marxist. Consider the case of George Bernard Shaw, who in the original *Fabian Essays* employs the term of 'social democrat' to designate 'the man or woman who desires through Democracy to gather the whole people into the State, so that the State may be trusted with the rent of the country, and finally with the land, the capital, and the organization of the national industry – with all the sources of production, in short, which are now abandoned to the cupidity of irresponsible private individuals'.[2] The legitimation is democracy but the proposal involves collectivisation on a scale that would make more sense to a Lenin than it would, say, to a Wilson or a Callaghan. Irrespective of what Labour was later to become, what is undeniable is the extent to which the roots of the Party extend back to the nineteenth century's search for a divisive surplus that had to be eliminated.

The Labour Party in the inter-war years was the heir to the past and the witness to the present. A pamphlet published by the Party in 1935 gave voice to a view which was hardly a minority opinion in the polarised Britain of the time – that socialism means 'public ownership of the entire productive machine', that socialisation is productive of a nation in which none is 'able to live on the value produced by the work of others': 'The main result is a society in which the work of all kinds of workers is organised, planned and welded together on a national scale for the production of general abundance for all.'[3] Impressed by the argument that ethics and efficiency alike pointed to the need for the State, the Labour Party committed itself to the early nationalisation of the basic industries and the public utilities. Its targets included power, transport, iron, steel, coal, water and land. It also set its sights on the City.

Even the young Clement Attlee had supported the nationalisation of finance in the 1930s – not just of the Bank of England, moreover, but of the discount houses, accepting houses and other monetary intermediaries as well. Elizabeth Durbin quotes from a memorandum in which Atlee states: 'It is, I think, now beyond doubt that the position of London as the centre of world capitalism is incompatible with a socialist regime or even a "moderate" Labour Government. "The City" in the middle of a socialist state is as anomalous as would be the Pope in Moscow.'[4] The acquisition of the banks, it was argued, would give the government control over the money-supply and the credit-multiplier. It would facilitate the pursuit of macroeconomic and regional objectives (including those which rely heavily on the investment-primed expansion of income and expenditure); and it would give the State the power to direct savings into socially-valued if also commercially less-attractive loans.

The young Hugh Gaitskell is known to have accepted, with reservations, the analogy between the nationalisation of the Mint and the public ownership of the joint-stock banks.[5] The young Anthony Crosland wrote from Oxford to report that the 'finance-capitalists' were 'obviously quite hopeless': 'The only thing to do with them is to nationalise the banks as quickly as possible.'[6] The young Harold Macmillan wanted to spare the more commercial of the intermediaries but to buy out the Bank of England: 'Obviously the time has come when the Central Bank should become, openly and in fact, the public utility institution which it has already virtually become in practice.'[7] Macmillan also proposed that the generation of electricity be 'partly owned and completely dominated'[8] by a State-sector Electricity Board and that the essential activity of coal-mining be taken out of the hands of private enterprises notorious for their lethargic adaptation, multiplicity of units, and low-waged labour force: 'I believe that a stage has been reached when coal mining itself should be rationalised under public utility ownership and control.'[9] Macmillan was a Conservative whereas

Attlee, Gaitskell and Crosland were Labour. Nationalisation was widely accepted in the 1930s, however, and so was the image of a State gearing itself up to leadership in war. Macmillan's *Middle Way* put into print what was in the air, that 'it is both possible and desirable to find a solution of our economic difficulties in a mixed system',[10] to combine the best of private-sector drive and initiative with the best of public-sector husbandry and stewardship. Macmillan's *Middle Way* demonstrated just how favourable to State ownership a thinking Conservative could be in the troubled era when even the Right looked Left in search of hope.

The Labour Government of 1945–51 appears in that sense more the actualisation of an on-going consensus than a radical breach with the past. The Bank of England was nationalised (but not the other City intermediaries), and so were the commanding heights of energy, iron and steel, and transport. The model adopted was that of the semi-independent public corporation. The Left Wing of the Party would have preferred direct ministerial control to the arm's-length autonomy of the London Passenger Transport model; and many there still were who continued to believe in the workers' control that had been championed by Penty in *The Restoration of the Gild System* (1906), by Cole in *Self-Government in Industry* (1917), by Tawney in *The Acquisitive Society* (1920). The winning coalition had, however, little time either for continuous accountability or for cooperative control. The Labour Right under Atlee was not motivated to fall back either on Gosplan or on the kibbutz.

By the end of the 1940s a significant number of the traditional targets had been taken. The result, Crosland said, 'is something of an intellectual void'.[11] Those words are virtually the first that the young moderate ever published on the future of socialism. Dating from 1950, from the year in which the Fellow of Trinity entered Parliament for the South Gloucestershire constituency, they indicate an openness to new theories which contrasts sharply with the reproduction of the tried-and-tested that was the instinctual response of the Party's mainstream. *Labour and the New Society*, also published in 1950, contained a declaration of intent which could largely have been taken from Party statements made two decades before: 'Public ownership is the most effective form of public control because it makes industry directly accountable to the people. When coal was nationalised, democracy was extended.... People cannot be expected to develop a sense of social responsibility and unselfishness while private gain is held up as a dominant motive in society. Public ownership gives an opportunity to replace the bad old incentives of fear and greed by the better incentives of responsibility and service to the community.'[12] *Labour and the New Society* preached more of the same. So did

Challenge to Britain. Submitted to Conference by the National Executive in 1953, it contained the reminder that the market sector was irreversibly over the top: 'British capitalism long ago entered its decline.... The attempt to restore free enterprise is impractical.'[13] Crosland identified an intellectual void even before his Party began thirteen years of opposition in 1951. The Party's mainstream, on the other hand, was obviously not persuaded that its conventional wisdom was losing touch with a reality that was stubbornly moving on.

The wilderness years of the 1950s forced Labour to re-think. It must not be assumed, however, that the reconsideration universally favoured the revisionists' cause. Many socialists re-thought and concluded that the old theories were the best theories after all. One of those traditionalists was Aneurin Bevan, who just after the leadership contest told an audience in Manchester that socialism to him remained inseparable from Clause IV: 'If the Labour Party is not going to be a Socialist Party, I don't want to lead it.... If it is not that, I am not interested in it. It loses its appeal when some people go about saying we are going to investigate industries, one by one, to see whether they qualify for nationalization! I regard that as a retrograde step. The National Health Service would never have been established in 1948 in the mood of the movement in 1956.'[14] Bevan, it would be fair to say, looked at the issue of public ownership and saw no sign of an intellectual void.

Bevan was prepared to be tolerant of a minority private sector made up of small competitive businesses: 'The kind of society which we envisage, and which we shall have to live in, will be a mixed society, a mixed economy, in which all the essential instruments of planning are in the hands of the State, in which the characteristic form of employment will be by the community in one form or another, but where we shall have for a very long time the light cavalry of private competitive industry.'[15] Bevan did not demand the early nationalisation of the sum total of British property-rights. No advocate of a public monolith, what he did demand was a continuance of the transfer of title until such a time as the State was in a position to command: 'It is clear to the serious student of modern politics that a mixed economy is what most people of the West would prefer.... In almost all types of human society different forms of property have lived side by side without fatal consequences either for society or for one of them. But it is a requisite of social stability that one type of property ownership should dominate. In the society of the future it should be public property. Private property should yield to the point where social purposes and a decent order of priorities form an easily discernible pattern of life.'[16] Bevan was not incapable of finding reasons for specific de-

privatisations: advocating a State buy-out of Imperial Chemical Industries, for example, he pointed to ICI's near-monopoly position and to the central role of the product in the modern economy. As important as the logic was, however, the passion. Public ownership for Bevan was an absolute principle and an article of faith.

Bevan was fond of presenting himself as a Tredegar miner whose political education had been a mix of industrial injury ('My father ... died in my arms in 1925, choked to death by pneumoconiosis. No compensation was paid him by the mine owners.'),[17] Baptist Wales ('I do not claim to be a very religious man; I never have. But ... Christ drove the money-changers from the Temple. He did not open the doors wide for them to enter.')[18] – and Marx, Engels and Lenin: 'In so far as I can be said to have had a political training at all, it has been in Marxism.... No serious student who studies the history of the last half century can deny the ferment of ideas associated with Marx, Engels and Lenin. Their effectiveness in arming the minds of working class leaders all over the world with intellectual weapons showed that their teaching had an organic relationship with the political and social realities of their time.'[19] Bevan, never distinguishing clearly between the various sources of his socialism, almost certainly exaggerated the influence upon him of the Marxian classics in a manner that in turn exaggerated the significance of the revisionists' campaign to bend back the bent rod. Be the substance as it may, the shadow of the Marxians is unmistakeable in the socialism of Bevan and his fellow fundamentalists. Marx had said that capitalist ownership was incompatible with a socialist future. Labour's Left was able to invoke the authority of the tradition in arguing that socialism was just a word in the absence of continued nationalisation.

Labour's Left in the 1950s showed the influence of a surviving Marxism. So, interestingly, did John Strachey, by that time back on the middle ground. Strachey the revisionist retained his commitment to the socialisation of capital even when, a regular broadcaster on Radio Free Europe, he had long since abandoned any claim to be Strachey the Marxist.

With respect to the objectives to be pursued, Strachey's *Contemporary Capitalism* is clearly from the same stable as Crosland's *The Future of Socialism*, published in the same year: 'The ideal of democratic socialism may be thought of as the attempt ... to realise a liberty that will not turn into the liberty to exploit, an equality that will not contradict variety, and a fraternity that will not become its opposite by striving to impose cooperation by force.'[20] In agreement on liberty, equality and fraternity, still the two authors went their separate ways with respect to the status of nationalisation as a means. Crosland denied that the collectivisation of capital was

a precondition for the classless society. Strachey the revisionist (conspicuously recycling a form of words that had been employed by Strachey the
Marxist some two decades before) was more extreme: 'If Socialists lose
sight of the central importance of the ownership of the means of production', he warned, 'they will cease, in a very real sense, to be Socialists at
all! They will subside into the role of well-intentioned, amiable, rootless,
drifting social reformers.'[21] Reviewing *The Future of Socialism* in the *New
Statesman* in October 1956, Strachey the revisionist made clear that there
was one issue at least on which he still stood shoulder to shoulder with his
earlier incarnation as Strachey the Marxist: 'I shall continue to believe that
the ownership of the means of production is the most important single,
though certainly not the sole determinant of the structure of society. I shall
continue to believe that the social ownership of the decisive part of the
means of production is the only permanent basis for a Socialist, classless
society.'[22] Crosland when he wrote about property was addressing himself
not least to the nationalisers within his own Party. On the Left like Bevan,
of the Centre like Strachey, what is clear is that many remained persuaded
that Marx had been on the right track in linking ideals so intimately to
ownership.

There was a further argument in the nationalisers' arsenal; and this
involved the presumed effectiveness of Soviet planning. The Webbs, first
in 1935 and again in 1947 had, in *Soviet Communism: A New Civilisation*,
put the administrator's seal of approval on the Eastern system of coordination by command. They were not alone in accepting that, just as
Keynesian demand-management could wipe out involuntary unemployment, just as Beveridge's welfarism could see off the Five Giants, so the
directed economy could grow faster than its anarchic competitor. Harold
Wilson, part-time consultant on East-West trade to Montague L. Meyer
Ltd, visited the Eastern bloc on a number of occasions in the 1950s. Ben
Pimlott writes as follows of the Oxford economist's impressions following
one such visit in 1957: 'Eurasian Communists had a bigger impact on him
than American capitalists: he returned with his faith in the efficacy of the
command economies of East Europe and China further reinforced.... The
Soviet Union was, itself, economically more healthy than the United
States.'[23] Wilson, a democrat, a supporter of NATO and of a British
nuclear capacity, was not in any sense a fellow-traveller or a Marxisant
manqué. An economist and not an ideologue, Wilson knew a success
when he saw a success. Like the Webbs, he visited the realm of bureaucratic centralisation and liked the performance that he saw.

So did his close collaborator, Richard Crossman, who in 1960 attacked
Crosland's revisionism for what Crossman asserted was Crosland's

'failure to observe the terrifying contrast between the drive and missionary energy displayed by the Communist bloc and the lethargic, comfortable indolence of the Western democracies.'[24] The Communist bloc had long promised that it would catch up with, then overtake, the market economies. Richard Crossman was a Western democrat who took the boast to be a forecast. Crossman was prepared to make the prediction 'that the whole Western world will face a grave crisis as the balance of power shifts and the countries which rely on planning and nationalisation catch up on our rich and easy-going economies'.[25] Crossman was prepared to warn of change 'as the Communist countries demonstrate with ever increasing force the efficiency of nationalisation': 'Progressively year by year we shall see that, judged in terms of national security, scientific and technological development, popular education, and, finally, even of mass living standards, free enterprise is losing out in the peaceful competition between East and West.'[26] Crossman, in short, was prepared to tell his Party that efficiency meant State and that the economic future was heavily invested in Clause IV: 'It would be strange indeed for the Labour Party to abandon its belief in the central importance of public ownership at the precise moment when the superiority of socialised economies is being triumphantly vindicated in world affairs.'[27] Crosland, in contrast, was not in the least persuaded that planning was being vindicated, the market discredited. Crossman did not review *The Future of Socialism* when it appeared in 1956. He did, however, write privately to the author to say that he had taken from the book a message undeniably different from that which had been intended: 'As you know, I was never a very keen nationaliser; but, when I see the substitute you provide for wholesale nationalisation, I must admit that the case for the latter is somewhat strengthened.'[28] When at last he did address Crosland's revisionism in print, Crossman made clear that he was strongly in favour of public ownership. He cited the economic success of the Communist bloc in triumphant vindication of his view that the moderates simply did not go far enough.

Crossman was a democrat and not a totalitarian. It was his assertion, indeed, that dictatorship was not so much a cause of affluence as a brake on progress: 'Our whole Democratic Socialist case is surely based on the contention that those who combine planning *and* free choice, social discipline *and* civil liberty, a strong Executive *and* independent justice, are not only better but stronger than their totalitarian adversaries.'[29] Crossman prudently avoided the question of how a planned economy can also allow for decentralised choice; or whether personal liberty is not *ipso facto* infringed by exchange controls, manpower policies and permits to trade; or to what extent the judges can protect the individual from the State when it is the Cabinet that dominates the flow of new statutes. Crossman may have been too hasty in his recourse to the *and*, but the thrust of his argument is clear – that representative democracy plus public ownership adds up to an unbeatable combination.

Nye Bevan himself had said the same: 'We will never be able to get the economic resources of this nation fully exploited unless we have a planned economy in which the nation itself can determine its own priorities.'[30] Never an admirer of a leadership lacking in popular legitimation, Bevan was, like Crossman, a strong believer nonetheless in the economic efficiency of the Soviet-type system. Addressing the Party Conference in the wake of the 1959 defeat, Bevan made clear to the compromisers and the orthodoxy alike that the future in his view could only lie with the East: 'The challenge which is going to take place in the next ten years is not going to come from Harold Macmillan…. The challenge is going to come from Russia. The challenge is not going to come from the United States. The challenge is not going to come from Western Germany nor from France. The challenge is going to come from those nations who, however wrong they may be – and I think they are wrong in many fundamental respects – nevertheless are at long last being able to reap the material fruits of economic planning and public ownership.'[31] Clause IV, Bevan emphasised, was economically as efficient as morally it was sound – the sole response, indeed, to the gauntlet thrown down by the East: 'That is where the challenge is coming from, and I want to meet it, because I am not a Communist, I am a Social Democrat. I believe that it is possible for a modern intelligent community to organize its economic life rationally, with decent orders of priority, and it is not necessary to resort to dictatorship in order to do it. I believe that it is possible. That is why I am a Socialist. If I did not believe that, I would be a Communist; I would not be a capitalist!'[32] Nye Bevan, Shadow Foreign Secretary and Deputy Leader of Crosland's own Party, had obviously not been much influenced by *The Future of Socialism* that had been published three years before. The wilderness years of the 1950s forced Labour to re-think. It must not be assumed, however, that the reconsideration universally favoured the revisionists' cause.

Crosland's adversaries were real and not imaginary. Stephen Haseler has said that Labour's supporters tend to be natural Gaitskellites: 'The vast majority of the Labour Movement has always identified the Labour Party with social-democratic reforming ideals.'[33] Even in the 1950s and early 1960s, Haseler asserts, 'the vast majority … had never, in practical terms, taken Party rhetoric, including Clause IV, seriously'.[34] Perhaps he is right; but the fact remains that an activist minority can exercise an influence on Party policy that is disproportionate to its numbers. Crosland recognised that the debate over public ownership had not ended with the historic nationalisations of the 1940s. Fearful lest the Left use the arguments of an earlier period to shape a Britain that had significantly changed in nature, Crosland issued a warning to socialists looking backward that the time had come to consolidate the irreversible gains of the Atlee government rather than to rush without consideration into new acquisitions that might do little to advance the socialists' cause.

Marxists and militants, Crosland said, tended to pyramid their predictions on the assumption 'that the pattern of ownership determined the character of the whole society'.[35] Their monism was over-simplified and naive: 'Ownership, while it can influence, does not uniquely *determine* the character of the society.'[36] Extensive collectivisation had been urgently required in the economic and social conditions of 1945. Aggressive nationalisation had become all but an irrelevance in the altered circumstances of 1956: 'A higher working-class standard of living, more effective joint consultation, better labour relations, a proper use of economic resources, a wider diffusion of power, a greater degree of co-operation, or more social and economic equality – none of these now primarily require a large-scale change in ownership for their fulfilment; still less is such a change a *sufficient* condition of their fulfilment.'[37] Always a means and never an end, common ownership beyond some point is unlikely to be of more than marginal significance to the nature of the surrounding society. Crosland as early as 1946 had sought, presciently, to establish the level of the crucial threshold: 'I am ... doubtful as to how far nationalisation needs to go. We must, of course, get the great concentrations of economic power in our hands, but when we have done that we shall only have nationalised about 20 per cent (quantitatively) of industry. Where do we go from there? In other words, does nationalisation stop after the 2nd. five years? I don't think I should be worried if it did.'[38] Socialism would continue to presuppose redistributive services and levelling regulations (including, with respect to property, 'inheritance laws that made the handing down of large private business impossible').[39] The required minimum of nationalisation achieved, however, ownership, beyond the crucial threshold, loses its urgency as a major determinant of a society's character.

Advocates of public ownership tended to advance the further defence that nationalisation was needed in order to equalise unwarranted disparities in income and wealth. Crosland did not deny the appeal of the defence, in an early letter describing it as 'the only real argument in favour of far more wholesale socialisation'.[40] What he did deny was its continuing relevance in a reforming Britain of fiscal socialism and the welfare state. Taxes and services could level outcomes without the need first to take over capital: 'Western social-democracy to-day has more in common with modern-style welfare capitalism than with Soviet Communism.'[41] Public ownership had not delivered the equality promised in the countries of the East: 'I think that public ownership is not a sufficient definition of socialism. If it were, we would have to say that Soviet Russia and all the communist Eastern European countries simply because they have public ownership [of the] means of production were socialist countries. I don't consider that they are, because they combine public ownership with a very high degree of privilege and inequality and all the things that matter to me.'[42] Public ownership had not shown itself significantly more egalitarian in the British compromise from Attlee to Heath: 'We can have a great increase in public ownership without any increase in equality, and indeed we have had since 1945.'[43] Nationalisers should never forget the lesson of Dalton and Jay, that full compensation paid to erstwhile shareholders in the form of interest-bearing bonds must mean that investors' purchasing-power will only very slightly be reduced – and that expropriation without compensation is not an option which the Labour Party has ever seriously entertained as just. Thence the conclusion, that equality is the end but public ownership no longer the obvious means. As Tony Benn states, Crosland believed that 'there was no link between public ownership and equality, no link between powers and control'.[44] There being no link, Crosland saw no need to support wholesale socialisation with the objective in mind of a more equal Britain.

Nationalisers tended also to argue that a more harmonious atmosphere in industry, a closer personal identification with wider social purposes, was likely to be a consequence of the elimination of the profit-seeking poison. Crosland himself had employed this argument in 1946 in the Oxford Union. Then, debating the coal industry against Harold Macmillan, just elected for Bromley, Crosland had presented a straightforward labour-capital explanation of 'sullen resentment', 'hostility', 'intense hatred & bitterness v. the owners' in terms of a direct response to 'low wages, excessive hrs., totally inadequate compensation for industry, frighteningly high accident rate': 'The result was an almost permanent state of guerilla warfare.'[45] The problem was capitalism, the solution a State that treats its workers with respect: 'It isn't concerned to make monopoly profits, but merely pay its way, so that the incentive to exploitation is just not there.'[46] Crosland in 1946 told the Oxford Union that miners' cooperation was not to be expected under profit-seeking capitalism: 'You can't & won't get that cooperation except by nationalisation.'[47] A decade later, the profit-seekers bought out, he was still waiting for an end to the tensions associated with 'the persistence of obvious class inequality', to the discontentment born of 'the suspicion that wages are not getting a fair deal':[48] 'The miners and railwaymen are in fact working for the public good as well as for themselves, and for an extremely urgent public good; and there are no shareholders or private profits to "expropriate" any of the fruits of their labour. Yet this appears to make only a limited psychological difference; and neither industry has a contented atmosphere.'[49] Objectively speaking, public ownership does not necessarily satisfy social objectives: 'Not all nationalized industries have flawless records on safety, the control of pollution or even incorruptibility. The British Government is itself the largest single employer of low-wage workers.'[50] Subjectively speaking, the transfer of title does not necessarily replicate wartime's sense of national solidarity: 'The simple act of replacing individual by group or collective relationships does not necessarily make people more contented, or fraternal, or amiable.'[51] It is, Crosland maintained, not enough merely to tell the workers that antagonism gives way to cohesion the instant that the State takes over the capital: 'They must see it, and feel it, themselves; and it is not easy to create the institutional framework within which they will.'[52] It is not easy to create the institutional framework within which people, overcoming greed, will feel at one with the national whole. It is much easier, being negative, to say what institutional changes will prove inadequate with respect to integration. Nationalisation will prove inadequate: 'the money incentive is just as persuasive',[53] the industrial atmosphere not significantly less confrontational. The socialist would in the circumstances be well advised not to expect the improbable from a simple change in the name of the boss.

Last but not least there was efficiency. Supporters of the State tended to put forward the view that public ownership would prove economical and productive. Their logic was rich and it was powerful. Nationalisation would eliminate parallel structures and the consequent under-utilisation of plant. It would discipline natural monopolies with technical economies of large scale. It would protect domestic supplies of essential commodities (and, of course, the jobs and communities that depended upon them). It would direct scarce savings into socially-valued investments. It would substitute coordination and combination for the unplanned chaos of competitive search. The economic logic was rich and powerful; and it was not without its appeal to the young Crosland. Crosland in 1946 had explained the 'incompetence', the 'inefficiency', the 'mismanagement' of the British coal industry in terms of capitalists and markets – in terms, in other words, of 800 pits owned by no less than 400 firms, most of them 'too small to be efficient', most of them 'too small to afford the risk'.[54] What was needed, Crosland said, was the amalgamation of units and the injection of public money. If the State was to unify and to pay, Crosland inferred, then the State should also own.

Crosland in 1946 endorsed the nationalisation of the coal industry and referred specifically to economic efficiency: 'We believed that by restricting the liberty of a few, we cd. increase the prosperity of all.'[55] Even in the 1940s, however, he was making clear that he had significant doubts as to the magnitude of the benefit: 'I have still to be convinced that the buying out of the shareholder is a necessary corollary of increased efficiency. Nor do I think, as a layman, that the nationalisation of the mines would produce even an extra 1000 tons a week from the industry. The question of management is really quite separate.'[56] Even in advance of nationalisation Crosland was not one to exaggerate the benefit. Nor was he prepared to do so after the event. The private sector, he consistently said, was tolerably efficient, 'the record of the nationalized industries ... at least not beyond reproach':[57] 'We have not yet succeeded in making the existing nationalized industries accountable in any satisfactory sense – certainly not to the consumer.'[58] Looking backward, Crosland in the wilderness years of the 1950s accepted that Labour had done right to take coal and gas, rail transport and telecommunications into public ownership. Looking forward, however, Crosland was adamant that the obvious bastions had largely fallen and that the old logic was increasingly inappropriate in the changed circumstances: 'The efficiency criterion ... does not point clearly to further large-scale nationalization.'[59] Looking forward, Crosland argued, there was an urgent need for Labour to reassess its techniques in the light of the objectives that it wished to attain.

4.2 LOOKING FORWARD

Crosland preached caution. He also believed that caution was more and more the people's choice: 'A democratic society is what we want and therefore we have to be in tune with the mood of the country which is towards the Centre.'[1] Emotion was giving way to consensus, Crosland said at the start of what he predicted would be the tranquil, rational decade of the 1960s: 'It is perfectly clear that there is going to be a decline in passion, a decline in militancy.... We are clearly going to have fewer demonstrations, fewer hunger marches, fewer crowds in Hyde Park.'[2] Extremism was giving way to agreement, Crosland said; and that meant that no Labour Party which remained doctrinally committed to all-out, one hundred per cent nationalisation of the means of production, distribution and exchange would stand a chance of winning elections in the 1960s.[3] Crosland had expressed his own conviction as early as 1946 that '100 per cent Socialism' was something 'we certainly don't want'.[4] The electoral defeats of 1951, 1955 and 1959 appear to have indicated to him that, precisely because of the convergence at the Centre, the voters did not want it either: 'Large-scale further nationalization would not be electorally popular'.[5] Richard Crossman made an identical assessment of the mood of the nation in the decade of the three defeats: 'Let me admit at once that Revisionism faithfully reflects the political mood of Britain during the last eight years.'[6] Richard Crossman, of course, saw the swing as a fluctuation. Anthony Crosland believed it to be a trend.

Crosland throughout his career took the view that the commitment to extensive further nationalisation was likely to cost Labour its well-deserved success. The last election he ever fought demonstrates the tenacity of his revisionist moderation. Before the election of 1974 he advised the Party, at a meeting at the Churchill Hotel, that 'the public would accept nationalisation in individual cases but not as the general case'.[7] After the election of 1974 he announced that the success had confirmed what he had predicted all along: 'Nationalisation is irrelevant and in constituencies that have nationalised industries, Labour did very badly because the industries are so unpopular; we only did well where they were lame ducks.'[8] Crosland preached caution. Crosland the theorist of consolidation and Crosland the vote-seeking politician were evidently in complete agreement on the need to make haste very slowly indeed.

Crosland preached caution but he did not preach inaction. A self-styled radical and not a conservative, Crosland would not have accepted that he was opposed to change where there was a need for change. Simply, it was Crosland's position that Clause IV took too much on trust when the premium instead ought to be on proof. Towards the beginning of his career Crosland made clear his view that redeployment and restructuring, married to socialisation in the specific case of coal, could in general terms be 'more or less successfully carried out under either public or private ownership': 'On the purely economic side, no simple slogan or formula makes any sense…. It is silly to take an extreme position, and argue *a priori* that one or other form of ownership is essential to the redeployment of resources.'[9] Towards the end of his career Crosland indicated that he retained his commitment to the cause of the open mind: 'I have long believed that no generalization was possible about the relative efficiency of publicly-owned and privately-owned industry. Each case has to be considered pragmatically on its merits.'[10] There was nothing in Clause IV about pragmatism. There was nothing in Labour's Constitution about the need to think things through.

Crosland looking backward had expressed his doubts about the across-the-board relevance of the old-style arguments. Ownership can influence but it does not determine. Equality neither presupposes nor is produced by socialisation. Co-operation and cohesion are not much affected by the title to capital. Economic efficiency is sometimes improved and sometimes is not. Crosland looking backward had reached the conclusion that the old-style arguments gave no more than limited guidance to a future of nationalisation that could only be specific and could never be general.

Yes nationalisation there would have to be; and Crosland, looking forward, was able to name new candidates for public ownership. These candidates will be examined respectively under the headings of Industry, Housing and Land. Crosland in the *New Fabian Essays* said of nationalisation that 'the long-run case for it remains extremely strong'.[11] Always specific and never general, what is striking is the constancy of his commitment to State ownership once he had convinced himself that private ownership consistently meant worse.

(a) Industry

Despite Clause IV (and the popular perception of Clause IV) Labour in the 1950s, vacillating and indecisive, had lost its way. In the 1950 campaign Labour set its sights on sugar and cement: they were nowhere to be seen in 1955 and 1959. In 1955 chemicals went on the shopping-list: not mentioned in 1950, the proposal had vanished by 1959. At various times the leaders and the activists flirted with the nationalisation of insurance, meat-wholesaling, building, land, mining machinery, aircraft, heavy electrical engineering, machine-tools and something evocatively known as the '250 major monopolies'. Only water figured in the programmes of 1950, 1955 *and* 1959. Labour in the circumstances was believed not to know its own mind. Labour was also feared: split by ideology and in-fighting, there was always the threat that Labour would sweep through the whole of corporate capitalism with the legitimation of its Clause IV. Labour in the 1950s clearly needed both to say where it stood and to convince the business community that investment would be safe in its hands.

Crosland was a participant in the debates of the 1950s. He was also an intellectual sceptic, committed to pointing out that the old-style certainties were losing their cutting edge at the margin: 'If the Party were to proceed with nationalization, using the obvious criterion of size, the next industries on the list (automobiles, aircraft, chemicals, shipbuilding, radio, electrical equipment) are not "natural" candidates.... They are neither public utilities, nor basic industries (in the sense that coal and railways are basic), nor natural monopolies, nor in need of central coordination; moreover, they have indistinct boundaries, and they are heavily involved in export markets.'[12] Size, Crosland had said in 1946, is of importance first and foremost because of its cross-correlation with command: 'Our real case for socialisation is less that it leads to more obvious efficiency than that without it a social & economic democracy is impossible. So I fancy we must go for industries roughly in order of their total importance to the country's essential economic life.'[13] Size, Crosland implied in 1959, had ceased to represent a social problem of concentrated power. Attlee's seizure of the commanding heights had effectively seen to that. Size might still point to State where the industry was basic to economic survival or where a forward-falling supply-curve favoured a single firm with a natural monopoly: 'I think a mixture of the monopoly and the essential-public-service criterion', Crosland had written in 1946, 'will have in fact to be our guide.'[14] Size might also speak for State where there was a need for a nationally-planned network or grid; or where it was not economies of scale *per se* so much as lack of competition from foreign suppliers that gave domestic corporations their opportunity to make windfall gains. Size, Crosland emphasised, had effectively identified good candidates for nationalisation in the past. The present, however, was different: lacking a clear and simple standard, the socialist had no choice but to monitor performance rather than seizing upon a distinguishing characteristic that might, like size, attract the nationalisers to the social benefactors and not only to the social pariahs.

Crosland for his own part had taken the trouble to look the candidates most carefully in the mouth. It was in that way that he had made up his mind in respect of steel. Nationalised in 1951, de-nationalised two years later, Crosland in 1953 announced that 'even to the layman the case for re-nationalizing steel is clearly made out'.[15] The case in question was the straightforward one of market failure in the economists' tradition of Marshall and Pigou. There was, Crosland said in *Britain's Economic Problem*, a 'congenital terror of under-utilization'[16] in an industry that was by its nature heavily dependant upon fixed capital. The steel-producers lived in apprehension of idle plant. The result was too little investment, a permanent shortage of capacity, and therewith an endemic lack of an essential commodity. The deficiency was a real one – and the answer was the State: 'When the government is willing, but private enterprise is not', Crosland declared in *The Future of Socialism*, 'it must be a government responsibility to ensure, where necessary by nationalisation, that the industrial base ... expands fast enough to support the expected rise in total output.'[17] The mine-owners in the 1940s had had to be bought out because of their reluctance to sink new pits, their attachment to obsolete equipment and dilapidated structures. The steel-producers in the 1950s were condemning themselves through the sheer lack of steel to the same inevitability of a State prepared to achieve. Crosland's confidence in nationalised industry may perhaps have been exaggerated; and he ought no doubt to have acknowledged that the uncertainty about the locus of ownership must in itself have been a significant cause of the reluctance to invest. Even so, his message at least is not in doubt. Britain needs its steel. To get its steel, it must turn to its State.

The Future of Socialism also endorses the nationalisation of the machine-tool industries. As with steel, it is efficiency and not ideology that dominates Crosland's argument when he seeks to show that excessive competition works to the detriment of the consumer's welfare: 'In such cases, the public acquisition and subsequent amalgamation of a number of separate firms might greatly improve the structural fitness of the industry.'[18] In such cases, in other words, even the staunchest Tory would do well to vote Labour in self-interested pursuit of technical economies unalloyed by the monopolist's commercial incentive to over-charge.

Crosland anticipated that nationalisation in the future would very often have to proceed on a firm-by-firm and not an industry-by-industry basis. In order to facilitate the fine-tuning and the selective targeting, he called for the creation of a publicly-owned investment trust, 'provided with public funds but independent of the Government, with instructions simply to make a profit by buying, establishing, or selling productive concerns. It would act, in effect, like a take-over bidder, seeking out inefficient firms, assets that were wrongly or under-utilised, slothful managements, and opportunities for new production.... Its choice of firms to acquire would be justified on clear commercial principles; and no question of compulsory, legislative discrimination would arise.'[19] Actively engaged in picking winners and spotting under-valued potential, faster than private predators in putting in bids for businesses that were not doing their best, prepared to sell at a profit as well as to snap up a bargain, one is tempted to ask why the managers of such a trust should want to be civil servants at all when they could in all probability command several times their State salary by trading entrepreneurially on their own. Crosland does not make clear why public ownership rather than a more competitive market should be the proper way to improve the performance of inefficient businesses or of lazy managements. Nor does he acknowledge that the take-overs he envisages (bereft as they are of 'compulsory, legislative discrimination') might be commercially sound but also at variance with a wider social interest that ranks over-manning above redundancies, a congenial workplace above a ruthless speed-up. His proposal for a publicly-owned investment trust has, on the other hand, the interesting feature that it enlists a singularly *micro*-economic perspective in the determination of the public sector. It is, after all, single firms and not whole industries that are to be identified as under-performing and made the wards of the economising State.

Creeping nationalisation can proceed through the intermediation of a State-owned trust. It can also be the consequence of the horizontal and vertical expansion of existing undertakings, of corporations already public due to scale or to monopoly. Crosland cites with approval the initiative shown by the Swedish railways in buying up private bus companies; and he also encourages the government to supply risk-capital in order to make possible the acquisition of neighbouring activities such as these. Crosland would not have proposed that the nationalised industries be allowed to swallow up their commercial competitors if he had believed that the outcome of the purchase would be to the detriment of the consumer. His argument will have an immediate appeal to readers who think that choice, quantity, quality and price will be significantly improved once the Post Office has bought heavily into the courier market as well.

The case for creeping nationalisation would be that much more persuasive were the pragmatist, more open than was Crosland to the democratic desirability of reversing what the past had done, to insist on permanent reappraisal in recognition of permanent change. New technology can undermine old conclusions by opening up what had previously been a natural monopoly to a viable number of active competitors. Rigorous logic can put paid to the inference that, because there must be a single supplier of railway track, so too must there be a single supplier of station-buffets and station-hotels. Strict egalitarianism can challenge the complacency of cross-subsidisation by uncovering instances where the rich person's loss-maker is paid for out of the poor person's surplus. The case for creeping nationalisation would be that much more convincing, in short, were Crosland to have provided a pragmatist's defence of creeping privatisation as well. Lacking such a defence, the danger is real that Crosland's State will travel down a one-way street as if guided by an invisible ratchet that is unprepared to reconsider a decision once a verdict on relative performance has after careful study been set in stone.

(b) Housing

Speaking of the ownership of industry, it was Crosland's message that the imperative had been shunted by Atlee's nationalisations from the centre to the periphery: 'Frequently public ownership is much more urgent in what one might call the social field, land and housing and so on, than it is in the field of manufacturing industry, which is where it attracts much the most attention inside the Labour Party.'[20] The old targets had descended into marginality. The new targets, on the other hand, had not received the socialism they deserved. Accommodation is a case in point.

Delivering the Herbert Morrison Memorial Lecture in 1971, Crosland said that the market had proved a success in the case of cabbages and cars, but that housing was a different matter. Pointing to the persistence of 'homelessness, overcrowding and slums',[21] Crosland concluded that an adequate supply at a reasonable price had not been forthcoming in respect of privately-owned accommodation for rent. The failure was endemic to the service; and that is why there was no alternative to socialised provision if there were to be a victory in the war against 'poverty and squalor which it is Labour's first objective to eliminate'.[22] Convinced that the market sector was doomed to inadequate supply at an unreasonable price, Crosland looked forward with hope to a more socialistic future in which 'local authorities will become the main provider of unfurnished rented accommodation'.[23]

Economic inefficiency, Crosland said, is compounded by an imbalance of power: 'The relationship between landlord and tenant is too unequal; and the landlord wields a degree of power over his tenant's life which is unacceptable in a democratic society.'[24] The landlord, laws against harassment and eviction notwithstanding, is able with remarkable ease to get rid of his tenants should he wish to convert and sell. The high-income tenant will at least be in a position to afford alternative accommodation. The low-income household will be more vulnerable to insecurity. In that sense the power-imbalance will be a vertical inequity as well. Unacceptable inequalities evidently reinforced the inference drawn by Crosland from market under-supply, that 'private landlordism is not an appropriate form of house-ownership in an advanced society'.[25]

Some observers, no doubt, would say that the real deficiency in the area of rented accommodation was neither economic nor ethical but rather political. The suspension of rent-control might have succeeded in expanding the supply of units. The restriction of improvement-grants to owner-occupiers might have stemmed speculative conversion made possible by regressive subsidy. Rent-rebates to deprived households, enforceable covenants governing improvements and repairs, statutory notice-periods but not absolute protection for the sitting tenant – these and other interventions might adequately have expanded the liberty of the have-nots without the need for the State actually to purchase and to let. Crosland did not believe that the State (through excessive restriction or through unwise intervention) had been a significant cause of the problem which he called upon the State through public ownership to resolve. A spokesman for the open mind, it was nonetheless his practice to assume that it is the private sector that is normally the source of the failures, the public sector that must be relied upon for the defence of the public interest.

(c) Land

Land scheduled for building or rebuilding had been subject to the speculative abuse of escalating values: 'Economic prudence, as well as social justice, demands a final solution in this field.'[26] By nationalising land for development, the State would stem the rise in ground-rents and the cost of property. It would also block off the opportunity for greedy profiteers to amass huge fortunes by means of buying and then of selling on. A betterment-levy would force the speculators to share their windfall gains. Public ownership would do more: blocking off rather than taxing away, it would compel the alert to channel their initiative into more productive employments.

Besides that, 'taxation doesn't give you one of the advantages of public ownership, that is that ownership does enable [you] to plan much better'.[27] Taxes and controls in a system of private ownership are infinitely preferable to the *laissez-faire* outcome of a free market in land. Yet the charge imposed or the permission denied must pale into insignificance when compared with the power of direction, encouraging and not blocking, positive and not negative, that is acquired by local or national government once it has taken into the public sector the ownership of the asset. In the case of manufacturing industry the requisite leverage can typically be exercised without any need for the capital to become the property of the State: 'From the present character of large-scale industry to-day, i.e. from the joint-stock form, it follows that the issue of "pure" nationalisation is largely irrelevant. All we need or want is public control.'[28] In the case of development land the position is different. Government controls and government spending will do what they can to address the challenges of congestion and transport policy, urban and rural planning. What they can will frequently not be enough unless and until the State has the courage to own the land as well: 'Therefore these are issues which ought to be easier for the Left to articulate than for the Right to articulate.'[29]

Efficacy points to State. So too does ethics. The moral shortcoming in the case of land involves the unearned reward, the demand-driven increment, that accrues to the passive recipient of the pure rent in consequence of the appreciation in the value of a stock of which the physical quantity is absolutely fixed in supply. Since land normally appreciates at a faster rate than does the average asset, it becomes over time an increasingly large part of the total national wealth. Such a growth-dividend is ethically suspect in so far as it is 'private value due to public causes'.[30] Nor should it be forgotten that the 'public causes' engendering the spillover need not be as general as the income elasticity of demand. They can be as specific as the windfall gain that is the free gift of industrial zoning and the protection of the green belt. Such politically-induced betterment was clearly a matter of concern to Crosland when, Secretary of State for the Environment as well as socialist intellectual, he wrote as follows of unde- served prizes handed out by interventionist governments: 'It is quite unac- ceptable that restrictions imposed by society for the general good should create huge unearned gains for capriciously-selected individuals.'[31] It had not escaped Crosland's notice that the individuals might be random but that the classes were not: the rich owned significantly more land than the poor and were therefore significantly more likely to reap the unearned gains. More disturbing still is the fact that so much of the disproportionate entitlement was the result of parentage and not of achievement: 'Inherited wealth of this kind is especially offensive to Socialists, particularly when, as with land, it is *undertaxed* inherited wealth.'[32] The accident of birth thus accentuates the moral shortcoming of the situational rent. Fiscal socialism can alleviate the abuse. Fiscal socialism cannot eliminate it.

That being the case, one would have expected Crosland to recommend the nationalisation of all land, not simply of development land. In places, indeed, he does appear to be very much in sympathy with proposals significantly less moderate than those officially endorsed by the Labour Party.[33] On balance, however, he was reconciled to the survival of privately-owned land for the usual purposes of agriculture, commerce, industry, owner-occupied accommodation. Perhaps he hoped that at some time in the future the development land nationalised would become the nucleus around which further acquisitions would come to cluster. Meanwhile, it should be noted just how radical were the recommendations that Crosland actually made – and how late in his career he was continuing to call for public ownership. The subject was the centrepiece of his Rita Hinden Memorial Lecture (on 'Socialism, Land and Equality') of 1974.

In attacking the pure rent that accrues to development land, Crosland was building on the activity-orientated judgementalism of earlier socialists such as Gaitskell, Tawney and, of course, Shaw. Shaw knew the differ- ence between productive work and slothful ease. He was able in 1889 to pass the following sentence on the free-riding landowners and their demand-led increment: 'What the achievement of Socialism involves economically, is the transfer of rent from the class which now appropriates it to the whole people. Rent being that part of the produce which is indi- vidually unearned, this is the only equitable method of disposing of it.'[34] Shaw's puritanical conscience was evidently revolted by a state of affairs in which, however functional the rent itself as an indicator of relative scarcity, still the rent-*recipient* performed no duties such as might give him a moral right to claim a reward. Here as elsewhere, in Shaw's own words, the Fabians' proposals 'have on them that stamp of the vestry which is so congenial to the British mind'.[35] As with Shaw, so with Crosland, who shared the Fabians' overall disapprobation of the something-for-nothing culture that separates the exertion from the share.

Crosland advocating nationalisation was more frequently critical of the over-payment of the passive than he was of the under-payment of the productive. Crosland advocating nationalisation was evidently taking as his enemy not so much active entrepreneurship in the sense of the Dark, Satanic Gradgrind as the absentee landowner in the sense of Henry George. Yet Henry George's something-for-nothing can hardly be said to arise nowhere else than in respect of land: 'The development over the years of the joint stock company and the increasing size of the business undertaking has meant that most owners of industrial shares are as passive or functionless as Henry George's landowners, and indeed far more so than the owners of agricultural land.'[36] That statement, by Hugh Gaitskell, shows that even revisionists opposed to across-the-board socialisation still recognised a Pandora's Box when they saw one.

Tawney, of course, had gone further in his call for a Functional Society determined to 'remove the dead hand of private ownership, when the private owner has ceased to perform any positive function'.[37] Later Galbraith was to propose the public ownership of all business corporations where the shareholder had sunk to the status of a 'purely passive recipient of income', where the management had in consequence elevated itself into a 'self-governing, self-perpetuating bureaucracy.'[38] In contrast to Tawney and Galbraith, however, the revisionists were quick to identify the functionless claim but slow to propose its socialisation. Thus Evan Durbin had called for greater State control over industry but was not ready to recommend the euthanasia of the absentee interest that he himself had termed 'parasitic', the abolition of private shareholding that he himself had branded 'useless', 'worse than indefensible', the termination of the *rentier* income that he himself had said 'is paid, collectively, for nothing'.[39] Douglas Jay, similarly, had regarded the corporation's capitalists as in effect devoid of function but had nonetheless taken the view that the modern socialist would do well to change the subject: 'Socialists have been mistaken in making ownership of the means of production instead of ownership of inherited property the test of socialization.'[40] Like *The Politics of Democratic Socialism*, *The Socialist Case* does not defend and it does not excuse. What it does do is to compromise by focusing the attack not on the capital itself but instead on its intergenerational transmission. The 'central aim' of socialism, Jay said, 'must be the abolition of all inherited incomes rather than all large incomes or all incomes that can be called "profit"'.[41]

Marx and Engels wanted private ownership to be ended because it was inseparable from the alienation of surplus. Tawney and Galbraith were favourable to nationalisation of share-titles where corporate capitalism had outgrown its function. Durbin and Jay wanted controls and taxes.

Controls (on mergers, on safety, on disclosure) combined with taxes (the capital gains tax, the estate duty) were Gaitskell's answer to the challenge of the private shareholder. They were Anthony Crosland's answer as well. The functionless rather than the exploitative having become the primary focus for moral outrage, the emphasis having shifted from capital in the sense of Marx to land in the sense of Ricardo, one would have expected Crosland like other revisionists to have seen in the ownership of shares the same lack of legitimacy that he had identified in the ownership of land. Possibly he did; but the recommendations he made were not of equal force. In the case of land, Crosland believed nationalisation to be appropriate. In the case of shares he was prepared to be satisfied with controls and taxes. Strachey the revisionist was less satisfied. Convinced that *The Future of Socialism* was 'a major work' ('No-one must in future take part in the current and, I trust, growing controversy on Socialism without having read it'), Strachey the revisionist contended in his *New Statesman* review that he could see little logic in dividend payment that was subsequently re-claimed by fiscal measures: 'Why ... pay the functionless owners their money in the first place?'[42] Strachey the revisionist still believed, of course, that ownership shapes superstructure. Crosland the revisionist did not: 'The ownership of the means of production is not now, in our view, the key factor which imparts to a society its essential character. Collectivism, private ownership or a mixed economy are all compatible with widely varying degrees of equality, freedom, democracy, exploitation, class feeling, industrial democracy and economic growth.'[43]

Property matters, Crosland said; but so do the many other influences that play their part in making us the nation that we are. That being the case, Crosland reasoned, it may be a minor inconsistency but it cannot be a major omission to tolerate the functionless shareholder while at the same time threatening the functionless landowner. The compromise that Crosland ultimately struck was therefore the same as that of Durbin and Jay. He advocated controls and taxes. Then he changed the subject.

4.3 PERFORMANCE AND POLITICS

Nationalisation will sometimes be the first step. It will never be the last. Crosland believed that the extension of public ownership would be inadequate so long as it was not accompanied by a clarification and a codification of the relationship between the State as owner and the businesses to which it holds the titles.

The first consideration involves variety, plurality and competition. In the case of industry this would at the margin mean a patchwork quilt of public and private: 'In the light of the evident disadvantages, outside the public utility field, of state monopoly and enormous scale, the method should be to take over not whole industries, but individual firms, leaving others still in private hands: or to set up new government-owned plants to compete with existing private firms.'[1] In the case of housing the council-owned rented sector would co-exist with owner-occupation, cooperative accommodation, housing associations and private lets: 'The object should be the maximum degree of choice, muddle and variety.'[2] In the case of land some plots would be owned by central government, some by local government, some by households, some by firms, some by the Forestry Commission, some by the National Trust. The result, here as elsewhere, would not be the intolerance of the single-valued solution but rather 'a diverse, diffused, pluralist, and heterogeneous pattern of ownership'[3] such as would increase the options and extend the possibilities.

What Crosland envisaged, in other words, was a genuinely mixed economy. Sometimes public and private would operate in different branches (the Metropolitan Police, the corner newsagent) and sometimes they would co-habit the same sectors (building, oil). Sometimes public and private would even be in joint ownership of a single undertaking: this would come about where a National Insurance Fund held investments in equities as well as gilt-edged, or where the government making a loan demanded voting stock and profit payment in return, or where shares ceded in liquidation of tax liability were held by a specialist parastatal such as the Dalton-like Death Duty Commissioners. The model, in short, is mix. The economy as a whole should be a mix of public ownership and private enterprise. The public sector should be a mix of devolved municipalities and central bureaucracies, arms-length corporations and operationally-independent funds. The private sector should be a mix of venturesome entrepreneurship and corporate capitalism, trades-union initiative and self-help endeavour. Mix means mix. Crosland on the middle ground was most definitely in favour of mix.

He was also in favour of active competition in those areas of social activity where he believed this to be a viable proposition. Development land is economically destabilising if priced by rivalry and council rents must not be set by supply and demand: where active competition was in his view inappropriate, Crosland was content to call for variety and plurality without at the same time insisting upon the market test of relative achievement. Where the active competition of public with private made both sectors more sensitive and more cost-conscious, however, there Crosland showed a marketeer's preference for the invisible hand. Nationalisation, he believed, must not absolve the State-owned businesses from the need to price sensibly in order to sell. Nor, importantly, must it lead the public corporations to expect privileged treatment from the government that holds the equity: 'There must be no favouritism in the allocation of contracts, raw material or labour; comparative performance must be the sole test – if the public companies cannot compete on equal terms, they do not deserve to be set up. This also means that new capital should not be supplied on tap from the Treasury at gilt-edged rates'.[4] Comparative performance must be the sole test. Public sector or private sector, the success-indicator must be the economic return. Lame ducks worth saving and public service worth fostering will be the exceptions. The exceptions must not be neglected, but nor should they be confused with the rule. That rule at its most modest was to be self-financing survival ('taking one year with another').[5] At its grandest it was to be the market victory of the fittest competitor.

Crosland consistently expressed great confidence in the publicly-owned enterprises. He looked to them in the 1970s as he had done twenty years before 'to act as highly competitive price-leaders and pace-setters, provide a yardstick for efficiency, support the government's investment plans, and above all produce a better product or service'.[6] In 1974 as in 1956 Crosland left the reader in no doubt as to the continuing economic case for 'an active policy of competitive public enterprise': 'A number of British industries call out for aggressive public competition – for example, construction, machine-tools, pharmaceuticals, the insurance companies and the building societies'.[7] A number of British industries would evidently benefit from the inter-sectoral competition of the publicly-owned alternative. Shaw had defended what he believed to be the natural monopoly of the Post Office with reference to what he believed to be the welfare of the consumer: State ownership had 'not only shown the perfect efficiency of State enterprise when the officials are made responsible to the class interested in its successes, but had also proved the enormous convenience and cheapness of socialistic or collectivist charges over those of private enterprise.'[8] Crosland reached a similar conclusion on the competitive public enterprise and the genuinely mixed economy. State-owned firms, he observed in 1961, had a tendency, 'by the force of example and competition',[9] to upgrade the standard of business competence in the industries in which they operated. The comparative performance of Renault in France,

of Volkswagen in Germany, seemed to symbolise to Crosland the economic attractiveness of competition and mix.

Comparative performance must be the sole test – and that is why Crosland
was a strong advocate of managerial autonomy. If the State-owned firm is
to be in a position to complete, Crosland said, it is clear that it must be
able to make its own decisions without that 'excessive mucking about'[10]
on the part of politicians that is so damaging to the alertness and the adapt-
ability of the administrators. Arms-length independence was in Crosland's
view the precondition for managerial effectiveness. Public ownership *per
se* was not: 'Efficiency has little to do with ownership because in the
modern corporation ownership has little to do with control.'[11]

Arms-length independence is operational independence, day-to-day
independence and not complete independence. A sensible government will
ensure that managers are free from parliamentary scrutiny and Cabinet
directives when making short-run choices involving marginal changes. A
sensible government will by the same token ensure than managers are
given adequate guidance when seeking to steer their policies by long-term
national objectives. Particularly is political leadership likely to be of economic value in the basic industries and the public utilities, where capital
and coordination argue persuasively for a unified mission: 'The most
common motive for nationalization is in practice not any desire to achieve
the ideal output in decreasing-cost industries, but a general belief that
greater efficiency will result from public ownership, i.e. that some
economy of central planning and control exists. It is most unlikely that a
government which has just socialized an industry precisely to secure its
central planning and administration will immediately devolve so fundamental a matter as price policy on to a large number of plant managers.'[12]
A sensible government will give the managers the freedom they need to
maximise the allocative efficiency of a given endowment. A sensible government will not interpret the doctrine of autonomy as endorsing the consistent devolution of price-policy: that way lies balance of payments crises
and wage inflation, quantity imbalance and oligopolistic cartel.

Ever the pragmatist, Crosland early decided that managerial autonomy in
the basic industries and the public utilities must not be allowed to mean
absolute freedom with respect to price. Presumably he believed that managers ought to enjoy a greater discretion in the case of competitive public
enterprise operating in a genuinely mixed economy. In-house price determination has an obvious appeal where National Savings is constantly being
challenged by the banks and the building societies, where a British Rail

hotel has a close substitute in the private hotel across the road. Price-setting could presumably be devolved in non-monolithic areas such as these even if the State as owner must be asked for a lead in the presence of economies of size and of natural monopoly. Crosland did not at any rate explore in any detail the question of pricing among the small. He said somewhat more about the large socialised industry – and about the need for the Standing Committee and relevant Minister to take an active interest in price.

That price, Crosland said, ought to cover the cost of production. Not the marginal cost, moreover, but rather the average cost. Many of the nationalised industries were subject to increasing returns, Crosland re-iterated in a contribution of 1950 in the *Oxford Economic Papers*. To price by the incremental and not by the representative value in such circumstances would be to build in a permanent subsidy from the Exchequer. So constant a drain would be incompatible with the overall commitment to self-supporting public enterprise that Crosland believed to be of such importance for the economic efficiency of the State-owned firm.

The price set, needless to say, was to be high enough to provide a surplus of internally-generated revenues that could become the basis for expansion and growth: 'A higher price for coal and steel might do something to encourage both investment and consumption.'[13] Funds would have to be earned by virtue of the fact that they would only exceptionally be donated by the State. Nor was there any reason why the surplus ought not to be a maximum, the outcome of prices that are the highest that the traffic will bear. Markets, Crosland emphasised, will only clear where the prices are indicative not simply of cost of production but of effective demand as well. Besides that, it is unfounded and erroneous to treat under-pricing as if it were necessarily an egalitarian social benefit: 'It is only rarely that the consumers of a nationalized product will be a class whose income it is desired to raise at the expense of other classes; and it would in any case be undesirable that this method should be at all widely used, in view of the great practical drawbacks of a large-scale subsidy policy.'[14] Very occasionally the subsidised price will be the optimal policy: 'In a small number of cases, where the product is mainly consumed by the lower-income groups, this must stand as a possible exception to the rule that total costs should be covered.'[15] In normal circumstances, however, pricing and redistribution should be regarded as two separate challenges – and socialists should not be afraid to say that the market ought to clear.

Crosland looked to political leadership for guidance on big issues such as the validation of public utility prices. He also looked to managerial autonomy for administrative rationality and even the occasional flash of insight. He did not require of the nationalised industries that they raise a fiscal surplus to cross-subsidise the social services. Nor did he reassure the nationalised industries that they would automatically enjoy the bail-outs in the absence of which their private-sector counterparts would rightly fear the bankruptcy courts. Perhaps simplistic in the light of electoral sensitivities, marginal constituencies, tinkering opportunists and vote-motives, what is clear from Crosland's submission is that the State should deal with the framework parameters, the managers should concentrate on the operational choices – and each group should in the short-run take care to mind its own business.

Public accountability was Crosland's answer to the vacuum of capitalism without capitalists, to the problem of power without property. In the entrepreneurial firm the principal clerks are accountable to the profit-seekers who own the assets: the demand-led supply that follows from the obsession with money-making may not be morally acceptable to the citizen who denies that spendable assets can ever legitimate social outcomes, but at least it is the consumer and the owner who collectively shape the allocations. In the managerial corporation the position is different: the dispersion of shareholding ensures that lucrative markets can safely be neglected, decisions are taken 'by self-perpetuating managerial oligarchies responsible to no one',[16] and the threat is real of target-setting in the interests of a small group rather than in the service of the public welfare. Before managerialism the business climate may have been ruthless and predatory but it was also responsive and efficient: that at any rate is the 'private vices, public virtues' message that is the core theology of the microeconomics textbook. Since managerialism the administered enterprise has come to pursue managerial objectives that are all-too-often a synonym for restrictive practices and conservative inertia: 'The managers, no doubt, achieve their desired goals of security and a quiet life; the nation loses a large amount of potential output.'[17] Crosland, in contrast to Galbraith, saw this waste as growth that could not be spared. Thence his plea for public accountability: the State should use the full panoply of laws and taxes at its disposal to compel the managers, eschewing the private pursuit of prestige, promotions, publicity and peace, to 'conform to its own positive views of what is desirable in the public interest'.[18]

Business accountability through State controls is, of course, Crosland's recommendation for the whole of the mixed economy. Obviously applicable in the case of the public corporation, the proposal is relevant to the entrepreneurial firm and the managerial corporation as well. The question then becomes whether the accountability expected from the nationalised industry ought to be greater than the State could reasonably require from the private undertaking that it did not own. Some socialists have said that the position is unambiguous: the capitalist will be driven by the 'age-old instincts of greed and personal gain'[19] but the community will favour a more imaginative mix of motives once it is itself in possession of the property. Other socialists have been more cautious about the conversion of State-owned industry into a *de facto* social service. Anthony Crosland belonged to the more cautious faction. Accepting as a fact that nationalisation 'does represent, in the last resort, an increase in the economic power of the State',[20] he nonetheless expressed a general preference for a looser rein.

Crosland wanted cautious State ownership but he did not want *laissez-faire* State ownership. His general preference may have been for laws and taxes but he was also prepared to support the socialisation of decision-making alongside the socialisation of property-rights where the looser rein by itself would not be enough to secure the public interest. Indicative of his lifelong status as a political animal was his undergraduate speech to the Oxford Union on the Labour Government's proposed nationalisation of coal: 'The real reason why we supported the Bill was this: we thought that there was a bit too much liberty lying around: that it was intolerable that a small group of Pte. individuals, responsible in the nature of things to no one but their shareholders, should be making decisions affecting not only the lives & labours of 600,000 workpeople, but virtually affecting the whole level of economic activity in the country. These were decisions that ought to be made by responsible servants of the State, & made in the interests of the nation.'[21] Because managers and shareholders were shunting the car on to a wrong line, because laws and taxes were not sufficient to shunt it back, therefore the State should do what was needed and give guidance on policy. Crosland wanted to make the government and not the management the ultimate arbiter of the prices charged by the public corporations. He expected the State as the relevant capitalist to take a constructive lead in discussions involving pit-closures and steel redundancies, on-the-job training and worker-consultation. He was not opposed to public sector pay restraint despite the objection of the nationalised executives that this anti-inflationary expedient was a burdensome tax on public corporations obliged to be appraised on the stern commercial principle that 'comparative performance must be the sole test'. In these and other ways Crosland showed that, sympathetic as he was to competition and decentralisation, even so he was of the opinion that 'complete devolution and fragmentation of economic activity down to a local level' was not a practical proposition in an era of large-scale enterprise: it 'simply will not happen, and could not work, in an advanced industrial economy. It is not merely that the result would be a catastrophic fall in living standards, but that one cannot turn back history in this way, or reverse the underlying social and technological trends.'[22]

Crosland was of the opinion that public ownership might reasonably be accompanied by public directive to an extent that would be impossible where the State, limited to laws and taxes, had not taken the big step and nationalised the assets. Given his diagnosis that the 'temperamental affinity'[23] between the corporate manager and the civil servant nowadays deprives the private sector of its profit-based teleology, given his warning that 'with the managerial revolution, there is a vacuum in accountability',[24] one might in the circumstances have expected that Crosland, reaffirming his faith in the economic efficiency of the public corporation, would have recommended that the State should issue even more directives in defence of the collective purpose. One might have expected that Crosland would have come down in favour of even more political leadership, even more social guidance, in order to ensure that public enterprise should not follow private down the narrow road that leads to organisational self-seeking. One would have been mistaken – since it was the cautious democrat's guarded inference that public opinion and State intervention will not necessarily point in the same direction: ' We must not … assume that more state power automatically brings greater democratic accountability.'[25]

Central to Crosland's reservations about accountability through politics was his belief that 'effective Parliamentary control is a myth': 'Parliament can never effectively control the nationalized industries. It lacks the time…. It lacks the objectivity…. It lacks the requisite caliber of M.P.'[26] The legislative timetable is too crowded for proper discussion. Party loyalties distort politicians' judgements. Not all members are commercially experienced or properly informed. Ministers have too many duties to make themselves responsible for continuous supervision. Parastatal holding-companies and semi-autonomous councils 'are not properly accountable to any elected body'.[27] Local government operations exchange a reduced risk of 'bureaucracy and Whitehall control'[28] for an increased danger that the parts will be at variance with the harmony of the whole. What all of this adds up to for Crosland is the non-controversial truism that 'governments do not always see the public interest so much more clearly than private firms'[29] – and the exceptionally controversial deduction from that truism that the State ought therefore to trust the managers day-to-day to look after the shop.

5 Control

Crosland was a selective nationaliser with a lifelong commitment to a substantial public sector. His early statement on pay-settlements well illustrates how much in sympathy he was with the Left's advocacy of an owning State: 'What is required is not a literal 100 per cent degree of socialisation, but a degree such (and it can hardly be less than 50 per cent.) that it is the public and not the private sector which sets in these matters the general tone.'[1] The public sector was to be the pacemaker and the model – and to exert the leverage it had to be large.

Crosland believed in State ownership as a means to State control. Equally, however, he believed that collectivist leadership was a practical possibility even where the producer remained private: 'Post-war experience demonstrates conclusively that governments now have sufficient weapons of control broadly to enforce their will (provided they have one) on private industry.'[2] Crosland's insistence on regulation and reform even within the confines of the British mixed economy served as a useful reminder to contemporaries less familiar with the classic texts of Pigou and Dalton that social power and social property need not in a well-managed future inevitably mean the same.

Crosland's political economy of steering and channelling is the subject of this chapter. The discussion is divided into five parts. Section 1 deals with the principles of control, section 2 with industrial policy, section 3 with the environment, section 4 with macroeconomic policy, and section 5 with the principles of de-control. The theme of the chapter is the need for a middle way that Crosland had identified while still an Oxford undergraduate: 'On the one side the harsh pressing over-weighted regime of Soviet Russia, where the state has run riot, & individual freedom has been swallowed up in the orgy of planning.... On the other hand America, where the executive is so weak, so timid, that at the slightest sign of crisis it disintegrates into impotence. The world doesn't want to choose between these alternatives. It wants a middle way, which will combine the advantages of a planned economy & a firm executive with those essential personal liberties which it needs now more than ever before.'[3] The world wants a middle way, neither unfree like the planned dictatorship nor uncontrolled like the anarchic marketplace. Crosland intended that his political economy of direction and guidance should make its own contribution to the cultivation of the fertile valley that lies in the shadow cast by the two barren peaks.

5.1 THE PRINCIPLES OF CONTROL

The Road to Serfdom in 1944 had warned the well-intentioned that personal freedom and the leaderly State were nothing other than mutually exclusive: 'It has been well said that while the last resort of a competitive economy is the bailiff, the ultimate sanction of a planned economy is the hangman.... The conflict with which we have to deal is indeed a quite fundamental one between two irreconcilable types of social organisation, which, from the most characteristic forms in which they appear, have often been described as the commercial and the military type of society.... We face here a real alternative.... There is no third possibility.'[1] Watching the world through the prism of *The Man versus the State*, Hayek looked at the social democrats and saw the National Socialists. He therefore warned against the middle way lest it begin with the Health Service and end up with the concentration camps.

Twelve years after the *Road* came the *Future*. Twelve years on from a *Serfdom* that excluded all compromise came a *Socialism* that sought to calm the exaggerations of the hysterical with a dose of common sense and a nice cup of tea: 'No one of any standing now believes the once popular Hayek thesis that any interference with the market mechanism must start us down the slippery slope that leads to totalitarianism. This was an implausible enough view, in a British context, even when it was first advanced; it has been thoroughly discredited now that we have experienced a decade of varying degrees of government control, with no sign of a weakening of our democratic fibre.'[2] In his refusal to accept that every Attlee harbours a bloodthirsty Stalin struggling to burst forth, in his perception that, the British not being foreigners, it can't happen here, Crosland's verdict on the 'nervous professor' closely resembles that of Tawney who had said that no 'British socialist of standing' seriously expected that a monstrous despotism would arise out of British Rail, the registration of aliens and the restriction of child labour: 'We, in England, have repeatedly re-made the State, and are re-making it now, and shall remake it again. Why, in heaven's name, should we be afraid of it?'[3]

Tawney did not live in fear of 'the appalling *débâcle* foretold by Professor von Hayek'[4] but put his faith instead in the wisdom of the good: 'It is as possible to plan for freedom as for tyranny',[5] he once observed. Tawney's confidence that the road to Westminster need not inevitably lead on to the Gulag was shared by the optimistic Crosland, who concluded that the British evidence lent little support to the Hayekian threat: 'It is very significant that the last 100 yrs. have seen a simultaneous growth of the extent of our political liberties on the one hand, and the power of the executive on the other, which suggests that these two are not so irreconcilable as people often suggest.'[6] Controversial though such a complacency will appear to a Right sceptical about political discretion and concerned about minority viewpoints, to a Left convinced that State regulation does no more than paper over the cracks of class and exploitation, what is of the essence to Crosland's middle way is the democratic underpinning of Crosland's principles of control.

Thus Crosland intended that the direction and the guidance should not be imposed top-down by a vanguard but should rather be organically embedded in a social order that consults and involves. Such an order would boast an impartial judiciary, independent of the political executive; a free press that does not bow to political censorship; a civil service with a disinterested ethic; a political opposition and a cycle of general elections. Above all these there should be not so much a written constitution (witness the sad fate of the Weimar Republic) as an unwritten constitution made up of convictions and attitudes: 'The real guarantee lies in the spirit of the entire people: it lies in the implicit but immensely binding agreement amongst all men of all parties to use the democratic method in the conduct of political affairs, & above all to use it when in power.'[7] Some countries, politically under-developed, are lacking in the democratic traditions that could predictably evict a ruling-group and replace it with a more congenial leadership. Russia was such a country, and the result was government by a Communist Party monumentally indifferent to the presence or absence of mass support: 'Given the lack of democratic tradition + inculcation of Leninist notions + needs of governing a backward country + the natural power-preserving and power-building psychology of any *untrammelled* ruling group, this type of revolution is bound to turn into Stalinism. And personally I am quite sceptical about the possibility of peaceful democratisation from within.'[8] More advanced Britain presented, however, a significantly different set of challenges and opportunities. There managed capitalism had come to co-exist with what the Marxist-Leninists had called bourgeois democracy – and what Anthony Crosland regarded as the crucial mechanism through which political interference can ultimately be labelled morally legitimate.

Just as Crosland eulogised the constructive contribution of the voter-citizen, so he emphasised the legitimating force of the paying customer. The economic market as well as the political market was evidently to take its cue from demand and only in exceptional circumstances from supply. Crosland had a libertarian's confidence in the value of individuals' judgements: 'These judgements, every radical and social-democrat must passionately endorse.'[9] Even, it would appear, when planning democratically to control.

John Stuart Mill was an English individualist who in 1859 had written as follows in defence of sovereign choice: 'The only purpose for which power can be rightfully exercised over any member of a civilized community, against his will, is to prevent harm to others. His own good, either physical or moral, is not a sufficient warrant.'[10] Anthony Crosland was an English socialist who in 1956 joined his voice to that of the earlier liberal in pleading an economist's case for the tolerance of diversity: 'The consumer is the best judge of how to spend his money; and even if he were not, the principle of individual liberty would still require that he should be left free to spend it, subject only to ... social service considerations.... What is profitable is what the consumer finds useful; and the firm and the consumer desire broadly the same allocation of resources. And while paternalists may dislike this allocation, wishing that less were spent on drink and pools and television sets, they must swallow their dislike in the interests of personal freedom.'[11] Paternalists such as Galbraith complain that they can find no genuine satisfaction of need in 'a lawn mower that can be guided by transcendental meditation'[12] or a pop-up toaster that embosses each surface with 'an appropriate devotional message from the Reverend Billy Graham'.[13] Crosland like Mill, however, is committed to the more tentative position that one person's frivolity is another person's necessity and that each consumer must normally be respected as the best judge of that consumer's interest.

Because he believed that individuals were capable of rational choice, Crosland rejected what he regarded as the patronising elitism of theorists of manipulation and contrivance such as Galbraith. *The Affluent Society*, published in 1958, particularly angered Crosland with its denial that consumers' wants remain genuine and intrinsic once food, clothing and shelter have become generally available: 'We may say that the marginal utility of present aggregate output, *ex* advertising and salesmanship, is zero.'[14] Crosland took advantage of a BBC broadcast on 'private affluence, public poverty' (a former classics scholar, he was able to recognise in Galbraith's unaccredited duality the 'habemus publice egestatem, privatim opulentiam' of Cato the Younger) to distance himself from a misguided welfarism unjustifiably derived from the 'dangerous argument'[15] that desires are not authentic and markets not spontaneous, that efficiency is therefore yesterday's priority and growth no longer a proxy for well-being. Crosland in his broadcast played down the alleged effectiveness of the hidden persuaders: the producers and the sellers will understandably seek to mould and shape, but their image-creation and product-promotion will despite their attempts not meet with real success so long as the consumers' rationality is not adequately engaged. The same, he said elsewhere, is true of the political market as well: 'Increasingly, voters are swayed by what governments achieve and not what politicians promise.'[16] In the on-going struggle between populism and propaganda, Crosland like Tawney remained unrepentantly on the side of the common man.

An advocate of State control who is also a supporter of decentralised choice is obviously faced with the difficult task of reconciling loyalties which to some will appear contradictory. Later sections will consider the extent to which Crosland succeeded in formulating a political economy of direction and guidance which was at one and the same time consensual and democratic, individualistic and libertarian. What is required here is a *caveat* about the distribution – or the maldistribution – of the spendable resources that make up the market mechanism's much-vaunted effective demand. That *caveat*, that exchange value and aggregate utility might not have the same philosophical implications in the light of the predetermining allocation of purchasing power, was evocatively given meaning by Shaw even in advance of the economic theories of Marshall and Pigou: 'A New York lady … having a nature of exquisite sensibility, orders an elegant rosewood and silver coffin, upholstered in pink satin, for her dead dog. It is made: and meanwhile a live child is prowling barefooted and hunger-stunted in the frozen gutter outside. The exchange-value of the coffin is counted as part of the national wealth; but a nation which cannot afford food and clothing for its children cannot be allowed to pass as wealthy because it has provided a pretty coffin for a dead dog.'[17]

Laissez-faire is unlikely to bring about a maximum of happiness, Shaw warned, so long as income and property are shared out so unequally as to make possible such a disparity of experience: 'It is the habit of counting as wealth the exchange values involved in these transactions that makes us fancy that the poor are starving in the midst of plenty. They are starving in the midst of plenty of jewels, velvets, laces, equipages, and racehorses; but not in the midst of plenty of food. In the things that are wanted for the welfare of the people we are abjectly poor.'[18] Crosland would have been too tolerant of individuals' preferences to join Shaw (like Galbraith later) in dismissing the luxuries and conveniences of the richer consumers as 'only a monstrous pile of frippery'.[19] Unprepared to say that much of wealth might in fact be illth, where Crosland would have agreed with Shaw was on the need to postpone welfare judgements involving market outcomes until such a time as the distribution of demand had been brought into line with the convection of claims that the wider society wished to legitimate as equitable and right. That distribution of endowments could not be brought about by the invisible hand – the reason why the re-allocation of economic power was so high a priority for the democratic socialist. Acknowledging the impurity, it was Crosland's contention that supply and demand even in the less-than-perfect present day were nonetheless capable of providing reasonable data on price and output which no tolerant individualist had any right to ignore.

Crosland's political economy was democratic and decentralised. Favourable both to the citizen-led polity and to the consumer-led exchange, Crosland was in essence a reductionist whose first principles could only be those of the atomistic units. Where, therefore, he came to the defence of State controls, the reason for his recommendation must be sought in revealed preference – in the expressed want on the part of the community for politicised action such as moves the community to a plane of need-satisfaction higher than any that would be attainable through decentralised choice left to its own devices. Like the economic supplier, the political supplier may inform and even suggest. Ultimately, however, it must be bubble-up rather than trickle-down that reveals the preference that unleashes the State. Ultimately, in other words, it must be market deficiency, popularly perceived, that triggers the demand for the political corrective.

One instance where the State can complement the private sector and improve the performance of the economic system involves the rational coordination of discrete industries ignorant of one another's production-targets: thus there might be a role for a French-type indicative plan drawn up by the government 'in close consultation with public and private industry'[20] such as was in embryo the National Plan in Britain that occupied Crosland in the four months he spent at the Department of Economic Affairs. Another instance involves the Pigovian divergence of social from private cost: Crosland's illustrations include pollution, congestion, redundancy caused by the withdrawal of a dominant employer from a declining region, a balance of payments crisis necessitating a shift into import-substitution despite an anxious conservatism on the part of private enterprise. Sometimes the State will intervene to make the market economy less cartelistic and more competitive. Sometimes the State will act to restore full employment by means of fiscal and monetary measures. Sometimes the State will put a consensual demand for an equalisation of opportunity and of outcome above the extremes of social distance that are the unacceptable consequence of uncontrolled capitalism, of inherited privilege. In case after case there will be good grounds for the State to get involved. Always, however, the bias must be in favour of decentralised choice. The onus of proof must be on the planners to demonstrate that the market, normally the superior mechanism, tends in specific circumstances regrettably to fail.

Markets can fail, Crosland said. As indicated in the previous chapter, however, so too can governments. The debate about market failure must in that sense be regarded as a debate about the balance of failure, about two failures and not about one. The correction of one failure can open the door to an even greater failure: thence the need for a thinker's evaluation such as differentiates Crosland on control so sharply from the mechanistic technologies of more dogmatic social engineers.

Statistical information and administrative technique will always be imperfect. Aware as Crosland was of this shortcoming, the much-respected Economic Advisor to the Government was, not surprisingly, more aware still. Commenting for his former student on draft chapters of *The Future of Socialism*, Westminster's Sir Robert Hall gave the impression of an idealist beset with frustrations ('I am going to write a book against democracy one of these days') that Oxford's Mr Robert Hall would mercifully have been spared: 'One of the great arguments against detailed planning is that it needs detailed information, very clear directions as to the object aimed at, and some skill at the executive level in carrying out central instructions. In my experience the average civil servant isn't good enough to do as good a job as the business man.'[21] Crosland shared Robert Hall's reservations about information and administration. Similar doubts had been expressed by Eduard Bernstein in his attempt to introduce a note of realism into the debate about the centrally-directed economy: 'What abundance of judgement, practical knowledge, talent for administration, must a government or a national assembly have at its disposal to be even equal to the supreme management or managing control of such a gigantic organism!'[22] Richard Crossman, philosophy don and student of Plato, had said far more about the opportunities than about the limitations in his *Government and the Governed* (1939) that Crosland read while still an undergraduate. Anthony Crosland was too much the economist to neglect what the philosopher-rulers are all-too-prone to ignore – that statistical and administrative deficiencies severely restrict what even the best-intentioned can reasonably hope to achieve.

Nor should it be assumed that all politicians will necessarily be philosopher–rulers. Crosland tended to reason that good leaders are rather like good dentists, that it is the responsibility of the rational shopper to pick out the best: 'If socialists want bolder planning, they must choose bolder Ministers.'[23] Crosland also accepted that the bold had very frequently been pushed out by the irresolute, the weak and the opportunistic whose unique distinction would appear to have been a decisive lack of 'will-power and determination – in the face of vested interests, pressure groups, indifference, electoral opinion, and back-bench revolts. That is, the failure was essentially a *political* one, which reflects the difficulty of planning in a democratic society.'[24] The pressures tend if anything to escalate over time as the satisfaction of one need after another gives rise to overload, inconsistency, and often simple rapacity: 'People make more and more incompatible (and often unreasonable) demands on government.... They grow sullen when their expectations, which they now see as entitlements, are not met.'[25] Electoral rents and party unity, buying votes with uncapped deficits and bribing voters with inflationary projects – Crosland placed his trust in the bold and the strong but others will express the fear that political failure is inseparable from an unstable equilibrium in which no supplier who wishes to please can afford too frequently to say no.

Political failure can be a result of excessive sensitivity to citizens' demands. It can also be a result of excessive detachment. Some interventionists have expressed only residual reservations about the exercise of discretionary power. Making much of the service ethic and the self-denying incorruptibility of the British politician and the British civil servant, such thinkers have tended to argue that the replacement of the non-specific remit by the written-down right is a constitutional acknowledgement of societal breakdown that lawyers will welcome but moralists can only deplore. Other interventionists, more sensitive to the arrogance of secretive office-holders, more sympathetic to the confusion of submissive citizens denied a contract or a charter, have been less sanguine about controls that empower agents without protecting principals. Anxious lest like be treated *ad hoc* and not as like, fearful lest the appointed and the elected regard the public as a problem and not as a privilege, such theorists have wanted to expand and enrich the network of non-market guidance but also to ensure that no responsible adult be debased into the passivity of the baby whose bathwater is best regulated by guardians.

Anthony Crosland was in favour of a citizen-State nexus that was two-way and transparent. The following, from 1956, is indicative of his contractarian bias: 'There is substance in the contention that the State's relations with its citizens should be regulated by the law, so that everyone knows where he stands, and what behaviour is reprehensible and what is not, and not by a system of Government agents with no fixed terms of reference, and hence invariably arbitrary in their decisions.'[26] Hardly a full declaration of support for a British bill of rights (let alone for a written constitution), such a statement is nonetheless an important reminder that Crosland had no real admiration for controls where they were purchased at the price of clarity, enforceability and the rule of law.

Thus Crosland was opposed to controls exercised by means of government-appointed directors, placed on the boards of private corporations and briefed to speak in defence of the public interest. An even-handed policy that does not discriminate between the firms in an industry does not distort their competitive relativities or arouse unnecessary resentments. Selective regulation, differently practised by different outsiders despite identical circumstances is, however, a different matter and a less acceptable proposition. Treated with respect, modern managements are 'normally attentive to government policy (that is, if there is one), and try consciously to act in the public interest'.[27] Offered partiality in place of the rule of law, the contemporary corporation will almost certainly not manifest so sensitive an attachment to the public purpose.

Crosland was an advocate of a political economy of direction and guidance that was democratic and decentralised, citizen-led and consumer-led, realistic and equitable. In all of this his views resembled those of Hugh Gaitskell, who had made the word 'uncontrolled' the essence of his critique of the capitalist order: 'So long as production is left to the uncontrolled decisions of private individuals, conducted, guided and inspired by the motive of profit, so long will Poverty, Insecurity and Injustice continue.'[28] Gaitskell had no objection to privatised agenda-setting so long as the outcome retained its appeal to the consensus. Where, however, a more attractive package was believed to be on offer through the State, Gaitskell called upon the controllers to mould and shape.

The approach is means–ends, the recommendation performance-related, the model a mix. Intended to combine the best of both worlds, the guided mix is, however, open to the charge that it is a pusillanimous utopia, stronger on consensus than it is on economics. That, for example, was the verdict of Aneurin Bevan on the revisionists' enterprise: 'Gaitskell wants to make capitalism work better – but with controls. That's what makes him so dangerous. He wants capitalism to go on existing – but without the prizes which capitalism earns for itself. Of course this is impossible. It cannot work.'[29] In his recognition that market capitalism is economically productive precisely because it is a system of profit and loss, Bevan resembled Hayek, who had written as follows of the incompatibility of freedom and regulation: 'Both competition and central direction become poor and inefficient tools if they are incomplete; they are alternative principles used to solve the same problem, and a mixture of the two means that neither will really work and that the result will be worse than if either system had been consistently relied upon.'[30] Bevan wanted more nationalisation, more control, whereas Hayek wanted less – in that very obvious respect the two thinkers were poles apart. Where they were united was in their shared perception that the middle way was no way at all – and that Tawney's early observation had not been undermined by the revisionists' specious casuistry: 'Hybrids are apt to be sterile. It may be questioned whether, in drawing the teeth of private capitalism, this type of compromise does not also extract most of its virtues as well.'[31]

The controlled economy might not be the efficient economy. Worse still, the controls selected might not be powerful enough for the lead required. Just as the planners can be daring and imaginative, after all, so they can be timid and reluctant. With respect to controllers such as Crosland and his fellow moderates, Stuart Holland on the Left had no doubt at all that there had been a general unwillingness to do anything in particular beyond the marginal and perhaps even the token. That timidity, that reluctance, Holland said, had not only stranded the economy without a rudder but had also caused the electorate to vote against what it correctly perceived to be weakness at the top: 'The fact is that Labour lost the 1970 election on the Croslandite social democratic policies it had attempted in 1964.... Because it failed to secure control over leading private enterprise by leverage from public enterprise, it never made itself master of the strategic sectors in the economy. It could only lament "being blown off course" because it had never determined the course in the first place.'[32] The Croslandites lacked the vision to see what was needed and the strength of purpose to force a confrontation. Trapped between a cup of tea and a cricket-match, Holland insisted, the Croslandites had demonstrated clearly if unintentionally the inadequacy of weak controls. Since they also refused to endorse the stricter controls that alone would have made the direction and the guidance effective, Holland was able to reach the following conclusion about Anthony Crosland's economic policies: 'It is on this key question of state power and government control that the Crosland analysis has been proved wrong, and with it the "revisionist" thesis of which he has remained the foremost advocate in post-war Britain.'[33]

Holland believed that adequate State control presupposed additional public ownership. Crosland did not. Crosland accepted that leverage was an impossibility in the absence of nationalisation: never a regulatory socialist and nothing else, he denied that legal restriction (of maximum hours and minimum pay, of child labour and occupational health) could, welcome though it was, prove an effective substitute for an ambitious State portfolio. What Crosland asserted, however, was that more and more ownership did not necessarily promise more and more control. Enough was as good as a feast. Enough had arrived, in Britain at least, by the end of the Atlee Government. To reverse what had been done would be to weaken the State's power in the mixed economy. To do more, on the other hand, would not be so significantly to boost the State's influence as to be deserving of the expense. The State could already set an example through pay-norms and investment policies, worker-consultation and responsible pricing. The State could already exert pressure by refusing to buy from suppliers who sweated labour in multinational subsidiaries, by favouring retailers who eschewed predatory pricing and abstained from market-sharing. The State could already do a great deal through the leverage of the assets that it had socialised. The State would not be in a position to do a great deal more were it to transfer additional assets from the private into the public sector.

Private corporations could be large, private industry could be concentrated: in 1953, Crosland recorded, the 100 largest companies accounted for 31 per cent of total industrial profits. Big Business was a fact. A fact, certainly – but not a threat: 'Broadly, any government can now impose its will (provided it has one) on the private corporation, and the actions even of a Conservative Government do in practice impinge on industry to an extent which would have been thought outrageous a generation ago. This new economic activism of governments profoundly affects the policies, and restricts the autonomy, of the large British corporation.'[34] Recent British experience had showed just how toothless the private sector had become in the face of a governmental challenge: 'Industry was quite unable to prevent the nationalization program of 1945–51, the postwar laws against monopoly and restrictive practices, and a level of profits taxation which continues to be described as "penal"'.[35] Industry had had its successes as well as its failures: Crosland's anecdotalism would have appeared less selective to a Left afraid of scale if he had included the de-nationalisation of steel and the absence of a training-commitment in what would then have emerged as a more considered balance-sheet. Be that as it may, Crosland's own assessment was a confident one. Crosland contended that the influence of private ownership was neither decisive nor dangerous when confronted with the power of a determined State.

State control had not always been so free from private impediment. In the past the old-style capitalist had occupied a position in society and polity which, for men like Morgan, Rhodes, Rockefeller and Leverhulme, had been substantial indeed. Adequate nationalisation, the strength of organised labour, the death of *laissez-faire*, had all contributed significantly to the weakening of that position. Importantly, too, the robber baron had fallen victim to the powerful logic of capitalist evolution which is prone to separate control from ownership not only in the outside mixed economy but also within the private corporation itself. Profit-seekers give way to office-holders, the adventurous to the conservative. Owner-entrepreneurs have a pecuniary reason to be thrusting rather than frightened. Cogs in a chart have more of an incentive to avert personal risks

than to maximise the gains that go to others: 'Jelly-fish where their prede-
cessors were masterful, they are slaves to their public relations departments, constantly nervous lest some action may provoke a parliamentary
question, frowns in the Board of Trade, trouble with the Unions, or criticism in the Press.'[36] The old-style capitalist was capable of bullying and
bribing in pursuit of favourable exemptions or attractive subsidisation.
Where, however, the manager on a salary approaches a politician in a Pall
Mall club or a civil servant at golf, he is far more likely simply to state
that his company has targeted that good publicity that is the reward for full
and complete cooperation.

Campaign contributions may buy access and perhaps even honours.
Policies, however, are traded in a different currency: 'Private business has
plenty of funds, which the Tory Party thankfully receives at election times;
but it has very few voters.'[37] The vote-motive is the reason why rational
politicians keen to be re-elected cannot allow their policies to be warped
by a money-motive that is always and everywhere short-sighted.
Crossman accused Crosland of being 'strangely unaware of the threat to
freedom presented by the irresponsible concentrations of power which
characterise the modern oligopoly'.[38] Crosland, on the other hand, accused
the nationalisers of being strangely unaware of the threat to business
power presented by the democratic consensus in a nation in which the
voter and not the capitalist will have the upper hand on the important issue
of control.

5.2 INDUSTRIAL POLICY

Centralised direction on economic grounds had appealed to Barbara
Wootton in her *Plan or No Plan* (1934), to G.D.H. Cole in his *Principles
of Economic Planning* (1935), to the Webbs in their *Soviet Communism*
(1935). A representative rejection of Mandeville and Smith on the unintended benefits of the maximiser's cupidity would be that of Herbert
Morrison in his *Easy Outline of Modern Socialism* of 1938: 'The important essentials of socialism are that all the great industries and the land
should be publicly or collectively owned, *and* that they should be conducted (in conformity with a national economic plan) for the common
good instead of for private profit.'[1] Schumpeter, no socialist himself, had
reached the conclusion in his *Capitalism, Socialism and Democracy*
(1942) that productive efficiency could be boosted through a greater
reliance on 'the superior rationality of the socialist plan': 'Socialist management may conceivably prove as superior to big-business capitalism as

big-business capitalism has proved to be to the kind of competitive capitalism of which the English industry of a hundred years ago was the prototype.'[2] Pigou, never a Labour man, had said much the same in his *Socialism versus Capitalism* (1937): 'The system of socialist central planning, if it could be effectively organised, would be in many respects preferable to our existing capitalist system.'[3] When Crosland returned to Oxford from the War, it must be emphasised, the term planning was not synonymous with slow growth, economic stagnation and *The Road to Serfdom*. For many, it is clear, the term still recalled the competence of Keynes's experts and of Beveridge's professionals that was believed to have contributed so powerfully to Churchill's wartime successes – and to those of Stalin's Soviet Communism.

Centralised direction was in the air in 1945. So too, however, was a recognisable scepticism about the viability of administered controls. Whether as flexible as Dickinson's market prices (standing proxy for social valuations) or as dominating as Cole's Ministry of Economic Planning (paralleling, like Wilson's Department of Economic Affairs, the Treasury's authority over finance and budgets), the statist proposals of the 1930s and early 1940s had given rise to a formidable challenge in the form of works such as Hayek's *Collectivist Economic Planning* (1935) and Robbins's *The Economic Basis of Class Conflict* (1939). No less important than the counter-attack from the Right had been the sheer confusion on the part of the Left as to how actually to operationalise the abstractions of Lange's two *Review of Economic Studies* papers (1936, 1937) or of Lerner's *The Economics of Control* (1944). There is clearly not much point in arguing that planners' prices ought to be *as if* set by supply and demand or that inputs should be moved into areas of maximum productivity if one is obliged also to concede that inadequate information makes such efficiency-enhancing intervention a practical impossibility. Pigou was only one among many to make the obvious inference, that planning as an ideal is technically superior to decentralisation but that the market in the real-world darkness will normally prove the more reliable compass: 'To solve a small number of simultaneous equations in a short time is one thing; to solve thousands and thousands of them is quite another.'[4]

Pigou came down in favour of second best because he believed first best to be unattainable. Ian Little came down in favour of market-clearing mechanisms, in opposition to continuous centralised direction, for essentially the same reason: 'Given that more or less full employment is maintained, by fiscal and financial policy, and given a suitable measure of income redistribution, it is claimed that, for the rest, the unimpeded price mechanism is pretty good at solving the economic problem, and that planning will distort the allocation of resources in an irrational or uneconomic manner.'[5] Little's *Critique of Welfare Economics* (1950) is not opposed to intervention where control is needed to correct a specific, named failure. What the *Critique* does oppose is across-the-board management such as is likely to magnify existing imbalances and make economic performance worse. Little says that he is 'specially indebted'[6] to Anthony Crosland for reading the *Critique* in draft and making comments on it.

Crosland warned against large-scale interference and day-to-day guidance. A complex network of licensing and rationing would mean 'an excessive growth of bureaucracy' and even the 'concomitant dangers of petty tyranny, graft, and corruption';[7] it would be accompanied by mistakes, bottlenecks, black markets, breakdowns in coordination; and it would on balance contribute less to the efficient production of 'the great bulk of consumer-goods and industrial capital-goods'[8] than would a reliance on the free market. The primacy of the consumer being a socialist objective, economic growth being the necessary condition for improving the social services, Crosland therefore advised that the committed socialist ought to oppose 'an increasing proliferation of controls' and to call instead for an industrial policy aimed at making the private sector 'as competitive as possible'.[9]

Douglas Jay in the 1930s had early articulated the revisionists' *credo* that the bias must always be in favour of spontaneity: 'The wiser course would thus seem to be not, like the Russians, to abolish the price system outright and then reintroduce it wherever its absence was obviously disastrous, but rather to preserve it and to modify it bit by bit in all those ways in which modification is indisputably justifiable.'[10] Anthony Crosland in the 1950s continued the defence of decentralisation in his contribution to the *New Fabian Essays*. There, not yet completely free from the countervailing attraction of the wartime plan, he had this to say about the directing State versus the checks and balances of supply and demand: 'Within the framework of overall government planning, the proper way to make the private sector responsive to the needs of the community is to make it competitive. The failure to do so was perhaps the greatest single failure of the post-1945 Labour administration.'[11]

Crosland's contention, that recent socialism's 'greatest single failure' was perhaps Labour's failure to make capitalist markets sufficiently competitive, will probably have had a greater appeal to economists and libertarians than it did to social planners and leaderly militants. It had no appeal at all to R.H.S. Crossman, who was later to write as follows about

Crosland's enthusiastic endorsement of automaticity and interest: 'What saddens me about Mr Crosland is that, instead of joining in the assault on economic orthodoxy, he seems to be advising the Labour Party to come to terms with it. Whereas, for example, *The Affluent Society* mercilessly exposes the vulgarity, the wastefulness, the incompetence, and the inherent contradictions of Western capitalism, Mr Crosland's *The Future of Socialism* is chiefly concerned to emphasise its stability and strength.'[12] Crossman criticised Crosland for making the competitive game a central part of the socialist order. Unafraid of the self-regarding orientation, committed to the welfare-enhancing outcome, it was Crosland's reply to his critics that State intervention to make markets free would more often serve the public's interest than would an industrial policy that constricts and constrains.

Crosland made clear the essence of his bias in his paper in January 1950 to the second of the Buscot conferences on 'Problems Ahead'. Still an Oxford don, he began by distancing himself from the economics of perfect information, rational choice, powerless automatons and Paretian optimality that he was presumably obliged to teach to his students: 'All talk about the optimum allocation of resources or the delicate mechanism of the price-system is rubbish.'[13] Optimality, he said, is rubbish. Second best, he continued, is not: 'Nevertheless, especially given an effective attack on monopoly restraints, the free movement of relative prices is a reasonably efficient *broad* guide to what consumers want and what is the real cost of different types of resources.'[14] Adequacy, he concluded, is preferable to nothing where the ideal is unattainable: 'Therefore (subject to the right level of monetary demand being maintained) we should allow a fairly free movement of prices over the economy as a whole, in order to ensure maximum flexibility, but be perfectly prepared to intervene with price control in any particular case in which free prices give results we do not like.'[15] The bias must always be in favour of spontaneity. The controller should nonetheless feel free at any time to plead an exception to the rule.

The bias must always be in favour of spontaneity. Thus it was that Crosland defended the work of the Monopolies and Mergers Commission that had been set up by Labour in 1948. Ever the pragmatist, he said that it was the great advantage of the British system over its American counterpart that the fact-finding investigation was able to distinguish good monopolies from bad whereas the blanket prohibition had no choice but to throw out the economies of scale even as it struggled against the single seller's exploitative charges. In his 1951 paper on 'Legislating against Monopoly', he marked the occasion of the Commission's first report by calling for increased staffing and additional referrals.[16] Even if no redress were subsequently to be forthcoming from the politicians, the young economist reflected, at least the case studies would gradually build up a picture of efficiency versus abuse which would help to guide future thinking on the question of industrial concentration.

Crosland also advocated legislation to abolish the practice of resale price maintenance: 'The important thing is to be quite clear and forthright: to announce that in future this particular restraint on freedom is a criminal offence.'[17] Observing that the Labour Government had proposed such a prohibition in its White Paper of 1951, Crosland in 1955 averred that the Conservatives were too close to the business interest to make so consumer-friendly a change: 'No doubt this is too much to expect from a Conservative Administration.'[18] Crosland in 1955 implied that Labour was the party that promoted libertarianism and competition, experimentation and novelty, whereas the Conservatives were the party of price-fixing and entry barriers, lower productivity and slower adaptation. It is unusual to think of Labour as the party of business efficiency, the Conservatives as the party of frightened minimax. It is even more unusual to treat all Conservatives as nervous stability-seekers, to assume that no socialists feared price-cutting chaos and the withering-away of the smaller retailer. Cautious Conservatives there undoubtedly were who defended the umbrella-price imposed by the risk-averting manufacturer. Yet there were also pro-market Conservatives like Edward Heath and, later, Margaret Thatcher who, encouraged by the lead of the United States and Sweden, were ultimately to outlaw resale price maintenance in 1964 and a long list of analogous restrictions after 1979. Whatever else may have divided the Croslandites from the monetarists, an attraction to the equity of exchange will at least have brought them together. RPM made markets uncompetitive. RPM had therefore not to be taken over by the State and its planners but rather abolished altogether in favour of the self-stabilising market.

Crosland was opposed to the ring-like, cartel-like abuse of organised power on the part of intra-industry bodies such trade associations and producers' boards: 'Nobody doubts that producers' boards are vitally necessary to improve the efficiency of the marketing process, but it is quite wrong that they should also have monopoly powers over price and output.'[19] He was an advocate of 'keen competition from imports'[20] though liberalising agreements such as that which established the European Free Trade Association. He defended infrastructure (such as new roads and additional housing) that *inter alia* broke up local monopolies by facilitating the mobility of outputs and inputs. He called for laws that would make more meaningful the informed exercise of the consumer's judgement – legislation on the labelling and description of goods and services, say, or binding instructions to broadcasters (private-sector and BBC alike) to report the results of independent tests such as those of

Michael Young's Consumers' Association. He advocated State subsidies and grants for research and development that would in effect make the smaller firm more competitive by virtue of the external economy and the sharing of overheads. Through the breaking up of positions of dominance, through the public provision of pro-competitive complements, it would be possible, Crosland believed, for State regulation not to repress the consumer's freedom but rather to extend it.

Crosland was no supporter of the exploitative power, the inflexible inertia, that could, he recognised, easily result from industrial concentration. Nor, however, did he hold any brief for firms that were too small to be productive, industries too fragmented to be up-to-date. Where *too little* competition meant few alternatives and high prices, he reasoned, there the State would do well to provide a stimulus to rivalry and choice. Where *too much* competition imposed an analogous tax, he added, there the State should emulate the wise doctor who treats different diseases with different medicines. Just as the British socialists were clearly wrong to regard nationalisation as an ideal and not as a means, Crosland suggested, so too were the American free-enterprisers seriously at fault when they assumed that more competition must always and everywhere lead to value for money.

Schumpeter had shown that perfect competition could be a cause of technological stagnation and wasted opportunities: 'In the last resort, American agriculture, English coal mining, the English textile industry are costing consumers much more and are affecting *total* output much more injuriously than they would if controlled, each of them, by a dozen good brains.'[21] Schumpeter's conclusion on the subject of economic progress was more than favourable to 'the large-scale establishment or unit of control': 'It has come to be the most powerful engine of that progress and in particular of the long-run expansion of total output.... In this respect, perfect competition is not only impossible but inferior, and has no title to being set up as a model of ideal efficiency.'[22] Schumpeter's favourable verdict on the dynamism of size was reinforced by the view of J.K. Galbraith that, large tasks presupposing large organisations, 'King Canute looks down on those who administer our antitrust laws with the utmost understanding and sympathy':[23] 'A slight continuing loss of efficiency, as compared with ideal performance, from the possession of market power is regularly offset and more than offset by large gains from technical development.'[24] Schumpeter and Galbraith were in agreement that the giant organisation and its collegial bureaucracy were very frequently, in present-day economic conditions, not the brake on development but rather the motor of change. Their perspective was shared by Anthony Crosland, who wrote as follows in support of size: 'The fact is that advances in productivity and technical innovation today do not come characteristically from the small man working in a highly competitive industry, but from the large, semi-monopolistic firm with huge resources: not from the gifted individualist, but from the organised research team: not from people working for individual profit, but from people working on a fixed salary in a large managerial structure: not from cut-throat competition, but often from cooperation – between firms, between industry and government and the universities, between management and labour.'[25] Economic reality has moved on since the time of Adam Smith; and nowadays it is organisation that is at the cutting edge of advance.

That being the case, it would clearly be wrong for politicians to impede mergers merely because of a dogmatic attachment to aggressive competition as a good thing in itself: 'In general, mergers are desirable if they lead to better management or genuine economies of scale without eliminating workable competition. In my view, more often than not, in Britain mergers will fulfil this condition.'[26] Such mergers benefit the consumer, make British exports competitive in world markets and speed up the rate of growth. Fully in the public interest, the process of rationalisation ought not to be discouraged by a government that has failed to move on from Smith to Schumpeter: 'In the case of monopolies and mergers there is no presumption in the law that market power works against the public interest.... In particular situations market power may be a necessity.'[27] Proposals that would merely redistribute economic welfare in favour of the new-dominant should be decisively rejected by a careful State that considers each application on the basis of the plus-sum probabilities. Proposals that would inject new life into old businesses should, on the other hand, be rewarded with the unreserved approbation of a thinking leadership that demands results and takes not ideology but 'the best allocation of resources and the largest improvements in efficiency'[28] as its guiding light.

Sometimes, indeed, a discretionary polity should actually initiate the sequence by acting positively to bring about the requisite marriages: witness the useful contribution of the parastatal Industrial Reorganisation Corporation, 'which is doing an excellent job in restructuring many sectors of British industry'.[29] The market failure that the IRC was addressing so well was precisely the fact that the private sector was unwilling to move into the Big Business phase that the Marxians had long asserted it was desperate to do: 'The Government do not believe that the unaided working of market forces will always be sufficient to bring about the needed rationalisation of industry.'[30] Industrial policy can evidently serve the community by uniting the under-developed as well as by keeping apart the predatory. Crosland in Cabinet is known to have practised what he preached. His support in September 1968 for the merger of General Electric and English Electric is a case in point: 'Tony Crosland warned us that we should sanction it without reference to the Monopolies Commission, arguing that any reference would take six months and hold up development at a critical stage. He concluded that the merger would certainly have to be approved in the end.'[31] Concentration and not competition was the better servant of the public interest – and the politician must move with the times.

Crosland found it unacceptable that allocative and dynamic efficiency should be conceptualised by policy-makers in terms of arbitrary categories such as percentage market share or combined assets per take-over. Even two firms can compete violently, he said, while even an industry of one can be frightened into moderation by the threat of a new entrant or the presence of a close substitute. Evidence and analysis are indispensable, Crosland concluded, if industrial policy is properly to chart a middle course between *too little* competition and the analogous tax of *too much*.

The approach is clearly that of an academic mind accustomed to making fine distinctions. Not entirely convincing, however, is the intellectual's confidence in the ability of practical policy-makers successfully to pick potential winners and to spot non-accountable abuse. Crosland's own eagerness to rush through the Electricity merger without waiting for the Commission's report testifies to an optimism about the competence and motivation of politicians which not all members of the community will necessarily be able to share. Besides that, Crosland's enthusiasm for size causes him to play down the valuable innovations that still originate in the small-firm sector while under-estimating the welfare loss that can so easily be the consequence of implicit cartelisation and sleepy toleration, discriminatory pricing to keep out new entrants and patent-hoarding to retard the pace of change. Crosland seems at times almost to have become the victim of a 'big is beautiful' lobby that, glossing over the take-over of viable competitors, eulogises the economies of size without saying why a concentrated industry should inevitably share its advantages with a consuming public that is notoriously deficient in countervailing power. Opposed as he was to State sector planning of prices and qualities, the check that Crosland had in mind was that of 'workable competition'. His argument in support of size would have been considerably strengthened had he said what steps a socialist government should take beyond the ultimate deterrent of a reference to the Monopolies Commission to defend that workability from the ever-present threat of managed markets and private-sector control.

Concentration means oligopoly and oligopoly means salesmanship. Some critics have contended that commercial advertising, more manipulative than informative, is a waste of resources and a source of distortion. Galbraith in particular has objected that the sales effort makes consumers more acquisitive, choices less rational, than would have been the case in the demand-led sequence of the perfectly-competitive model. Crosland's position, as was indicated in the previous section, was significantly more relaxed. Arguing against the exaggerated fears of those who credit the 'want-creators' with dissatisfaction, materialism and moral decay, arguing in favour of Mill's individual sovereignty and Tawney's Henry Dubb, Crosland made the point that the sales effort is inseparable from the productive scale and the technological advance that confer such benefits upon the consumer: 'It is one of the factors which help to create and sustain the modern mass-production and mass-distribution economy – an economy characterised by large units, long production-runs, heavy capital investment, lavish expenditure on research, and a rapid rate of innovation.'[32] Advertising is socially beneficial where it makes possible a rise in living standards in consequence of the launch of new products and the exploitation of capital-intensive technologies: 'The firm will take the risk only if it can be reasonably certain of a fairly rapid mass demand; and this can be ensured, in most cases, only by a prodigious initial advertising campaign.'[33] Even defensive advertising can be in the public interest, where the unintended function of the zero-sum reallocation of a fixed product demand is to ensure the survival in the imperfect market of more than a single monolithic seller: 'If advertising is the price we have to pay for retaining competition, it is usually worth paying.'[34] Advertising, in short, is fully compatible with initiative, enterprise and price-reduction in a world where word of mouth is too haphazard for efficient operation – and where the consumer, nobody's fool, remains the rational arbiter of the individual's needs.

One objective of industrial policy was, in Crosland's socialist future, to provide a stimulus to competitive capitalism. A second objective was to encourage cost-cutting concentration and to abet economical mergers. Third and last was the residual objective – to shape and tailor the course of demand and supply in order that economic outcomes should be in full conformity with a social consensus that does not stop short at the power of the purse. There is much that an interventionist government can do to correct the moral failures of an irresponsible market: the prohibition of slavery is a persuasive illustration of a popular measure that altered the rules of the game. It is surprising in the circumstances that Crosland had relatively little to say about socialist engineering by means of industrial policy. His philosophical position is clear enough: 'No one today (except for a lunatic fringe in the United States) believes that the economy should be wholly unregulated and the pattern of production entirely dictated by market forces.'[35] His precise proposals for all that are by no means all-embracing.

Most prominent among his recommendations are those that have a discriminatory bias in favour of the less-advantaged. Restriction of working-hours and of child labour, health and safety regulations to shield the shop floor, payments to lame ducks where the alternative would be redundancies, tax-concessions to firms relocating in unemployment black-spots – measures such as these reflect a desire not so much to improve the competitive efficiency of the economy as to redistribute the endowments of social power. The liberal democracy has long maintained that the law is the bulwark of the have-nots against the depredations of the powerful.[36] The socialist democracy extends that principle from the courtroom to the factory by insisting on new laws aimed specifically at the protection of the vulnerable. Simultaneously, of course, it must take a tough line with respect to powerful special pleaders such as Cunard, starved of cash but still able to launch the QE2: 'Tony at first held out firmly and said he didn't see why we should spend a lot of money putting Cunard to rights. Let them go bankrupt and afterwards the Government could buy up the remains cheaply.'[37]

Discrimination aside, there are further proposals in Crosland's political economy which are intended to challenge the verdict of demand (suitably corrected by progressive tax) and supply (subject always to statute on disclosure and contract). The short-term capital gains tax would discourage speculative take-over bids followed by large-scale asset-stripping. The two-tier corporation tax would provide a motive for dividend control and ploughing-back. Town and country planning would influence the location of industry. Prices and incomes policy would impose ceilings on negotiated agreements. Crosland on industrial policy cannot evidently be reduced to competition and concentration, to market incentives and nothing more. As attractive as he believed free enterprise to be to the median British socialist, what is clear is his willingness to involve the government where he believed that consensual objectives such as growth, equalisation and welfare were better served by direction than they were by the minimal State.

Striking, therefore, is Crosland's decision to cut short his list of proposals at a point when the guidance he supports is by no means all-encompassing. The managerial revolution leaves business decision-makers

accountable to no one but themselves. The suppression of the profits maximand frees firms from the single-minded pursuit of satisfied customers.
Croslandite arguments such as these suggest that industrial regulation will
have to be relatively continuous. In the event the policy proposed turns out
to be relatively loose. National planning turns out to be French-style
indicative forecasts, matrices drawn up 'in close consultation with public
and private industry'[38] that are in every sense the amicable product of
'cooperation and consent'.[39] Manpower planning turns out to be the State
sector's passive acceptance of the skill convections that are identified for it
by public and private employers who do not pay *pro rata* for the education
supplied. Crosland could clearly have said more about socialist engineering and the governmental lead. The fact that he opted not to do so is an
important reminder that by and large he was content to leave to industry
itself the choices that would influence its performance.

5.3 THE ENVIRONMENT

Crosland was Secretary of State at the Department of Local Government
and Regional Planning in 1969–70. In that capacity he stopped plans for a
third London airport at Stansted, saved historic buildings such as Norman
Shaw's Scotland Yard, and set up a Royal Commission on environmental
pollution. Returning to government as Secretary of State for the
Environment in 1974–76, he opposed the construction of a new airport at
Foulness (Maplin); he was displeased with the destruction of homes for
motorways and the damage to the coastline; and he took a personal interest
in vertical take-off aircraft which he believed might be a technological
solution to the problem of runway congestion. Crosland, it is clear,
regarded the protection of buildings, countryside and amenities as a proper
concern for a socialist politician: 'I am, and always have been, a passionate supporter of most conservation and environmental causes.'[1]

As a trained economist, Crosland will have recognised the environment
to lie in the textbook territory of social costs and common benefits, neigh-
bourhood externalities and third-party spillovers: even in economic equilibrium, the influential Pigou had reasoned, still the uncorrected
diswelfares of river pollution or factory noise must mean that the felt well-
being of the community as a whole could be raised to a higher level if
some restriction were to be placed on the invasive liberty of the individual
tort-feasor responsible for the smoking chimney's noxious emissions.
Crosland was a dynamic thinker who believed that the need for intervention was growing more urgent and that more social control, not more

laissez-faire, was the hope for the future: 'We shall.... need more regulation as society grows more complex and interdependent.'[2] Crosland, importantly, was also an egalitarian socialist, determined that the protection of the environment should simultaneously be an exercise in levelling up: 'It is the less well-off who work and live in the worst environment; the rich can purchase a good environment for themselves.'[3] The rich are often able to purchase a private escape-route from industrial effluent and tree-less estates; 'only social action can give the less well-off the same protection';[4] and thus it is that the 'increasing degree of social and institutional control'[5] which is unavoidable must carefully skew its interventions towards the deprived in a manner which is not unavoidable but rather the socialist consequence of a conscious choice.

Crosland, an egalitarian *as well as* an interventionist, was in the circumstances hostile to those environmentalists whom he believed to be the friends of the rich at least as much as they were the friends of the earth. One school which he criticised was that which sought to protect ecological balance by means of a slow or a zero rate of economic growth. The anti-growth conservationism of Galbraith, Doomwatch and the Club of Rome, Crosland said, is unacceptably smug, 'indifferent to the needs of ordinary people': 'This attitude is (a) morally wrong when we still have so many pressing social needs, and (b) self-defeating since without growth we shall never find the huge sums of money which we desperately need to cure pollution and improve the environment.'[6] A second school which he criticised was that which, conservative with respect to open doors and pro-gressive inclusion, was attracted by the man-made obstacles proposed by authors such as Mishan when, in *The Costs of Economic Growth* in 1967, that defensive conservationist mooted 'an international ban against all air travel'[7] in order to contain over-grazing through mass tourism. Such environmentalists, Crosland said, were reactionary elitists whose attitude to the aspirations of the majority was self-protectively to pull up the ladder and declare the craft to be full: 'Yes, indeed, the rich would proceed in leisurely fashion across Europe to the Mediterranean beauty spots where they would park their Rolls Royces and take a boat or horse-drawn vehicle. As for my constituents, who have only a fortnight's holiday, let them eat cake and go back to Blackpool.'[8] Crosland felt strongly about shaky democrats who, in his view, were utilising environmentalism in a bid to prevent the debasement of their own privileges. It is an indication of how strongly he felt about this capture of cause by class that he in 1974 cited as threats to 'the stability of democratic society' the agitation of 'angry workers, students, squatters' – and of 'middle-class amenity groups'.[9]

Crosland did not regard slow or zero growth as an acceptable solution to the problem of the environment: fumes and dirt are bad, he argued, but slow or zero growth in public spending on housing, health and education must be acknowledged to be a pollutant as well. Nor did he welcome the moratorium on change that would *de facto* exclude the less-advantaged from advance and access: the greenbelt protected, he pointed out, is also the slum overspill denied convenient rehousing. Attracted as he was to the environmentalist's crusade, Crosland was clearly not prepared to sacrifice the war on poverty or the minimisation of inequality simply in order to retard resource-depletion or to ensure aesthetic surroundings. Intervention, in other words, was necessary but what mattered too was the social bias of the instrumentality selected. What Crosland wanted was environmental control that not only looked after the wildlife and the plant-species, the historic railway-stations and the majestic Victorian warehouses, but also balanced claims in such a way as to ensure that the working classes and the socially-deprived were not inequitably forgotten in the scramble for law.

Crosland's environmentalism is interventionist, committed to 'an allocation of resources which is not determined by market forces but reflects our social priorities': 'God alone cannot create an Alkali Inspectorate or stop the barbaric depredations of profit-hungry property firms.'[10] Crosland's environmentalism is also socialist. In that sense it is directly concerned with under-privileged people and only secondarily with badgers and geese.

One dimension of Crosland's environmentalism involves the location of activity. The private sector, uncoordinated, cannot possibly be in a position to take the broader view: 'Market forces work well enough in the field of ordinary consumer goods. But they work ruinously in the field of land-use and buildings.'[11] Town and country planning has the attractive property that it is able to think big. The *tabula rasa* of wartime devastation represented to the young Crosland 'an overwhelming argument' for a leaderly State: 'In the blitzed towns of Britain to-day we have an absolutely unique opportunity of planning new communities which will be a joy to live in & a credit to our country: we have a chance to replace some of our grey drab over-crowded streets with wide spacious & prosperous cities: & we just can't afford to allow any individual property-owner to stand in the way.'[12] Opposed to automaticity and in favour of control, Crosland's commitment to a policy on location was to last him a lifetime.

Thus he recommended that the government compel the dispersion of employment by means of limiting the office-building it permits in crowded municipalities such as London. He suggested physical quotas on new jobs in urban areas where the land-shortage caps the housing-stock. He endorsed the economic deterrent of a differential tax on floor-space or a payroll-tax on staff in geographical circumscriptions which the policy-makers believed to be over-expanded. The incorporation of (liberal) pricing alongside (*dirigiste*) restriction no doubt owed much to the economist's logic of David Henderson and Ralph Turvey, who were advising Crosland when he wrote that 'we must always seek to harmonize private and social costs by influencing charges and prices'.[13] Since charges and prices can prove a regressive burden on the less well-off, since State directive is clearly the more finely-tuned instrument, the reader who suspects that Crosland talked pecuniary inducement but preferred political targeting may not in the event be all that wide of the mark.

Locational planning to Crosland meant directive but it also meant money. A generous provider as well as a sensible guide, the State, he said, should take the lead in the construction of new towns. Financial aid should be made available for the revitalisation of declining regions and the upgrading of infrastructural services. Development land should come under public ownership lest greedy speculators 'furiously rebuild the urban centres with unplanned and aesthetically tawdry office-blocks'.[14] Favourable to a future that had room for public goods like parks and small businesses like second-hand bookshops, Crosland, in short, looked to the State to prevent the urban blight that he associated with maximal return on capital investment: 'Whether we stave off the threat, or succumb to it, will depend on how far the country is willing to sacrifice private interests and unregulated liberty to social control and government initiative. There will be only too much to divide the socialist from the conservative in this field.'[15]

Closely related to a policy on location must be a policy on transport. While at Environment in the 1970s Crosland actively explored the nature of a socialist environmentalism that would embrace not merely the geographical dispersion of employment and housing but also the manner in which ordinary men and women satisfactorily reach their destination.

Growing incomes mean a rising demand for the private motor-car. Convinced that the desire of the working classes to accede to the independence and amenity of the better-off one step ahead was 'wholly legitimate and in any case inexorable', Crosland reminded present-day car-owners that it would be unacceptably intolerant to stand in the way of effective demand and mass consumption: 'It's extremely important for the affluent classes who've had motor cars for as long as they can remember to realise what an enormous increase in a person's subjective and objective standard of living a motor car represents. It would be a profoundly anti-democratic attitude for any government to be straight anti-motor car – or to try to limit the number of cars.'[16] Here as elsewhere, Crosland said, the affluent classes had no moral right to press the State for laws that would prevent the newly-upgraded from invading their existing privileges. Yet the problem then becomes the very real one of mutual frustration and traffic jams, of wasteful delays and crowded roads. Fred Hirsch emphasised the extent to which 'positional goods' like the private motor-car (goods subject to the spoiling property that 'what each of us can achieve, all cannot')[17] were in danger of becoming a resented social limit to sustained economic growth. Writing in Britain in the last years of Crosland's lifetime, Hirsch declared apocalyptically that 'the extension of middle-class objectives has outdistanced middle-class opportunities'[18] and that the fury of gridlock was just around the corner. Crosland was fully aware that more cars on the one hand, more congestion on the other, represented a serious threat to harmonious evolution – and that he was genuinely uncertain as to how best to reconcile the interests of the individual with those of the whole: 'I regard this as an unsolved problem in every advanced country.'[19]

Unsolved though the problem almost certainly is, Crosland was able nonetheless to make constructive suggestions for a national policy on transport that would, not banning the cars, still alleviate the crush. He was not opposed to the construction of new motorways: the champion of consumers' tastes, he could not honestly defend the cars while blocking the roads. What he did oppose was the *excessive* construction of new motorways, where the existence of the over-building was to be identified by the resultant decay in shared facilities: 'New roads mean less use of public transport. So services get worse and fares go higher and higher. Most of our people still do not have the permanent use of a car, and they are the sufferers. The pensioner is cut off from family and shops; the young mother finds it harder to get her children to school; the whole physical and social environment suffers.'[20] The crowding out of the buses and the trains, Crosland is saying, is analogous to a regressive tax which falls most heavily upon the least-privileged sectors of society. That in itself would be a socialist argument for lower fares and more reliable services which, directional and redistributive, is analytically separate from the across-the-board benefits of less congestion, less toxicity and less noise that cannot tell the banker from the ploughman in the rush-hour. The consciously targeted as well as the across-the-board is evidently a prominent topic in transport policy. Logically so; since it is Crosland's wish to equalise social distance as well as to defend the cause of access without crowd.

A further dimension of Crosland's environmentalism involves pollution and its prevention. Aware as he was that cleaner engines and expensive filters can put up prices in the shops and cost some workers their jobs,

Crosland made no secret of his belief that the socialist policy will often be no policy at all. On the one hand he personally shared the anxieties of aesthetically-minded pressure-groups such as the Ancient Monuments Society ('I have all my life been a passionate conservationist')[21] with respect to the anti-intellectualism and the ugliness, the 'architectural mediocrity' and the 'commercial vulgarity',[22] that he saw as inseparable from 'the power of the bulldozer, and the pressures that it represents, which can in five minutes destroy the heritage of five centuries'.[23] On the other hand he was prepared to accept that responsible adults, neither madmen nor children, might rank higher pay above designer surroundings, tower-block offices above inaccessible green fields, mass consumption clothing above juggernaut-free precincts, cheaper food above fresher air, less unemployment above less effluent. Choices must be made where consensus fails; and Crosland was adamant that the bias in the event of conflict should work to the advantage of the more deprived. An important implication is that the socialist policy will often be to tolerate the pollutants in order that the more vulnerable might be spared the disproportionate burdens.

Sometimes, however, it will happen that the democratic majority validates the green scenario and makes it legitimate for the State to get involved. There will then be several routes that a regulatory government will be able to explore. The first is land-use planning – the case of the outright prohibition to stop a noisy new airport, the zoning scheme to protect a historic site or a beauty-spot. The second is selective taxation – as where a lump-sum road levy is replaced by a *pro rata* petrol tax in a bid to ration discretionary motoring by means of price. The third is public subsidisation – the sponsorship, for example, of commercially-unattractive research into the pollution-free car or the silent aero-engine. Crosland does not rank the three routes in terms of their impact either on the quality of life or on the levelling of experience. What he does, however, is to invite others to build on his insights by formulating a socialist pollution policy that gives due weight not to one but to both of these two important considerations.

In taking responsibility for the environment, the State, Crosland argued, must see to it that the benefits of intervention are not dissipated through fragmentation of jurisdiction. What this means is that the State, committed as it is to the coordination of the private sector, must ensure that relevant public-sector choices are coordinated as well. The requisite planning is, Crosland maintained, difficult to achieve in the absence of inter-ministerial collaboration: 'There is no absolutely neat way to divide up planning responsibilities. But it will work if the departments have a sensible degree of cooperation.'[24] The requisite planning presupposes communication, in other words, and not simply control: 'We have as substantial a battery of pollution controls as any country in the world. But these controls are exercised by a large number of separate executive departments, as they must be; and so we need some central co-ordinating machinery to see if there are any gaps, to decide whether existing priorities are right or wrong, and to try to foresee future likely causes of pollution.'[25]

Collaboration and communication are necessary for an effective environmental policy. Necessary without doubt, they will not, however, prove sufficient so long as the division of labour remains no more rational than an illogical patchwork of historical accidents. Crosland in *The Conservative Enemy* had early on committed himself to the reappraisal and the consolidation of the independent sovereignties: 'A coordinated policy will be impossible so long as responsibility for transport, location of employment, housing, and town and country planning remains divided, as it now is, between three separate Ministries; a prior condition of effective planning is the creation of a single Ministry of Town and Country Planning responsible for all these basically inseparable functions.'[26] A decade later, still convinced that the environment required a super-ministry of its own, he was writing in The *Guardian* that Edward Heath, incoming Prime Minister, would do well to link together the overlapping portfolios in 'one department responsible for regional planning, local government and planning, housing, construction, and transport': 'Size is unavoidable, not only to achieve a smaller Cabinet but to secure coordination of planning.'[27] Crosland was speaking from experience in 1970 in a way that he had not been a decade before: in 1969–70 he had been the Secretary of State for Local Government and Planning, and as such been put in charge of all the functional areas (save transport and housing) that had figured so prominently in his proposals of 1960 for merger and expansion. His office in 1969–70 was the very room that had been occupied by George Brown at the Department of Economic Affairs – the ultimate federal ministry, the ultimate expression of Labour's belief in the 1960s that big is beautiful if backed up by science.

Housing, employment, pollution, conservation, roads and a variety of other issues are so closely related, Crosland said, that it makes little sense to parcel out the duties to independent and isolated administrations. The functional areas must be continually re-thought. So should the question of the geographical base that is the proper unit for the joint decision-making. Where people in the towns use the countryside for recreation, where people in the countryside commute to the towns for work, self-contained microcosms are simply unable to cope with the challenge: 'To try to administer town and country separately for planning, transport and development, as happens today, becomes more and more impossible.'[28]

One response would be to set up regional planning authorities (30, perhaps, in the nation as a whole) to ensure that arrangements proceeded not piecemeal but area-wide. Another response would be to diminish the numbers and increase the size of the local councils: neither so small as to be ineffectual nor so huge as to be unresponsive, Crosland told the House of Commons that he saw the ideal population for purposes of local government as lying in the range from large (a catchment of 250 000 persons) to very large (a circumscription rising to the million mark).[29] Bigger but fewer units, coordinated and orchestrated by central government, will presumably be a force for the diminution of inequalities as between the regions: to that extent Crosland probably saw them as moral and socialist, not only as technocratic and effective. Crosland does not consider the possibility that different localities might have different preferences or that the *de facto* concentration of control might be regarded as an external imposition by grass-roots advocates of democratic devolution. Confident that big is beautiful, Crosland was no less confident that wise leadership would have the ability sensitively to deliver an environmental policy that would prove as popular as it was effective.

5.4 MACROECONOMIC POLICY

There is a solid tradition in British political economy which looks to discretionary management and not to market flexibility for the ultimate guarantee of full employment and price stability. Anthony Crosland is a part of that tradition. The witness at an impressionable age to mass unemployment and the Keynesian revolution, a new MP in the wake of the welfare state and the post-war nationalisations, Crosland in his first 30 years had lived through a switch from bust to boom which was consensually accepted to have been the product of wartime activity seamlessly succeeded by a wise counter-cyclical Butskellism that piloted the ship of State along its chosen course. Well-informed leaders equipped with sensible macroeconomic strategies had learned to do what was needed, Crosland reasoned. The process was irreversible – and monetary and fiscal neutrality as much a thing of the past as the Great Depression which self-stabilising automaticity had failed to reverse.

Demand management was inevitable. So too was public spending and fiscal policy, given the Keynesian warning that the interest-rate and the money-supply were unlikely to be adequate to stimulate an under-employed economy that had drifted into excess capacity. Keynes had given hypothetical examples of 'fortuitous and often wasteful mitigations' which would have the multiplier function of combatting stagnation by means of boosting demand. The most famous of his illustrations was the following: "' To dig holes in the ground", paid for out of savings, will increase, not only employment, but the real national dividend of useful goods and services.'[1] Crosland, in favour of socialism as well as opposed to slump, was able to go beyond the arbitrary randomness of Keynes's pyramids and Keynes's monastic foundations. As Douglas Jay had done in 1937, Crosland recognised in counter-cyclical public spending policy a valuable opportunity to target the gaps in the social fabric that freedom of enterprise had condemned to neglect.

Thus he regarded the right to welfare as an end in itself, and not just as the means that made real the right to work: 'Generous social services and a more equal division of income will diminish the volume of savings and provide a permanent cushion of demand.'[2] Cold War defence, similarly, was both a necessary evil and a recession-proof stabiliser: 'Peace, alas, is a less good lubricant than war of the engine of social change.'[3] Then there was road-building and urban renewal, overdue and desirable: infrastructural investments such as these could be scheduled counter-cyclically to arrest a downturn. Macroeconomic stability and a generous State sector were, Crosland early concluded, not substitutes but rather complements. He was never to change his mind. The public debt as a brake on growth, the rediscovery of monetary policy, the ratchet effect in the government's budget, the political obstacles to deflationary cuts – these and related debates of the 1960s and 1970s all but completely passed him by. A Keynesian as well as a socialist, Crosland was consistent in his belief that public spending was indispensable if demand management was successfully to keep the economy on course.

Demand management to Crosland tends to be another name for slump-prevention. The asymmetry in the usage reflects the formative years of the 1920s and 1930s together with the widespread fears of the late 1940s and early 1950s that the market might be about to slide back into the pre-war depression. A socialist as well as a Keynesian, Crosland was understandably in sympathy with the marginal workers whose jobs were at risk in the down-turn and whose prospects would improve in the boom. His concern with the evil of unemployment reflects his formative years and his socialist sympathies. It also means that he was bound to have reservations about contractionary policies even after inflation had emerged as a major economic problem.

Crosland was not complacent about the damage that could be caused by rising prices. At his most anxious in the 1970s he was capable of condemning the new enemy in language as strong as that of any monetarist: 'Inflation is now the greatest menace threatening our society.... There is now a serious risk that we shall end up with a galloping inflation like a South American republic.'[4] In 1956 when *The Future of Socialism* appeared the rate of inflation was 3.3 per cent. In 1975, the year of Milton Friedman's *Unemployment versus Inflation?*, it was 26 per cent. Crosland was increasingly concerned about the harmful consequences for British economic and social life of a rise in the price-index that was so rapid and susceptible to such acceleration.

Inflation, Crosland believed, was inequitable and anti-socialist in its redistributive bias: while some welfare-claims are index-linked, while some property-contracts are fixed in value, it was Crosland's contention that the less-advantaged are more exposed on balance than are the rich to the erosion of purchasing-power. Inflation, moreover, was socially undesirable in so far as it represented a threat to growth (and therefore to public spending) and to jobs (most of all to the jobs of the most vulnerable) and to living-standards (and yet 'Labour.... is the party of the consumer as well as the worker').[5] Such stagflation in combination with such insecurity 'induces a mood of anxious yet militant resentment'[6] that is both destabilising in itself and a source of electoral unpopularity for a government seen to be unable to contain the rise. Crosland can hardly be accused of being soft on changes in nominal values. Nor can it be said that he failed to recognise the harm that such changes could inflict on the real variables of output and employment.

Crosland in the 1950s was optimistic about the possibility that a nation could secure full employment without a rise in prices and wages – and without a government policy to plan the magnitudes of those values. The following passage from the first edition of *The Future of Socialism* is indicative of his overall confidence in 1956: 'The case for a national wages policy is not definitely made out on the grounds that full employment must *ipso facto* induce an autonomous wage-inflation.'[7] Macroeconomic policy to trim demand to supply was likely to prove sufficient just as, even with controls, it must always prove necessary: 'A national wages policy must therefore fail if there is excess demand; and it is redundant if there is not. The wage problem is essentially a problem of preventing demand inflation.'[8] Those words appeared in *The Times Review of Industry* for August 1958, only months before A.W. Phillips was to reveal his fitted curve and the trade-off to which it pointed: 'If, as is sometimes recommended, demand were kept at a value which would maintain stable wage rates the associated level of unemployment would be about $5\frac{1}{2}$ percent.'[9] Crosland in the 1950s took a more merciful view of the macroeconomic options. Draconian unemployment victimises the weak while only postponing the rise until the end of the squeeze. A better choice would therefore be higher taxes (to reduce consumption) without higher interest-rates (to protect investment): productivity would then rise (thereby validating the rise in pay) but employment would not fall (since demand would be more nearly reallocated than reduced). Crosland's reasoning is suspect (his proposals appear to skew the excess but not to trim it) and his instruments are few (rejecting as he does both public spending cuts and interest-rate hikes). His policy-inference at least is a straightforward one. Macroeconomic policy is all that is needed to deliver the desired mix of low unemployment and low inflation – and 'the case for a national wages policy is not definitely made out'.

Those words on the subject of a wages policy do not appear in the 1964 edition of Crosland's *Future*. By the 1960s and most of all in the 1970s Crosland had become more interventionist, more committed to controls: 'An anti-inflationary policy is now the first priority for our country', he stated in 1972, 'and that means a prices and incomes policy'.[10] He did not welcome the inevitable with any real enthusiasm: 'Would that it were not so!'[11] What he did increasingly accept, however, was that the only alternative to the guidance of nominal variables would be the slower growth of real ones: 'As far as wage and price inflation are concerned, I have no doubts in my mind that we must have a prices and incomes policy. We must have it because the only alternative will be squeeze and deflation.'[12]

One advantage of a policy is that it contains inflation without creating unemployment. Guidance obviates the need for destabilising stop–go, it assists businesses to overcome uncertainty, and it protects that growth that even the most self-seeking of unions are known to favour: 'Neither Party nor unions can attain their goals without continuous growth; and we shall not achieve that growth without an incomes policy.'[13] Reconciling policy-objectives by means of an overall ceiling, the strategy has the additional advantage that it can be employed simultaneously to advance the cause of social justice through the twisting and re-shaping of earnings-differentials to the benefit of the lower-paid: 'Administered in cooperation with the trade unions, such policies have the further advantage of transforming wage bargaining from mere power bargaining to an exercise in the social determination of relative incomes.'[14] Egalitarian as well as effective, the democratic determination of *who* gets *what* transcends the possessive individualism of sharp elbows. It elevates consensus above market even in sectors of the economy where the ownership of capital remains decisively in private hands.

Yet the unions were by no means enthusiastic about the *de facto* nationalisation of a part at least of the substantial power that was conferred upon them by collective bargaining. Crosland was aware that the long-term success of a pay-policy was crucially dependent upon the willingness of the negotiators and the rank-and-file to settle for less than the market would bear. Never at home with the punitive sanctions of fines and imprisonment, it was Crosland's view that a programme of maxima and norms was unthinkable in British conditions so long as it was not buttressed by popular acceptance and shop-floor agreement: 'The ordinary union members must be convinced that such a policy is right and just.'[15] In that sense every incomes policy must ultimately be a voluntary one, crucially dependent upon 'a return to the old Cooperative Rochdale spirit – a sense of obligation to a wider good, thought for others as well as for ourselves, and a more Puritan self-government of our own desires and lives'.[16] Those words, dating from 1972, are a reminder that self-policing ethical standards (and not simply the cold efficiency of mechanistic structures) will frequently be an integral part of a successful macroeconomic policy. Sometimes the good society will presuppose no more than market-clearing rationality. Sometimes, however, what is required will be self-control and voluntary restraint instead. For a British incomes policy to have any chance of success, Crosland believed, it is the latter and not the former course that is the more likely to serve the public's interest.

The unions must volunteer, must hold back their claims. Concerned about the wage-differentials needed to correct manpower shortages and attract labour into mining, Crosland as early as 1947 was putting forward self-restraint as the ideal option: 'What is required, ideally, is a voluntary halt to all wage-increases save in this crucial sector – a halt lasting until the undermanned trades are firmly established in the leading positions.'[17] Crosland expected that the unions would agree to curb their demands, but only if capital could be persuaded to share their sacrifices. The *quid pro quo* of dividend-limitation that Crosland proposed in 1947 is the first reference in his political economy to the idea of an implicit contract as the basis for the calculus of consent.

The implicit contract of 1947 had the character of a two-team bargain. The contracting framework was that of the classical Marxian dyad. It was soon to be opened out. By 1951 Crosland, proposing an end to resale price maintenance and an increase in the food subsidies ('Subsidies benefit the poor much more than the rich, since they spend a larger proportion of their income on food'),[18] was expressing the hope that the unions would acknowledge the concessions made by the third party to the wage bargain: 'Would it then be too much to ask the trade unions, in exchange for this substantial programme of action on the part of the Government, to accept, even if only temporarily, a mild form of wages policy?'[19] Tentative, temporary and mild – Crosland despite his hesitation was articulating the principle that the new network of rights and duties was not a dyad of classes but instead a triangle of interests in which society itself would have to be treated as an equal partner.

Crosland's compact by the early 1950s had become tripartite and comprehensive, politicised and social. He never reverted to the old-style twin – or failed to criticise others for asking the workers for restraint without also tabling public policies in exchange. Edward Heath's wages policies were to him precisely the kind of short-horizoned interventionism that was unlikely ever to succeed: 'The first responsibility lies with the Government. It is no good asking the workers for restraint if rents are to double, if house prices go on rising at the present rate, if fantastic profits are made by property developers, if top salaries go up by 18 per cent. To make any policy acceptable, Mr Heath will have to reverse his entire ideology and substitute the politics of fairness for the politics of greed.'[20] It was the great shortcoming of Edward Heath's wages policies, Crosland argued, that they were myopic and partial, narrow where they ought to have been general. Labour would not make the same mistake. Speculative property-rises would be taxed and development land nationalised. Council rents would be contained and council housing expanded. Unemployment would be resisted and public transport improved. Policies such as these would redistribute life-chances and purchase cooperative attitudes. Edward Heath's victimisation of wages could only lead to confrontation and resentment, the desperation of statutory enforcement and the inevitable return to stagflationary waste.

A generalised *quid pro quo* is the precondition for an effective incomes policy. Yet there is something more, and that is a levelling tendency built into the package itself. Success through controls, Crosland said in 1971, 'is *only* possible within a framework of government policies for greater social and economic equality as a whole. It is no good simply asking the trade unions to cooperate in a prices and incomes policy against a background of reactionary social policies.'[21] *Only* means *only*: in that sense the pursuit of non-inflationary growth must be accompanied by the socialist's reduction in social distance. The two goals are indissolubly linked. They cannot be separated. In Crosland's words, speaking to a Fabian meeting in 1974: 'Of course most people do not want literal and total equality. But they want many fewer unjustifiable inequalities. They want a Labour Government to have, as someone has recently put it, a combined minimum income policy and maximum income policy. They want a sense of fairness and elementary social justice; and we shall not contain inflation unless we achieve it.'[22]

Fairness and justice through levelling and equality involve both a floor and a ceiling. In favour of the floor is the strong desire of the British people to raise up the least-advantaged: 'The British people are prepared to accept austerity – and even to make sacrifices – in order to help the worst off in our society. They support our policy of concentrating help on higher pensions, better housing and subsidies to essential foods.'[23] In favour of the ceiling is the counterpart desire of the British people to prune down the very prosperous: 'They will support us only if they are convinced that the rich are paying their fair share. They demand a redistribution away from those with very high incomes and ostentatious wealth. This will not release huge sums of money to help the poor; the spending of the rich in total is not high enough for that. But without such a redistribution we shall not command the moral authority to carry through our social programme.'[24] The floor protects the at-risk and shares abnormal handicaps: the altruistic desire of the British people to provide wheelchair access for the disabled and better schooling in the slums is a constructive impulse that reflects credit on the caring compassion of a united nation. The ceiling is more problematic: intended explicitly to punish the successful for their deviance from the median, a source of malicious *Schadenfreude* far in excess of revenues redistributed, the capping and the cutting down appear to be the close correlates not so much of 'moral authority' and 'the politics of fairness' as of immoral power and the politics of envy. Crosland, as would be expected, drew a different inference from what he took to be the felt wish of the British people for levelling down and not just for levelling up. Levelling down and not just levelling up would, he concluded, have in any case to be a part of any acceptable social contract that stood a chance of delivering the unions' voluntary restraint.

Crosland from the early 1950s had proposed a wide-ranging social contract. His suggestions clearly antedate the 1974 election and the adoption by the Cabinet (of which he was a member) of just such a multipartite arrangement in the years from 1975 to 1977. Intellectual influence is notoriously difficult to document; but it must be supposed that Crosland spoke very eloquently indeed in support of social policies supplied in exchange for trade union commitment and the spirit of Dunkirk. The period was one of rapid inflation and pressure on the pound; of bankers' demands for controls over pay and union militancy in the face of compulsion; of a popular perception that something had to be done and a socialist insistence that spending cuts would accentuate injustice. The Cabinet must in the circumstances have been abnormally receptive to any idea that might rescue British incomes policy from the guiding light, the legal norm, the early warning, the emergency freeze, the National Board that had in the past so conspicuously failed to deliver a long-term benefit. Advanced by Crosland or advanced by others, the social compact had the great attraction that it gave hope to a beleaguered Cabinet. Nor was the departure without precedent: it had been George Brown, after all, who in 1964 had brought together the Trades Union Congress (speaking for the workers), the Confederation of British Industry (speaking for the employers) and the Department of Economic Affairs (speaking for the State and the people) to hammer out a tripartite *Declaration of Intent* on inflation. To that extent the spending corporatism of the 1970s may be regarded as the logical next step on from the talking corporatism of the first Wilson mandate.

The social compact of the mid-1970s must have been very attractive to Anthony Crosland. In the years from 1975 to 1977 the TUC (which, admittedly, had no real authority to bind its member-unions to any specific covenant) recommended compliance with a voluntary pay policy in exchange for a 'social wage' payable in welfare (higher pensions and child benefits), legislation (against redundancies and unfair dismissals, in support of maternity leave and retraining schemes), microeconomic policy (to limit the rises in fuel and other public utility prices), macroeconomic policy (to create employment, to resist deflation). The *quid pro quo* of that experiment in interdependence was close indeed to Crosland's own proposals for a rights-and-duties solution. Nor did the course of events under the compact suggest immediately to socialists that the distinguished Labour theoretician might inadvertently have backed the wrong horse. The 1975 norm was a £6 limit – a percentage rise would have contributed less than a lump sum to the cause of equalisation. Inflation was halved to 12 per cent within a year – *prima facie* proof that a political solution could deliver an economic pay-off. Massive reductions in public expenditure had not been needed – and Crosland had consistently opposed such economies on the grounds that the incidence, unqually shared, falls most heavily on the jobs and services of the less advantaged.[25] The voluntary and cooperative principle had been upheld – and Crosland, even in the crisis conditions of 1966, had not compromised on his position that 'punitive powers should not apply on the wages and incomes side but only to prices'.[26] All things considered, therefore, both the theory and the practice of the 1970s compact must have been very attractive to Anthony Crosland.

Crosland intended that the pay norm backed up by the social wage should protect the public's interest in a stable level of prices. Control, he believed, would be a better guarantor of macroeconomic balance than would the market's uncoordinated free-for-all. The commitment to intervention is clear. Yet the argument appears to gloss over important difficulties. Crosland does not acknowledge that buoyancy of demand in exchange for moderation of claims can prove an unstable arrangement where leapfrogging employers in pursuit of scarce inputs have no option but to out-bid. He does not accept that higher public spending as part of a corporatist social package can only make demand-led inflation an even greater problem in the long-run. He does not anticipate the resistance of the electorate to higher deficits intended to stem excessive price-rises. He does not envisage the reluctance of the consensus to validate an appeasing package that makes no mention of strike-ballots and imposes no penalty on firms that exceed the norm. Complexities such as these make the reader wonder if Crosland's contract can properly be regarded as a permanent solution and not simply as a stop-gap palliative.

Union cooperation is arguably the ultimate question-mark. An old-school Englishman imbued with the seemly and the gentlemanly, a social-ist of sentiment with an emotive attachment to the stranger-gift, Crosland does not consider the possibility that practically-minded unions will, exploiting the State's promise of full employment at any price, systematic-ally abstain from voluntary restraint in order to negotiate the best deal they can for their members. Ethics will humanise economics, Crosland seems to be saying; and for that reason the unscrupulous blackmailer is unlikely to prove the typical member of the integrated community. The assessment is an encouraging one in the light of Crosland's insistence that the categor-ical imperative is needed to avert a market failure: 'The Social Contract asks all of us to recognise our dependence on each other. No man, no union, is an island. If the Social Contract were to be destroyed at the hands of a small minority, we should every one of us be the losers. It must not happen.'[27] Crosland, it would be fair to say, could not have foreseen that, in 1979, it was to be the unions and the strikes that would contribute so much to the electoral defeat of Crosland's own Labour Party. A moralist, a functionalist, a collectivist, he expected voluntary restraint in response to perceived inter-dependence. He treated selfish disruption not as the rule but as the exception.

Such an exception was the strike threatened by the National Union of Railwaymen in 1975. Crosland believed that the union was not living up to its social obligations. He also expressed the view that it would be a 'suicide course' for the State to pay above the norm: 'The National Union of Railwaymen must be clear on that point. Principles of social justice should determine the distribution of our national wealth. But all Government efforts to increase social justice are lost in the crazy haphaz-ard lurches which characterise pay settlements under conditions of such rapid inflation.'[28] The State as the owner of the nationalised industry should not capitulate to a bully who wanted to sacrifice the whole to the interests of a part. Nor should the railwaymen assume that it would necessarily be to their advantage if concessions were made that productivity could not justify: 'Fares would have to increase even more sharply. That would make rail less competitive, and ultimately it would mean a smaller railway industry and fewer jobs for railwaymen than would otherwise have been the case.'[29] The rise would mean cost-push inflation for Britain as a whole. It would also lead to a contraction of employment in the railway industry itself. Both the public bad and the private bad argue strongly in favour of reasonable claims and responsible attitudes.

The union should volunteer to hold back: its moral stance, generally adopted, will contribute to that plentiful stock of public goods of which the selfish free rider is known to be the natural enemy. The State should be resolute in its resistance. The titulary of the capital in question, *a fortiori* the regulator of private and public alike, the government must where necessary risk the unpopularity of a strike in order to demonstrate to the exploitative that the national interest is not open to challenge. Ideally, of course, even the Railwaymen will back down from the confrontation once they grasp that it is prices and jobs that their self-interest is so short-sightedly putting on the line: 'I have a great respect for the leaders of the railway unions, and a great faith in the common sense of the mass of their members.'[30] Yet a voluntary policy is dependent on volunteers; and sometimes it must happen that the government will wait in vain for sufficient signatories to subscribe to its implicit contract. Crosland does not say what should be done when morality fails. Others have filled the gap: compulsory conformity, punitive sanctions, demand deflation – and union reform.

Crosland in *The Future of Socialism* had praised the unions: seeing them as the legitimate voice of the working class, he had looked forward to the corporate society and 'high-level industrial democracy', to 'maximum Trade Union influence, though exercised from outside and not inside, at the national level of the industry'.[31] Crosland in the 1950s had welcomed the countervailing power as evidence that capitalists' dominance was at last being corrected: 'The Trade Unions, skilfully exploiting the existence of a seller's market for labour, have established a remarkable degree of control over those management decisions which directly affect the day-to-day life of the worker.'[32] Crosland by the 1970s had become less enthusiastic. Always in sympathy with worker consultation and collective bargaining, Crosland by the 1970s was openly expressing his reservations about the irresponsible exercise of power.

The unions, he claimed in 1974, were standing up not merely to bosses and managers but, increasingly, to elected governments as well: 'They wholly defeated the Labour Government, and effectively frustrated the Tory Government, in major confrontations over industrial relations legislation; while the miners and others, in an open battle over wages in 1972, forced Mr Heath into a humiliating reversal of his chosen economic policies.'[33] Trade union leaders, responsive to their narrow membership and insensitive to the wider community, were riding rough-shod over the interests of the excluded and the vulnerable: 'Competitive militancy wins the most for the best-organized and higher-paid; the strong become stronger and the weak become weaker, as after a Tory Budget. That is one (though not the only) reason why Labour must stand adamantly for an incomes policy.'[34] The unions pervert the course of political democracy. The unions bash the poor as if guided by a Tory Budget. One reason for an incomes policy is the need to keep the unions in line. Especially for a reformer whose socialism was perpetually politicised, never syndicalist, doubts such as these might be expected to have led to proposals and solutions. Not least would this be so in the light of Crosland's contention that effective action on inflation presupposes the voluntary restraint of precisely those economic units that had demonstrably been aggressive when they ought to have been cooperative. One might have expected proposals and solutions but one does not find them. A Labour man from the age of 16, Crosland approached the hurdle but he did not jump.

One possibility would have been legislation to temper the unions' hegemony. Aware as he was that industrial relations had fundamentally altered since the prosecution of the Tolpuddle Martyrs, Crosland could have expressed his opposition to the closed shop or asked for union power to be scrutinised by the Monopolies and Mergers Commission. Convinced as he was that union leaders on 'wider political issues' were frequently failing to echo the members' views, Crosland could have championed the internal election and the pre-strike ballot. The reality was somewhat different: Crosland (like Callaghan) opposed the proposals in Barbara Castle's 1969 White Paper *In Place of Strife*, which sought to impose legal limits (a 28-day cooling-off period, a curb on unofficial action, a check on inter-union disputes) in the sensitive area of industrial relations. Insisting that the measures were unwise and premature, Crosland in Cabinet 'made it perfectly clear that he wanted to see the penal clauses postponed'[35] without which a Bill would effectively have been a dead letter. Privately he was even more critical: he complained that the Prime Minister's 'unspeakable nature is one of the great facts of our political life'[36] and told Richard Crossman that he believed Harold Wilson to be cracking up. One can see his point: with 150 union-sponsored Labour members in the House, there was not the remotest possibility of a Bill becoming an Act and a climb-down was inevitable. On the other hand, Crosland shared with the advo-cates of the White Paper (Roy Jenkins among them) a suspicion that the unions were exercising more power than was equitable or efficient in a modern mixed economy. It is a surprise in the circumstances that he makes not a single suggestion of his own for a constructive alternative.

Not wishing to support legislation to temper the unions' hegemony, Crosland could at the very least have spoken out for a reconsideration of his Party's procedures. Since Giles Radice recalls him in the early 1960s as having described the union block vote at Conference as 'a historical anachro-nism',[37] since Tony Benn reports him in the early 1970s as having dismissed undemocratic unions as unpopular vote-losers ('Tony Crosland said at one of our Shadow Cabinet meetings that it wasn't Marxism that was the problem, because nobody really believed in Marx, but whether the Labour Party ought to be so tightly linked to the unions'),[38] one would have expected him at the very least to call for a radical reappraisal of the unions' special relationship. Crosland undoubtedly believed in the '60s of *Strife* and the '70s of Scanlon that interests were not congruent and could actually be conflictual: 'We must remember that the unions and the Party have their own distinct fields of responsibility, and their own distinct duties and obligations to their members and electors; neither is, nor should be, the creature of the other.'[39] Crosland can hardly have been comfortable with the antinomian defiance of hard-left shop stewards at odds even with their own central leadership; or with the Vietnam Years Trotskyism that looked to the unions not to support the capi-talist system but rather to subvert it; or with the insistence of militants like Tony Benn (supported by Michael Foot) that Conference decisions be made binding on the elected members of the Parliamentary Labour Party; or with the popular perception that Labour was, ideologically and financially, too close to the unions to be able to speak for the nation as a whole.

Interests were not identical, Labour was bigger than production line – and yet the future of socialism was in essence to mean more of the same: 'Labour's special link is, and must be, with the organized working class, and its solid base is in the trade union movement. Both party and unions represent the same aspirations of their members and their families; and the area of common interest and mutual need is, and always will be, enor-mous.'[40] That defence of cohabitation dates not from the age of Attlee (when the block vote was all but a rubber stamp for the PLP), nor from the years of high revisionism (when the unions, centrist on the whole, were disproportionately pro-Gaitskell), nor from the new dawn of the 1964 election (when 'beer-and-sandwiches' conciliation was expected by many to be Harold Wilson's alternative to strikes and confrontations). Rather, that defence of the special relationship dates from 1973 – from a time when union hostility had made punitive sanctions for pro-inflationary settlements a practical impossibility; when the old-fashioned morality of voluntary restraint had lost all legitimacy in the eyes of new-style leftists such as the miners' leader Mick McGahey. Crosland was not a union-sponsored Member of Parliament (albeit in his private capacity a member of the General and Municipal Workers Union). A respected senior moderate, he was in a strong position to recommend a radical reappraisal of the traditional linkages between a sectional movement and a political party avowedly responsible to the nation as a whole. It is a matter of record that here too he approached the hurdle but he did not jump.

Not wishing to support legislation to temper the unions' hegemony, not prepared to speak out for a reconsideration of his Party's procedures, there was a third option that Crosland might have wanted to select. That third possibility would have involved not the curbing of the unions' influence but rather the streamlining of the unions' organisation. In Britain, the large number of independent unions and the overall weakness of the TUC have meant that wage-bargains are uncoordinated and national guidelines easy to circumvent. In Scandinavia, Crosland appreciated, the institutional framework is more congenial to the consensual formulation of effective standards: there, he recognised, monolithic unions and representative bodies are at the forefront of consultation and cooperation. In Scandinavia, Crosland acknowledged, the tripartite principle has made wage-negotiation *de facto* a part of incomes-policy: 'With the full consent of the trade union movements, centralised bargaining procedures in which the government is directly represented have been accepted as the normal means of determining incomes.'[41] The Scandinavian machinery is eminently conducive to the attainment of Crosland's egalitarian and anti-inflationary objectives. Yet he neither endorses the adoption of the Scandinavian system nor advances ideas of his own for reform and overhaul. An incomes policy, Crosland seems to be saying, must start from here and not from the ideal. The conservative enemy will nod approvingly at this tolerant acceptance of the *status quo*. Crosland's friends, on the other hand, will wish that he had said more about the interface between industrial relations and incomes policy in a socialist future that need not mean more of the same.

Tony Benn wanted Labour to become ever closer to the unions: 'The trade union movement not only has to defend its own rights and should be supported by us but ought to have a joint programme with the Party.'[42] Anthony Crosland, Benn recalled, most certainly did not: opposed to the 'lurch to the Left'[43] that Benn believed to be the writing on the wall,

Crosland and his fellow moderates were men who 'hate the idea of the unions having a say'.[44] Benn, as this section has shown, is over-stating his case. Whatever Crosland may have said in private about obstructiveness and ungovernability, his public support for the unions as an integral part both of the Labour Party and of its incomes policy reveal him to have been a man of tradition and not a union basher demanding a divorce. Convinced that cost-push inflation had built market failure into British macroeconomics, Crosland sought to enlist the unions in his search for a solution. It is possible to say that Crosland was too generous to the agents that he believed to be at the root of the problem. It is less convincing to say that he, hating the unions, took steps to clip their wings.

5.5 THE PRINCIPLES OF DE-CONTROL

Twelve years before *The Future* had been *The Road*. Twelve years in advance of a *Socialism* that enlisted the State in the service of fairness had been a *Serfdom* that had seen every council-estate as a potential concentration-camp and regarded every Minister of Education as a propagandist, a brain-washer and a manipulator. Crosland cannot be expected to have been much in sympathy with an anxious author who had identified in every Atlee the slippery slope that must lead to Hitler and had insisted that there could be no middle way between the market and the Gulag. Crosland was a pragmatist who, acknowledging public-goods problems and third-party spillovers, was unable to accept that the invisible finger pointed inevitably to uncontrolled exchange. Unafraid to invoke State regulation where public authority would improve industrial performance, reduce environmental contamination and secure non-inflationary growth, Crosland was convinced that there were times when to refuse to intervene would be to deprive the community of its most congenial outcomes.

The Future legitimated control and *The Road* did not: to that extent the insights of the socialist and of the libertarian were mutually exclusive. Yet *The Future* also legitimated de-control; and there at least the pragmatist would appear to have joined his voice to that of the dogmatist in calling for *freedom from* and individual choice. No advocate of planning for the sake of planning, no paternalist offering repressive dominance in the name of leaderly wisdom, Crosland shared much with Hayek, just as he also shared much with Tawney. The eclecticism, the individualism, the willingness to compromise all reaffirm the quintessential case-by-caseness of Crosland's socialism. By the same token, they remind the reader just how difficult it is to situate in left-to-right space the intellectual position of a social thinker with a strong commitment both to State guidance and to the re-privatisation of autonomy that is the subject of the present section.

Crosland noted that past socialisms had tended to be ambivalent about *freedom from*: 'Of the various streams which make up the total socialist tradition, Leninism is profoundly anti-libertarian; the Fabianism of the Webbs (to put it mildly) could hardly be described as hostile to bureaucracy; and the pre-war Labour Party nationalizers instinctively favoured large scale and centralization.'[1] Socialists in the past had sought to produce the good society by means of public administration and scientific management. The vision, worthy but bleak, had rendered good service in disciplining the avaricious and assisting the forgotten. On the other hand, the pendulum had been allowed to swing too far and the individual was coming to feel stifled by the sheer weight of the collective: 'Society's decisions impinge heavily on people's private lives as well as on their social or economic welfare; and they now impinge, in my view, in too restrictive and puritanical a manner.'[2] The need in the past was undoubtedly for Blue Books and White Papers to stamp out the tuberculosis and the starvation, the slum housing and the sweated labour, that were the ugly characteristics of early *laissez-faire*. The need in the present is not precisely the same: 'Now the time has come for a reaction: for a greater emphasis on private life, on freedom and dissent, on culture, beauty, leisure, and even frivolity. Total abstinence and a good filing-system are not now the right sign-posts to the socialist Utopia.'[3] The need in the past was undoubtedly for control. The need in the present is for liberty as well: 'I should like to see action taken both to widen opportunities for enjoyment and relaxation, and to diminish existing restrictions on personal freedom.'[4] The need, in other words, is for selective de-control alongside the regulatory interventionism with which socialist reform has in the past so intimately been associated.

Britain, Crosland said, stood in need of the nationalisation of land and the control of incomes, State schools and welfare benefits. No less, however, was there a felt desire for the liberalisation of laws which had unwarrantably socialised the realm of the private. There were restrictions on homosexuality and abortion. There was censorship of films and books. There were licensing-laws that curfewed drinking-times. There were municipal injunctions that curtailed open-air cafés. Not advocating an across-the-board restoration of autonomy to the consenting adult, it was nonetheless Crosland's position that State intervention in personal areas such as these was little short of 'intolerable'. Such interference, he said, 'should be highly offensive to socialists, in whose blood there should always run a trace of the anarchist and the libertarian, and not too much of the prig and the prude.'[5]

Socialism, Crosland said, ought to take a principled stand in support of liberty. It had not always managed to do so, or to distinguish between 'a puritan government of one's own life, which is excellent, and a Pharisaical attitude to the lives of others, which is deplorable'.[6] It was not managing to do so in Crosland's own time: 'It is not only dark Satanic things and people that now bar the road to the new Jerusalem, but also, if not mainly, hygienic, respectable, virtuous things and people, lacking only in grace and gaiety.'[7] The road is barred by self-styled guardians who have taken upon themselves the pastoral function. The road ought now to be unbarred in order that the sanctimonious and the holier-than-thou should lose their dominion over the unique and the idiosyncratic.

Crosland believed that liberty enjoyed the support of consensus – that the ordinary man or woman wanted the individual to be free to choose. Even in Mr Wilson's Swinging London, however, and still less in Mr Macmillan's Done Thing, it is possible that the ordinary man or woman was far less tolerant of diversity than was the metropolitan intellectual. The unborn foetus will gnash its gums at the news that illiberal abortion-laws are 'prehistoric' and 'flagrantly unfair'.[8] The friend of the family will share the surprise of the low-paid labourer at the prediction that 'a time will come, as material standards rise, when divorce-law reform will increase the sum of human welfare more than a rise in the food subsidies'.[9] The advocate of traditional standards will regard lower penalties for the possession of cannabis (accompanied, admittedly, by higher penalties for trafficking and dealing)[10] as indicative of an unhealthy accommodation with aberrant permissiveness. The affectual communitarian will accept Crosland's view that, while solidarity, cohesion, neighbourliness and belonging are undoubtedly socialist values, so too are 'freedom, autonomy, and critical revolt' – but will most definitely reject the order in which Crosland ranks his preferences: 'I personally hold the latter values higher.'[11] The consensus, in short, might not validate Crosland's liberty and might opt instead for a cultural conservatism that Crosland himself would have found repressive. Repressive or not, he would have had no choice but to accept it as valid. Styling himself a democrat and not an elitist, Crosland was impelled by his methodology to reject middle-class decision-making processes such as 'require only the participation of *minority* groups': 'I am concerned with the views of the *majority*, and that our future policy discussions should pay attention to the wishes and aspirations of the *majority* of my working-class constituents.'[12] Should that majority insist on chapel when NW1 holds out for Sunday trading, Crosland would have had no choice but to swim with the flow and not with the anarchist and the libertarian whose rights, it would appear, are always contingent, never absolute.

Consensus will often be ambivalent about liberty where it is convinced that deviance will result from de-control. Crosland's attitude to the censorship of the media is in the circumstances of particular interest. In the country of Lord Reith's authoritarian tutelage, in a period when the Lord Chamberlain still censored the stage, Crosland's bias towards the demandled sequence is stark and striking: 'We are *not* proposing to ban by law the trivial and the vulgar, the escapist and the decadent – apart from the horrifying implications for liberty, we should hardly agree on what is trivial if we cannot even agree on what is pornographic.'[13] The media ought on balance to be tolerated, irrespective of the personal view that a critic might hold of the tabloids and the comics: 'Much of their present output.... is inane, banal, trivial, strident, mawkish or offensive; and scarce talent is wasted, and to some extent perverted, in producing it. But this seems to be what most people choose. And (quite apart from the democratic principle of freedom to communicate) why should not people freely choose their tastes and entertainment just as they freely choose their economic goods?'[14] Crosland knew what he liked – and what he did not like. At the same time, he was reluctant to stand in the way of the democratic mass in its rush to get its horror from *Clockwork Orange* and not from *King Lear*. His step-daughter was so repelled by the violence in *Clockwork Orange* that she had to leave the cinema. Crosland was not very much on her side when she told him of her trauma: 'That film has been described in every national newspaper. No one forced you to go to it. I haven't the faintest desire to see *Clockwork Orange*. That doesn't mean others shouldn't see it if that's how they want to spend their time.'[15]

Crosland's point was that the film did not libel or blaspheme; that the consumer had a shrewd idea in advance of what it contained; and that the potential of such a film to do genuine harm was in truth 'rather marginal'.[16] Crosland was able, in other words, to reassure the public that ordinary people were most unlikely to be depraved into emulation and corrupted into crime by the sight of violence on the screen. He said much the same about the contribution of commercial advertising to the increase in teenage lawlessness: 'Generally, a free society ... develops strong defensive mechanisms to protect its freedom of choice in the face of mass propaganda. It is a great mistake to take Madison Avenue at its own valuation.'[17] Commercial advertising undoubtedly exploits the search for status, the competitiveness, the acquisitiveness, the materialism of modern society. It appeals to cultural values but it is only marginally responsible for calling them into being: 'The media simply do not possess this overwhelming power to manipulate our tastes and deprive us of "free choice".[18] A society concerned about crime would therefore do well to blame itself, not want-creation and not *Clockwork Orange*, for the antino-mian attitudes that the media did little more than to reflect.

Stanley Kubrick was to take a stronger line on the artist as initiator. Alarmed by the incidence of copy-cat hooliganism, he ultimately prohib-ited all further screenings in Britain of the very film that Crosland's step-daughter had found so repellent. No anarchist, Crosland would have been more than prepared to close ranks with the censors and the shepherds if he had been persuaded that any but the pathologically suggestible were likely to be induced by media illustration into real-world cruelties that would oth-erwise have remained uncommitted. Crucially, however, he was not of the opinion that the typical Englishman normally needed the State's protection from his own darker side. Here as elsewhere, it would appear, Crosland was content to trust in the good sense of Henry Dubb. John Reith was not.

John Reith, creator of the BBC, its General Manager (from 1922 to 1927), its Director-General (from 1927 to 1938), imprinted the stamp of paternalism on the public broadcasting of Crosland's formative years. He regarded hot jazz as a 'filthy product of modernity' that the Nazis had done right to ban. He described televised dog-racing as 'degradation and prostitution' and Juke Box Jury as a 'manifestation of evil'. He instructed his subordinates to transmit what the masses needed and not to respond to popular preferences. By the mid-1960s, even he knew that the world had changed and that Sir Hugh Carleton Greene (divorced and an unbeliever) was not the Platonic guardian that the former Director had tried to be: 'I lead; he follows the crowd in all the disgusting manifestations of the age.... Without any reservation he gives the public what it wants; I would not, did not and said I wouldn't.'[19]

The BBC by the mid-1960s had effectively abandoned the idea that the Director-General had a right to ignore Dubb's priorities and a duty to lead Dubb instead. That is why Crosland felt able to play the devil's advocate to an extent that would have been too risky had the Reithians still been at the helm. Specifically, Crosland argued, there is a persuasive educational case for the State to offer 'a wider range of serious programmes than would be chosen by immediate majority vote; in the hope that over the years the public, having been offered this range, will more and more freely choose it.'[20] The argument is the same one that legitimates schooling (even com-pulsory schooling) in order to expand the lifetime range of potential choices. Here it is used with caution and presented as a compromise. De-control for the BBC means the transfer of initiative from supply to demand. It also means that from time to time the vendor will propose a product.

Democracy in the media is enhanced by competition and sustained by differentiation. That is why the State should do its best to encourage entry and foster alternatives. The BBC should pick up additional minorities by means of additional channels and local radio. Independent television should co-exist with the State network. The Monopolies Commission should scrutinise amalgamations that concentrate options and restrict variety. The ultimate objective was consumer choice:: 'Our aim should be the maximum degree of cultural pluralism and availability of different aesthetic goods.'[21] No strategy would prove capable of securing that end which did not include a commitment to de-control.

The State might wish to go further still. Interpreting de-control to imply empowerment, it might choose to impose a Marshall-type tax on the advertising revenues of long runs. The revenues raised could then be used to subsidise newspapers that could not rely upon economies of scale. At present, Crosland observed, 'the range and variety of independent newspapers are below the requirements of a healthy democracy'.[22] Consumer choice, he reasoned, would not adequately be met in the absence of a transfer from the State. In that sense *freedom from*, to have real meaning, must be accompanied by *freedom to* made possible by a Pigovian public subsidy.

Crosland endorsed a policy of *freedom from*. He also expressed the hope that free individuals would have the courage to have fun. Socialism in the past had all-too-often been associated with the Spartan imperative of 'hard work, self-discipline, efficiency, research, and abstinence',[23] with 'the dull functional nightmare which many fear.'[24] The ascetic and self-denying tradition of reformers like the Webbs was one which Crosland found 'hideously unattractive': 'We want less, not more emphasis on bureaucracy and collectivisation, but more radicalism and dissent of the sort they hated.'[25] The old socialism of early nights and early mornings had been overtaken by affluence, Crosland believed; and the time was right for a new socialism of 'lights, dancing, food, gaiety, culture', of excitement and pleasure unalloyed by the obsession with 'economics, politics, or the need for a new Fabianism'[26] that made the old emphasis appear so dated and so misplaced.

Crosland did not regard the de-controlled society as implying a bull market in uplifting things and community-based activities. Freedom from control, he believed, ought to bring with it a freedom from sober earnestness as well. A note to himself just before he entered Parliament well captures his vision of socialism as *joie de vivre*: 'And N. bloody B. this not mean Min. of Fine Arts & masses of pub. libraries & Fabian pamphlets on organisation of leisure. Much too much of all that. Nonsense to say people can't be perfectly happy on sex, gin & Bogart – and if that is what they want under Soc., well & good. I know many cultured people who want just that (e.g. me).'[27] Interested in food and drink, jazz and the Beatles, sport on television (which he would leave his own dinner parties to watch) and church architecture (which he fitted in with his Pevsner even when travelling to a ministerial appointment), Crosland appears indeed to have incorporated in his own lifestyle a considerable measure of the self-indulgent hedonism that he clearly believed to be an important element in the future of socialism. As the *Daily Mirror* put it in its 1977 summing up: 'Tony Crosland's epitaph is that he was an enthusiastic believer in the theory that there is a life BEFORE death…. He believed abundantly in all sorts of things: good jokes, good conversation, good cigars – and a good life for the people of this country.'[28]

Socialism in Britain had long enjoyed the reputation of not enjoying much at all. Richard Crossman's recollection of a dinner-gathering in 1953 gives an indication of what sensitive outsiders privately thought of Labour at the time when Crosland was beginning work on his revisionist classic: 'We had superb food and drink and a really old-time conversation, with Bob Boothby, John Strachey and Tony Crosland. Bob is convinced that Butler is on the up-grade…. Most of the conversation, however, was about the future of the Labour Party and Socialism, with Bob, as usual, talking like a Socialist but finally admitting that the reason he was a Conservative was that he was a Cavalier, while all the real Socialists were Cromwellians.'[29] The flamboyant sybarite's verdict on the dour and the drab must have seemed perilously close to the mark to a socialist of *joie de vivre* such as Anthony Crosland, already known as he was not for the woolly old red shirt so much as for what Brian Walden was later to call 'the outward trappings, the fine plumage': 'Great thinkers are usually depicted by Hollywood as short, bald, tortured men who sit unappreciated in garrets working by the light of an oil-lamp. Such caricatures stick in the popular mind, so that the tall, handsome, elegant, cigar-smoking Anthony Crosland, not infrequently found playing ping-pong, or watching *Match of the Day*, seems too relaxed, sleek and successful to be an intellectual heavyweight.'[30] Crosland was too much of a Cavalier to correspond to the popular image of what a Socialist was supposed to be. Herbert Morrison was more like the Cromwellian template of cold showers and grey suits. Crosland's commonplace book indicates that he found Morrison's asceticism singularly unappealing: 'No pte. life, or satisfying home, or family life: ? no sex with wife after v. early yrs.: no intellectual interests: wholly philistine in aesthetic or artistic matters.'[31] There was not much laughter in

Morrison's Socialism. Crosland's Socialism was self-consciously more Cavalier.

This is not to underestimate the self-discipline and the seriousness that were there as well. Brought up surrounded by Plymouth Brethren, on the Fabian Executive for 15 years, a trained economist, an active politician, it would have been impossible for there to have been little more to Crosland than a *Lebenskünstler* looking forward to lunch. People who knew Crosland comment unanimously on his assiduity and his energy as well as his ebullience and his love of life. It was this duality in his nature that led Roy Jenkins to describe him as 'a man of contradictions': 'He was a puritan with an inclination to self-indulgence.'[32] Susan Crosland has resolved the contradiction by suggesting that, Cromwellian when he had to be, he was profoundly unconvinced that denial of gratification was somehow a good thing in its own right: 'He saw no virtue in sitting on a bed of nails when there was a comfortable armchair in the same room.'[33] Socialism to Crosland was intended to be life-affirming and joyous. It was not intended to be the mortification of the flesh. Socialism to Crosland was intended to enjoy the 'moral-cultural-emotional appeal of the William Morris tradition'.[34] It was not intended to share the values of those '*v. admirable* characters', the Webbs, whose gift to British socialism had gone beyond their 'devotion & conscientious single-mindedness' to embrace 'their considerable indifference to all forms of art or culture, their lack of temptation towards any of the emotional or physical pleasures of life, their consequent priggish puritanism'.[35] Self-discipline and seriousness were to Crosland no more than the means to an end. They were never meant to be a pastime and a way of life.

Freedom from political restraint in combination with *freedom from* personal inhibition leads to a de-controlled culture of individual choice and the pleasure-principle – to a liberated culture of 'brighter and gayer streets at night, later closing-hours for public houses, more local repertory theatres, better and more hospitable hoteliers and restaurateurs, brighter and cleaner eating-houses, more riverside cafés, more pleasure-gardens on the Battersea model'.[36] Life is for living, Crosland said, and not simply for productive efficiency. After all, 'we do not want to enter the age of abundance, only to find that we have lost the values which might teach us how to enjoy it'.[37]

Crosland believed the de-controlled culture to be the culture of the future. The real question is whether it is a specifically *socialist* culture. The restless and the radical will deny that it is. Critical of working-class

conformity as well of the Reithian Sunday, hostile to the union demarca-
tionist as well as to the elderly Etonian, the faction of freedom will agree
with Crosland that the conservative must be the enemy but will deny for
all that that the socialist is likely to be a friend. Crosland, on the other
hand, appears to have held the double-barrelled conviction that *freedom
from* is a socialist value – and that a socialist party is the best guardian of
the libertarian inheritance.

The socialists were the libertarians because the Conservatives were the
conservatives: Crosland's stark characterisation of the Tories as blood,
horse and Church (together with his consistent refusal to acknowledge the
platform of the Liberals) meant that he was able to treat the Socialists as
the only party in a position to challenge the Lord's Day and the conventional order. His challenge could, of course, have been more aggressive:
he said little about women (apart from the occasional plea for the removal
of legal impediments to equal rights),[38] or about colour (despite the fact
that two years after *The Future of Socialism* Britain saw the eruption of
racial violence in Notting Hill), or about the House of Lords (save when,
in 1969, he was a member of the Wilson Government that made a half-
hearted attempt, later abandoned, to abolish the hereditary principle and
the delaying privilege). Even if the Conservatives were too conservative to
face up to these issues, it is by no means obvious that the revisionists were
willing to do so. Besides that, the Conservatives themselves were moving
into the libertarian camp. Less and less under the dominion of Colonel
Blimp and Sir Shirefox, more and more a party of grocers and estate-
agents, it was the Tories and not the Socialists who were ultimately to
become associated in the popular mind with the de-controlled culture.

Yet there is a further link between de-control and socialism; and here, it
must be accepted, Crosland's argument is somewhat more conclusive. De-
control in Crosland's world-view is not a thing apart but rather an integral
part of a wider whole. On the one hand the cleaner eating-houses, on the
other hand the cleaner streets. In the one sector 'better designs for furniture and pottery and women's clothes', in the other sector 'more murals
and pictures in public places'.[39] De-control to a socialist is evidently not
the same as de-control to an anarchist: not wishing to see the State wither
away, Crosland envisaged that control should accompany de-control in
order that the mixed economy should secure the benefits of a sensible
balance. A socialist libertarian thinks of the matrix, a non-socialist libertarian homes in on the atom. Both are individualists but still they are different. The latter frees and walks away. The former liberates but also
complements. It appears to have been a distinction of this nature that
Crosland was making when he defined his *freedom from* to be a socialist

freedom, Hayek's *freedom from* to be an organ cut loose from the organism which alone could sustain its life.

It is a recipe neither for the Command Economy nor for the Law of the Jungle. Industrial policy is the report of the Monopolies Commission, the ban on price maintenance, the indicative forecast. The environment is to be protected by zoning schemes, public transport, the selective subsidy, the occasional tax. Macroeconomic stability is ensured by fiscal Keynesianism, voluntary restraint and the social contract. De-control makes it easier to trade in the wife and to find a hospitable wine-waiter. Few calories will be lost in marching with Crosland from the *status quo* of his own times into a future of socialism that was intended to be an improvement. The model is the middle – and the middle is where we remain.

William Deedes, a Conservative, recognised in Crosland a man of moderation: 'Though instinctively at odds with his grand design ... I respect him as a silversmith on whose wares the marks mean what they say. He would be in most people's First XI for any Coalition.'[40] So did Christopher Fletcher-Cooke, centrist Conservative in the common-sensical Bow Group and open-minded collector of kindred spirits in search of compromise. Fletcher-Cooke examined Crosland's eleven-point challenge of 1962 (policies that 'no Tory could accept'[41] such as entry into Europe and the creation of a Greater London Council) and concluded that he had heard it all before: 'Of the eleven points that he mentions it is difficult to see any which could not be accepted by every member of the Bow Group and some of which have already been accepted by the present Government.'[42] Labour Right, Conservative Left – the middle is the middle whatever it is called.

Clarence Randall said it all: 'Here is an articulate British socialist an American business man would enjoy talking with over a lunch table.'[43] Clarence Randall was a retired industrialist. His article in the *Chicago Tribune* was headed 'A British Socialist on Ground Thought Reserved to Capitalism'. His conclusion was perceptive, that the ground was not reserved at all but was instead the common property of all reasonable middlists.

Including Herbert Schmertz. Herbert Schmertz was Vice President of the Mobil Oil Corporation. So impressed was Schmertz by the thrust of Crosland's *A Social-Democratic Britain* that he arranged for the key sections on the environment to be re-printed in a full-page advertisement which he and his colleagues placed in *The New York Times*.[44] Schmertz wrote to the Labour Member of Parliament to praise 'the cogency and spirit of your message.... We believe readers here will find it persuasive.'[45] It is unlikely that the Mobil Oil Corporation had ever before waxed so lyrical about a Fabian Society pamphlet. Middlists comes in all shapes and sizes.

Yet Crosland did not describe himself as a middlist and insisted that he was a socialist. Of course his revisionism was intended as a warning to the Left not to spoil the *quo* that had delivered the *status*: to that extent he was consciously defending the proven success against the ill-advised challenge of the nationalisers and the planners. On the other hand it was no less Crosland's wish to re-kindle the commitment of a complacent centre to the important objectives of equality and welfare that affluence and liberty would without State intervention be unable to satisfy. Arguably a middlist in the tried-and-tested realm of economic affairs, Crosland reveals himself to be a socialist of classlessness and redistribution the moment that the society and not the economy becomes the focus of his attention.

The posture is a familiar one, that self-seeking acquisitiveness can make us rich but that only conscious collectivism can make us just. Keynes glimpsed the duality with especial clarity: 'For my part I think that capitalism, wisely managed, can probably be made more efficient for attaining economic ends than any alternative system yet in sight, but that in itself it is in many ways extremely objectionable. Our problem is to work out a social organisation which shall be as efficient as possible without offending our notions of a satisfactory way of life.'[46] The same duality is at the heart of Anthony Crosland's economic revisionism. *Anthony Crosland: The Mixed Economy* would appear to have shown that Crosland was not irretrievably to the Left of Deedes and Fletcher-Cooke, Randall and Schmertz, in the future he envisaged for market capitalism, wisely managed. *Crosland's Future: Opportunity and Outcome*, on the other hand, shows that he wanted to see an active State, up and doing in the key areas of equalisation and welfare. Socialism or social-ism, what is clear is that Crosland on the middle ground cannot be situated very far from the Keynes who proclaimed the end of *laissez-faire* but nevertheless trumpeted the efficiency of the capitalist market.

6 Conclusion

Crosland's socialism is about equality of opportunity, equality of outcome, economic growth, the ownership of productive resources, the regulation of economic activities. Crosland's socialism is made up of five key concepts, five strands in a skein. Five central characteristics in turn mark out that skein as distinctive, a whole in excess of the sum of its strands. Those five dimensions of Crosland's methodology and approach – caution, multidisciplinarity, systematisation, pragmatism, hope above all – conclude this book with a reminder that Crosland's socialism is a playing-field for intellectual discourse just as much as it is a specified set of objectives and goals.

First, caution. There is in Crosland's socialism a sober and bounded vision of the New Jerusalem that was described by the young Asa Briggs in the following words: 'The very idea of a Utopia is repugnant to Mr Crosland. All that Socialists can and should do is to contrive social and economic rearrangements. They can redecorate the house, introduce new rooms and demolish cellars and top storeys: they cannot, or should not, exchange it for a castle in the air. They can assist us to become more contented and comfortable in our changed surroundings, but they cannot hope that living there will make us new people. Socialism lies in legitimate aspirations, not in dreams.'[1] Crosland could have put the cat among the pigeons by demanding the immediate closure of the public schools; by warning against the frenzied competitiveness of a maximising meritocracy; by questioning the value of consumer-led growth in a world of emulative preference-patterns; by recommending the re-privatisation of an industry such as telecommunications once technological advance had undermined the natural monopoly that had earlier forced the capital into the portfolio of the State. Instead Crosland put the pigeon among the pigeons by suggesting that structural discontinuities were no longer to be expected, that the economic and social system could be improved at the margin but was in no particular need of reconstruction or redesign.

Marx was a man of passion who waxed indignant at poverty, oppression, degradation and misery; and so were socialists of sentiment and outrage like William Morris, Nye Bevan and Tony Benn. Anthony Crosland was at some distance removed from the emotive involvement of the prophets and the evangelicals. As Lewis Coser once observed of

Crosland's middle book: 'Certainly, we do not find in *The Conservative Enemy* any of the passionate concerns at injustice and exploitation which formed the basis of the socialist ethos in the past. Instead, Crosland and his colleagues ... talk like conscientious and high-minded bookkeepers.'[2] Passages can undeniably be cited which illustrate the managerial socialism that Ben Pimlott once described as 'the civil-service Keynesian liberalism of Gaitskell and his later followers'.[3] One of those passages is the following, in which Gaitskell seems to be saying that the superiority of socialism would have one day to be demonstrated by means of economic and technical achievement above all else: 'The philosophical differences between the parties would gradually diminish and their rivalry would turn increasingly ... into a competition in governmental competence.'[4]

No one can fail to notice the importance of the bookkeeping and the competence in the work of Gaitskellites such as Crosland. No less important than the performance and the cost-effectiveness to the revisionists were, however, the concern with social balance and the valuation of social justice that gave mixed-economy socialism its *ought-to-be*. Thus Crosland, eschewing the nebulous and distant aspirations of comradeship and fraternity, did not eschew the more immediate morality that made him so hostile to untaxed capital gains, segregated secondary schools and development land in private hands. His sense of right and wrong pointed him in the direction of environmental protection that could in no way be reduced to the simple quest for productive efficiency. His ethical standards also led him to a defence of the autonomous individual by means of markets that leave people free to choose: 'What is profitable is what the consumer finds useful.'[5] Crosland, a socialist philosopher and not merely a high-minded bookkeeper, clearly approached the real world's shortcomings with a moral code and not simply a cookery-book of technocratic *how to*s. That said, Crosland's moral code demonstrably confined him to the middle ground and ensured that his socialism would not stray too far from an on-going way of life.

Second, multidisciplinarity. Crosland's socialism is characterised by an unhesitating recognition of 'the simple truth that economic change is inextricably bound up, both as cause and effect, with wider changes in society as a whole'.[6] Resistant to the maddening evasiveness of the textbook's *ceteris paribus*, attracted by grand theory and the wide-ranging synthesis, Crosland, reviewing Arthur Lewis's *Theory of Economic Growth*, found much to admire in the work of an economist who was unafraid to trespass into politics, history, anthropology and sociology in the pursuit of a total picture that refused to settle in a single area of academic discourse: 'It needed a book like this to make one realise just how circumscribed a subject economics had become. This was certainly not always so; all the great economists from Adam Smith to Marx, automatically took the whole of the social sciences as their province. But for 100 years economics has become more and more specialised; and only Schumpeter, amongst the great figures of this century, was willing to straddle many other disciplines besides his own.'[7] The parts had gone into separate collections and had in the interests of clarity to be reassembled: Crosland's political economy is imbued with the methodological organicism of a holist who believed that the breaking down had gone too far.

Crosland reassembled, but he also ranked. Marxians and other economic determinists had long regarded the productive base as the principal cause. Crosland, in contrast, treated societal facts – inter-generational mobility, the common culture, the self-perception of class – as independent variables, in no way to be cut down to the predetermined consequences of the economic structure. *The Financial Times* was in no doubt as to the importance of Crosland's revision: 'It is some innovation when a Socialist thinker removes economics from the pivot position in socialism.'[8] The causal independence is not complete in the sense that it is economic growth which is at the heart of occupational upgrading, cultural homogenisation, expanding State revenues to pay for expanding public services. Still, however, it is true that for Crosland the capitalist economy no longer had the power to dictate the contours of equality and welfare – and that society and polity were increasingly taking its place as the primary determinants of interaction and distance. In the words of Bernard Crick, writing in 1960 on the withering away of the economic imperative: 'The primacy of economics has been replaced by sociology at the centre of the socialist imagination.[9]

Third, systematisation. Crosland's socialism is thinking socialism, systematising socialism in pursuit of comprehensive principles that can situate the particular and instruct the pragmatic. Crosland's notebook for 1976 shows him to have taken particular pride while at Environment in ensuring that socio-philosophical considerations were not overlooked in the Transport Policy Review that was conducted by his civil servants in the course of that year: 'Certainly, outstandingly best & most analytical review of transport policy in living memory, & wd. not have been so without my work.... Was unusual systematic attempt to apply first principles (ec., soc., egalitarian, env.) to major sphere of activity.'[10] First principles have consequences – Crosland's defence of sound categories in 1976 recalls his earlier argument for ideas in systems in 1945: 'I am dismayed, as an ex-intellectual, by the bankruptcy of Soc. thought & theory. There is less unity on theory than there has ever been before, & there is a danger in becoming too pragmatic & empirical in our political thought.'[11]

Aware of the danger, Crosland deliberately set out to provide a framework for generalisation that would give isolated facts a context and would guide future investigators in their choice of relevant observations. The result was a schema that the particularism, the fragmentation, the reductionism of subsequent theoreticians, 'the over-great absorption with the snip-snap of periodicals rather than the long judgements of volumes'[12] (the phrase is from Bernard Crick), did not even try to match. Crosland in his later years is known to have been disappointed at the failure of a new generation of socialist *intellectuals* to come along. His disappointment at the lack of new ideas recalls that of the *Psalms*: 'Where there is no vision, the people perish'. It also recalls the pessimistic verdict of Stephen Haseler on the post-Croslandite generation of British social democrats, timid, conciliatory and confused: 'Most of Labour's moderate leaders today are so demoralised, so tame, so unsure of their own intellectual coherence and, above all, so frightened to incur the wrath of the movement that they give the appearance of political jelly. And jelly melts under heat.'[13] Crosland's thinking socialism, modest and marginalist though its domain may have been, was considerably more robust than that.

Systematising as he was, of course, Crosland was simultaneously preaching the virtues of real-world evidence and was disparaging pure speculation that neither emanated from facts nor ended up in action. His target being over-blown wishful imaginativeness as much as piecemeal, reactive short-termism, his intellectual system had to keep in touch with the raw data of experience if it was to be of any use to the reforming realist bent on mapping – and re-structuring – the outlines of the modern mixed economy. As John Vaizey writes: 'He was a great believer that if the *thinking* was got straight and the *facts* got right, then the machine could be made to deliver the goods. In essence, this is what his version of Socialism became. He was a Fabian in the true tradition – that is, not what it is erroneously supposed to be, right-wing moderate gradualism, but social enquiry followed by social action.'[14] No evolutionist, no determinist, Crosland believed that values could exercise a high-powered influence relative to alleged laws of historical inevitability – but only if the aspirations were firmly rooted in the politics of the practicable. His intellectual system was an intrinsic part of his campaign to decide what could and what could not be done. Michael Young was hardly alone in finding it a source of exhilaration: 'His voice carried conviction because it was always the voice of someone thinking out his position for himself.'[15]

Fourth, pragmatism. There is an acknowledgement in Crosland's social-ism that the pure free market is much of an ideal type as the dictionary's command economy, completely and totally planned. The mix being the norm, the study of production, consumption, distribution and exchange is then bound by its nature to be that of political economy and not of disem-bodied economics in its scientific void. In the words of Charles Lindblom: 'In all the political systems of the world, much of politics is economics, and most of economics is also politics.'[16] Such a conclusion would have appealed to Anthony Crosland, a political economist and an economist in politics who stood on the shoulders of Marshall and Pigou, Keynes and Beveridge, Dalton and Jay, to make pragmatic response the cornerstone for a mixed economy of managed capitalism that would in his view be a source of equality and of efficiency alike.

Nationalisation in the past had been a success: morale had been improved, competitive waste eliminated, natural monopoly made account-able, the Bank of England and the railways forced to face up to their non-commercial obligations. Nationalisation in the future, gradual, selective and case-by-case, would extend the benefits of public ownership to the machine-tool industries (in order to secure economies of scale by means of concentration) and rented accommodation (in order to ensure an expanded supply at a reasonable price). Convinced that regulation and control would often be sufficient to defend the public interest without an actual transfer of title, Crosland made his socialism of laws and directives an essential part of his mixed economy of power and influence: witness the restric-tions on market freedom that he proposed in respect of corporate mergers, environmental diswelfares and cost-push inflation. Crosland wanted to assist the private sector through indicative economic planning and even the liberalisation of superfluous legislative shepherding. It was his con-tention that the pragmatic mix of unfreedom and *laissez-faire* would make the economy more productive even as it made the community more inte-grated and more just.

A different perspective would be that Crosland somewhat misjudged the efficacy of the middle ground. Too interventionist to trust entrepre-neurial alertness to redirect resources in line with the signals of supply and demand, too hands-off to encourage elected politicians to fix the prices and coordinate the quantities in the course of democratic goal-setting, the criticism will invariably be made of Crosland's mix that it con-cedes too much to the pressure-group society and the inward-looking corporatism of managers and bureaucrats without also demonstrating that the public good of economic growth will not on the way fall victim to the neglectful inertia of the conservative enemy. Without economic growth there can be no socially-engineered progress towards the socialism of equality and welfare that in Crosland's view had to be built upon public spending and public services and not upon the hard-line expropriation of the capital-owning class. In that sense the consistent Croslandite must be especially sensitive to the criticism that social justice through Crosland's mix is being purchased at the cost of value added rather than complementing the sustained rise in living standards that to Crosland was the *sine qua non* for levelling without confrontation.[17]

Fifth, hope – all the hope and all the confidence of a socialist of dynamism and upgrading who believed that history was on his side. As Crosland said in 1975: 'My political misfortune is that I was born an optimist.'[18] By then the 1950s had most decidedly come to an end. The New Left activists were denying that there could be a meaningful socialism without the collectivisation of capital or that moderate reform could ever be the equal of the plutocratic enemy. The New Right Thatcherites were preaching liberalisation, tax-cutting, privatisation and competition in the interests of an affluent society that looked to individuals and not to States for the choices that shaped people's lives. Unemployment was back on the agenda after the oil-price shock of 1973. Stagnant growth accompanied by unacceptable inflation compounded the problem of the instability and the joblessness. Friedmanite monetarists challenged the belief of the Keynesian fine-tuners in the efficacy of macroeconomic guidance. Investigators like Peter Townsend and John Goldthorpe demonstrated the survival of poverty and inequality even in the British welfare state. Public spending had faced a measure of opposition in the years even of high consensus that, as David Marquand makes clear, Anthony Crosland had hardly been able to anticipate: 'In 1979, Britain's ratio of public expenditure to GDP was the second lowest in the European Community; only Greece had a lower one. Much the same is true of the rate of growth in the ratio. In the twenty years from 1960 to 1980 ... only France came below Britain.'[19] The public schools had not been abolished, the unions had become unpopular, the electorate was abstaining at elections, the student generation was saving the whales and not the homeless. The socio-economic world was in many ways quite a different place in the 1970s from the British conditions that had moulded and shaped *The Future of Socialism* two decades before.

Colin Welch, convinced that Crosland was an over-enthusiastic optimist who 'took too much for granted', speaks of 'a certain shadow' falling over the last years of Crosland's life: disillusioned, he was 'condemned to live in his own future. He saw it, and it didn't work.'[20] A more realistic view would, however, be that Crosland was aware that much had changed but that he continued to regard the core message as lasting and good. Crosland in the last year of his life told Roy Hattersley that he believed there was a need for a new theoretical work on the socialism of mix and justice. What he also made clear was that, much having changed, the middle ground remained nonetheless an intellectual position with a democratic appeal that the extremes would do well not to write off as *passé*: 'We have got to keep making the point that the far Left are not the only people who can claim a socialist theory while the rest of us are thought to be mere pragmatists and administrators.... It's not enough to disagree with the Marxists *et al*. The Centre must remember and keep reminding people that we are ideologists too.'[21] Crosland believed that revisionism had continually to be revised. He did not believe that social democracy in Britain had reached the end.

Notes and References

Abbreviations to Works by C.A.R. Crosland

CP   Crosland Papers, in the British Library of Political and Economic Science.

FS   *The Future of Socialism* (London: Jonathan Cape, 1956), reprinted as Vol. VII in D.A. Reisman, ed., *Theories of The Mixed Economy* (London: Pickering and Chatto, 1994). An abridged version of *The Future of Socialism* was published by Cape in 1964. The notes to the present book first give the reference to the 1964 edition and then (in brackets) the page-number in the 1956 original. A comparison of the 1956 and the 1964 editions will be found in D.A. Reisman, 'Crosland's *Future*: the first edition', *International Journal of Social Economics*, Vol. 23, No. 3, 1996, pp. 3–54.

CE   *The Conservative Enemy* (London: Jonathan Cape, 1962). Full references to reprinted papers are given when first cited.

SN   *Socialism Now*, ed. by D. Leonard (London: Jonathan Cape, 1974). Full references to reprinted papers are given when first cited.

1. Introduction

1. P. Jenkins, 'Socialism in our time?', *The Guardian*, 22 March 1974.
2. D. Leonard, 'In Memoriam: I' in D. Lipsey and D. Leonard, eds, *The Socialist Agenda: Crosland's Legacy* (London: Jonathan Cape, 1981), p. 9. The tribute first appeared, entitled 'Goodbye, Tony', in *The Economist* of 19 February 1977: Susan Crosland, in *Tony Crosland* (London: Jonathan Cape, 1982), p. 402, explains why what was clearly intended to be an obituary appeared, with her approval, two days before the life-support machine was actually switched off. D. Leonard was the Labour MP for Romford from 1970–74 and was Parliamentary Private Secretary to Crosland. Later he became a full-time journalist on the staff of *The Economist*.
3. C. Welch, 'Crosland Reconsidered', *Encounter*, Vol. 52, January 1979, p. 84.

2. Anthony Crosland

1. P. Williams, *Hugh Gaitskell* (London: Jonathan Cape, 1979), p. 750.
2. J. Vaizey, in M. Young, J. Vaizey and D. Bell, 'Memoir: Anthony Crosland & Socialism', *Encounter*, Vol. 49, August 1977, p. 89.
3. 'Anthony Crosland', *The Observer*, 25 July 1965, p. 10.
4. C.A.R. Crosland, notebook entry dated July 1973, in CP 16(8).
5. Ibid., entry dated 1974.
6. H. Dalton, *Practical Socialism for Britain* (London: George Routledge and Sons, 1935), p. 320.

7. R. Jenkins, 'C.A.R. Crosland', in R. Blake and C.S. Nicholls, eds, *The Dictionary of National Biography 1971–1980* (Oxford: Oxford University Press, 1986), p. 193.

8. This topic is examined in more detail in D.A. Reisman, *Crosland's Future: Opportunity and Outcome* (London: Macmillan, 1996), Ch. 2.

9. C.A.R. Crosland, 'The Labour Party and the War', unpublished manuscript dated January 1940, in CP 2(18).

10. Ibid.

11. Ibid.

12. Ibid.

13. C.A.R. Crosland, Letter to P. Williams dated 29 January [probably 1946], in CP 3(27).

14. C.A.R. Crosland, Letter to P. Williams dated 10 June 1945, in CP 3(26), Pt. ii.

15. Ibid.

16. Cited in B. Pimlott, *Harold Wilson* (London: HarperCollins, 1992), p. 42.

17. C.A.R. Crosland, Letter to P. Williams, date unclear [probably 14 December 1940], in CP 3(26), Pt. i.

18. C.A.R. Crosland, Letter to P. Williams dated 19 January [probably 1941] in CP 3(26), Pt. i.

19. C.A.R. Crosland, Letter to P. Williams dated 15 July 1941 and Letter to P. Williams, n.d. [probably 1940 or 1941], both in CP 3(26), Pt. i.

20. R. Jenkins, *A Life at the Centre* (London: Macmillan, 1991), p. 32.

21. Jenkins, 'C.A.R. Crosland', loc. cit.

22. W.T. Rodgers, 'Crosland: A Man of Suspended Judgement', *The Daily Telegraph*, 5 June 1982, p. 16.

23. S. Crosland, *Ruling Passions* (London: Weidenfeld and Nicolson, 1989), p. 83.

24. Ibid., p. 190.

25. C.A.R. Crosland, Speech to the Oxford Union, n.d. [probably late 1940s], unpublished manuscript, in CP 13(21).

26. Ibid.

27. Cited in S. Crosland, *Tony Crosland*, op. cit., p. 204.

28. Cited in ibid., p. 210.

29. T. Benn, *Against the Tide: Diaries 1973–76* (London: Hutchinson, 1989), p. 576.

30. B. Pimlott, *Hugh Dalton* (London: Macmillan, 1986), p. 424.

31. Cited in ibid., p. 509.

32. Cited in ibid.

33. Cited in S. Crosland, *Tony Crosland*, op. cit., p. 54.

34. Ibid., p. 49.

35. Cited in Pimlott, *Hugh Dalton*, op. cit., p. 588.

36. Jenkins, *A Life at the Centre*, op. cit., p. 89.

37. Cited in Pimlott, *Hugh Dalton*, op. cit., p. 588.

38. Cited in ibid., pp. 630–1.

39. Cited in ibid., p. 630.

40. Pimlott, ibid., p. 624. The other three were P.D. Henderson, I.M.D. Little and P. Williams. Robert Hall, Michael Young and J.H.Smith commented on individual sections.

41. R.H.S. Crossman, 'Angry Young Men', *The Guardian*, 7 December 1962.
42. 'New Jerusalem or Old Adam?', *The Economist*, 27 October 1956, p. 320.
43. D. Leonard, 'Foreword' to SN, p. 11.
44. C.A.R. Crosland, Speech in South Gloucestershire, n.d. [probably 1949], unpublished manuscript, in CP 13(21).
45. Ibid.
46. Cited in S. Crosland, *Tony Crosland*, op. cit., p. 65.
47. Cited in ibid., p. 147.
48. D. Jay, *Change and Fortune* (London: Hutchinson, 1980), p. 290.
49. C.A.R. Crosland, Speech in the House of Commons, 19 April 1950, *Parliamentary Debates (Hansard)*, Vol. 494, No. 151, Col. 183.
50. Ibid., Cols. 185–6.
51. Vaizey, in Young *et al.*, 'Memoir', loc. cit., p. 86.
52. 'G.C.', review of *Britain's Economic Problem*, *The Financial Times*, 1 June 1953.
53. Review of *Britain's Economic Problem*, *The Listener*, 11 June 1953.
54. D. Jay, 'Three Dangers for Britain', *Daily Herald*, 28 May 1953.
55. N. Kaldor, 'Britain's Economic Future', *The Manchester Guardian*, 27 July 1953.
56. Ibid.
57. 'G.C.', review, loc. cit.
58. Review, *The Listener*, loc. cit.
59. J. Strachey, 'Soldiers, Dollars and Funk Money', *Tribune*, 5 June 1953.
60. T. Balogh, 'Hamlet Without Claudius', *New Statesman and Nation*, 4 July 1953.
61. C.A.R. Crosland, Letter to P. Williams dated 5 July 1940, in CP 3(26), Pt. i.
62. C.A.R. Crosland, 'The Transition from Capitalism', in R.H.S. Crossman, ed., *New Fabian Essays* (London: Turnstile Press, 1952), p. 35.
63. FS, 1956 edition only, p. 13.
64. FS, p. 55 (91).
65. FS, p. 338 (494).
66. C.A.R. Crosland, 'The Principles of Cooperation', originally published as Ch.2 of the *Cooperative Independent Commission Report* (1958), in CE, p. 236.
67. C.A.R. Crosland, Letter to T. Herzl Rome dated 22 November 1961, in CP 13(4).
68. T. Herzl Rome, Letter to C.A.R. Crosland dated 15 December 1961, in CP 13(4).
69. See D. Bell, 'Politics' New Look', *New York Post*, 23 February 1958.
70. Rome also invited Crosland (who declined) to write an introduction for a reprint of Bernstein's *Evolutionary Socialism* that Schocken were publishing.
71. Crossman, 'Angry Young Men', loc. cit.
72. 'Labour's Liberal', *The Economist*, 17 November 1962.
73. Crossman, 'Angry Young Men', loc. cit.
74. The title of *The Economist* review, note 72, supra.
75. C.A.R. Crosland, Letter to G. Howard Wren dated 3 January 1961, in CP 13(4).
76. Cited in Rodgers, 'Crosland: A Man of Suspended Judgement', loc. cit.

77. Jenkins, *A Life at the Centre*, op. cit., p. 218.
78. C.A.R. Crosland, in E. Boyle and C.A.R. Crosland (with Maurice Kogan), *The Politics of Education* (Harmondsworth: Penguin Books, 1971), p. 187.
79. Cited in S. Crosland, *Tony Crosland*, op. cit., p. 148.
80. FS, p. 191 (261).
81. C.A.R. Crosland, notebook entry dated August 1967, in CP 16(7).
82. R.H.S. Crossman, *The Diaries of a Cabinet Minister*, Vol.II (London: Hamish Hamilton and Jonathan Cape, 1976), p. 454.
83. C.A.R. Crosland, Speech in the House of Commons, 20 March 1968, *Parliamentary Debates (Hansard)*, Vol. 761, Col. 454.
84. C.A.R. Crosland, Speech in the House of Commons, 30 April 1968, *Parliamentary Debates (Hansard)*, Vol. 763, Col. 1006.
85. See C.A.R. Crosland, 'Legislating against Monopoly', *Socialist Commentary*, January 1951.
86. SN, p. 18.
87. C.A.R. Crosland, Thames Television interview with Llew Gardner in the series People and Politics, programme 14, 1974.
88. R.H.S. Crossman, *The Diaries of a Cabinet Minister*, Vol. I (London: Hamish Hamilton and Jonathan Cape, 1975), pp. 305–6.
89. Pimlott, *Harold Wilson*, op. cit., p. 414.
90. Ibid., p. 421.
91. Cited in B. Castle, *The Castle Diaries: 1974–76* (London: Weidenfeld and Nicolson, 1980), p. 542.
92. Cited in Pimlott, *Harold Wilson*, op. cit., p. 354.
93. See C.A.R. Crosland, Speech in the House of Commons, 21 November 1967, *Parliamentary Debates (Hansard)*, Vol. 754, Cols. 1140–54.
94. Crossman, *Diaries*, Vol. II, op. cit., p. 646.
95. Ibid., p. 446.
96. Ibid., p. 550.
97. Ibid., p. 477.
98. Ibid., p. 532.
99. Jenkins, *A Life at the Centre*, op. cit., p. 217.
100. Ibid.
101. The phrase is that of Denis Healey, in his *Time of My Life* (London: Michael Joseph, 1989), p. 329.
102. Castle, *The Castle Diaries*, op. cit., p. 461.
103. R.H.S. Crossman, *The Diaries of a Cabinet Minister*, Vol. III (London: Hamish Hamilton and Jonathan Cape, 1977), p. 535.
104. Ibid., p. 545.
105. Ibid., p. 677.
106. C.A.R. Crosland, *A Social-Democratic Britain*, Fabian Tract 404, 1971, in SN, p. 71.
107. SN, p. 26.
108. SN, pp. 26–7.
109. SN, p. 29.
110. SN, p. 53. A similar condemnation of intolerant extremism may be found in C.A.R. Crosland, 'Socialists in a Dangerous World' *Socialist Commentary*, November 1968, in SN pp. 68–9, where he writes as follows about the authoritarianism of student activists: 'Violence is never justified unless it is

the sole method of establishing democracy; otherwise it becomes a weapon against democracy, reflecting a derision for the rights of the majority and a contempt for the right of free speech'. Democratic process must not be sacrificed, he is saying, even if the intended endstate is (like socialism) a desirable one. Extracts from the paper appeared in *The Observer* of 6 October 1968 under the title 'The future of socialism, 1968'.

111. SN, p. 24.
112. I. Rowan, 'Crosland: The Last Interview', *The Sunday Telegraph*, 20 February 1977.
113. SN, p. 37.
114. SN, p. 58.
115. FS, p. 357 (524).
116. C.A.R. Crosland, 'The Battle for the Public Purse', The *Guardian*, 24 March 1976, p. 14.
117. C.A.R. Crosland, 'Equality in Hard Times', *Socialist Commentary*, October 1976, p. 3. The (Reverend) John Lewis in question had been a Christian Marxist, active in the Left Book Club and its affiliated societies in the 1930s.
118. C.A.R. Crosland, 'What the Labour Party Must Do', *The Observer*, 21 January 1973.
119. C.A.R. Crosland, Paper to a Fabian Society conference, Oxford, January 1950, unpublished manuscript, in CP 13(23).
120. C.A.R. Crosland, Speech to the Grimsby Labour Party, n.d. [probably 1975], unpublished manuscript, in CP 13(24).
121. C.A.R. Crosland, Speech to the Tonbridge Labour Party, n.d. [probably mid-1970s], unpublished manuscript, in CP 13(24).
122. C. Tugendhat, 'Socialist Spokesman', *The Financial Times*, 21 March 1974.
123. 'New Jerusalem or Old Adam?', loc. cit.
124. D. Taverne, 'The philosophy of social democracy', *The Times*, 15 April 1974.
125. A. King, 'Philosopher King', *New Society*, 4 April 1974.
126. N. Kinnock, 'Crosland's civilised capitalist cocktail', *Tribune*, 5 December 1975, p. 5.
127. Ibid.
128. 'Great Britain: The Shock of Today', *Time Magazine*, 25 January 1963, p. 22. The cover-story on Britain's changing mood was overtaken by events: Gaitskell died only a week before it appeared. The article continues to describe Crosland as a 'pacemaker' in British politics.
129. Cited in S. Crosland, *Tony Crosland*, op. cit., p. 219.
130. C.A.R. Crosland, 'Britain, Europe and the World', *Socialist Commentary*, November 1976, pp. 9, 11.
131. Cited in Williams, *Hugh Gaitskell*, op. cit., p. 719.
132. Cited in ibid., p. 702.
133. Crosland, 'Britain, Europe and the World', loc. cit., p. 10.
134. Ibid., p. 14.
135. CE, pp. 7–8.
136. M. Postan, 'Political and Intellectual Progress', in W.T. Rodgers, ed., *Hugh Gaitskell 1906–1963* (London: Thames and Hudson, 1964), p. 62.
137. Ibid.
138. CE, p. 7.

139. C.A.R. Crosland, 'Radical Reform and the Left' (Original title: 'On the Left Again'), *Encounter*, Vol. 15, October 1960, in CE, p. 131.

140. C.A.R. Crosland, Speech at a press-conference held on behalf of the Labour Campaign for Britain in Europe, 3 June 1975, unpublished manuscript, in CP 13(27).

141. C.A.R. Crosland, Speech at a dinner held by the Labour Committee for Europe in honour of Roy Jenkins, 6 December 1976, unpublished manuscript, in CP 13(34).

142. Benn, *Against the Tide*, op. cit., p. 347.

143. An equally curious situation obtained in 1975 when the House voted on the renegotiated terms: then 137 Labour Members supported their Government, 145 voted against it, 33 abstained – and it was the support of the Conservatives that ensured the approval of Wilson's recommendation.

144. R. Jenkins, 'Anthony Crosland', in *Roy Jenkins' Gallery of Twentieth Century Portraits* (London: David & Charles, 1988), p. 67.

145. S. Fry, 'Crosland: An Appreciation', *The Sunday Times*, 20 February 1977, p. 4.

146. S. Crosland, *Tony Crosland*, op. cit., pp. 326, 337.

147. C.A.R. Crosland, notebook entry, July 1976, in CP 16(8).

148. Ibid.

149. Crosland, notebook entry, August 1976, in CP 16(8).

150. Ibid.

151. C.A.R. Crosland, *Britain's Economic Problem* (London: Jonathan Cape, 1953), p. 179.

152. Ibid., p. 204.

153. C.A.R. Crosland, *The British Economy in 1965* (Hugh Gaitskell Memorial Lecture) (Nottingham: University of Nottingham, 1965), p. 13.

154. Crossman, *Diaries*, Vol. I, op. cit., p. 567.

155. 'Is Industry Letting Britain Down?', interview with C.A.R. Crosland, *The Sunday Times*, 10 December 1975, p. 35.

156. Crossman, *Diaries*, Vol. III, op. cit., p. 232.

157. Crosland, notebook entry, July 1976, in CP 16(8).

158. Crosland, *The British Economy in 1965*, op. cit., p. 14.

159. Crosland, notebook entry, July 1976, in CP 16(8).

160. Ibid.

161. Ibid.

162. Crosland, 'Equality in Hard Times', loc. cit., p. 3.

163. Crosland, notebook entry, July 1976 (final six words dated 1974), in CP 16(8).

164. Ibid.

165. Benn, *Against the Tide* op. cit., p. 576.

166. C.A.R. Crosland, Statement in the House of Commons, 2 February 1977, *Parliamentary Debates (Hansard)*, Vol. 925, Col. 556.

167. J. Callaghan, Statement in the House of Commons, 21 February 1977, *Parliamentary Debates (Hansard)*, Vol. 926, Cols. 1034–35.

168. Leonard, 'In Memoriam: I', in Lipsey and Leonard, eds, *The Socialist Agenda*, op. cit., pp. 12–13.

169. Lord [Jack] Donaldson, 'In Memoriam: II', in ibid., pp. 16–17. In Government Lord Donaldson had been Parliamentary Under Secretary in

the Northern Ireland Office (1974–76) and Minister for the Arts (1976–79). Much earlier, he had been active in the South Gloucestershire Labour Party and in Crosland's adoption for the constituency in autumn 1949.

170. Jenkins, *A Life at the Centre*, op. cit., p. 103.
171. Ibid., p. 66.
172. Ibid., p. 30.
173. A. Watkins, 'The New Model Educator', *The Spectator*, 29 January 1965, p. 126. The article coincides with Crosland's entry into the Cabinet.
174. Ibid.
175. M. Young, in Young *et al.*, 'Memoir', loc. cit., p. 85.
176. Crossman, *Diaries*, Vol. II, op. cit., p. 614.
177. M. Falkender, *Downing Street in Perspective* (London: Weidenfeld and Nicolson, 1983), p. 244.
178. Ibid., p. 243.
179. The view of Denis Healey, in his *Time of My Life*, op. cit., p. 451.
180. Cited in P. Dunn, 'The Egg-Head Egalitarian', *The Sunday Times*, 3 September 1967, p. 11. The source is not named.
181. Cited in ibid.
182. Ibid.
183. D. Marquand, 'Inquest on a Movement', *Encounter*, Vol. 53, July 1979, p. 16.
184. Cited in ibid.
185. A. Watkins, 'Mr Crosland's Clarion Call', *The Spectator*, Vol. 219, 21 July 1967, p. 67.
186. Crosland, in *The Politics of Education*, op. cit., p. 156.
187. Ibid., p. 157.
188. C.A.R. Crosland, Speech in Grimsby, 7 October 1974, unpublished manuscript, in CP 13(29).
189. C.A.R. Crosland, Letter to P. Williams dated 13 March 1945, in CP 3(26), Pt. ii.
190. C.R. Atlee, Preface to *New Fabian Essays*, op. cit., p. ix.
191. B. Magee, 'Conservatism with a small "c"', *Socialist Commentary*, January 1963, p. 19.
192. B. Walden, 'Theory and Practice', *New Statesman*, 17 July 1970, p. 59.
193. Jenkins, *A Life at the Centre*, op. cit., p. 30.
194. Crossman, *Diaries* Vol. II, op. cit., p. 725.
195. Rodgers, 'Crosland: A Man of Suspended Judgement', loc. cit. Rodgers was Crosland's Minister of State at the Board of Trade.
196. Ibid.
197. Cited in Jenkins, *A Life at the Centre*, op. cit., p. 218.
198. Jenkins, *A Life at the Centre*, op. cit., p. 228.
199. Ibid., p. 218.
200. Castle, *The Castle Diaries*, op. cit., p. 282.
201. Ibid., p. 522.
202. Ibid., p. 440.
203. Ibid., p. 68.
204. Cited in ibid., p. 329. Owen was Crosland's Minister of State at the Foreign Office.
205. Healey, *Time of My Life*, op. cit., p. 457.

206. Cited in Crossman, *Diaries*, Vol. III, op. cit., p. 180.
207. Jay, *Change and Fortune*, op. cit., p. 401.
208. Crosland, in *The Politics of Education*, op. cit., p. 167.
209. Ibid.
210. Donaldson, 'In Memoriam: II', loc. cit., p. 17.
211. C.A.R. Crosland, notebook entry (1973), in CP 16(8).
212. C.A.R. Crosland, Letter to P. Williams dated 23 September [probably 1940], in CP 3(26), Pt. i.
213. S. Crosland, *Ruling Passions*, op. cit., p. 128.
214. Ibid., p. 345.
215. R. Berthoud, 'Mr Crosland: A strong personality who rarely seems to catch the public eye', *The Times*, 25 March 1976, p. 16.
216. Donaldson, 'In Memoriam: II', loc. cit., p. 17.
217. Falkender, *Downing Street in Perspective*, op. cit., p. 245.
218. R.H.S. Crossman, *The Backbench Diaries of Richard Crossman*, ed. by J.P. Morgan (London: Hamish Hamilton and Jonathan Cape, 1981), p. 686.
219. Ibid.
220. Cited in Pimlott, *Harold Wilson*, op. cit., p. 244.
221. Rowan, 'Crosland: The Last Interview', loc. cit.
222. Cited in Pimlott, *Harold Wilson*, op. cit., p. 305.
223. H. Pelling, *A Short History of the Labour Party*, 8th. ed. (London: Macmillan, 1985), p. 125.
224. Falkender, *Downing Street in Perspective*, op. cit., p. 244.
225. Pimlott, *Harold Wilson*, op. cit., p. 486.
226. Cited in ibid., pp. 25, 35.
227. Ibid., p. 488.
228. Ibid., p. 66.
229. Crossman, *Diaries*, Vol. III, op. cit., p. 535.
230. Crossman, *Diaries*, Vol. II, op. cit., p. 779.
231. Cited in P. Ziegler, *Wilson* (London: Weidenfeld and Nicolson, 1993), p. 295. Ziegler's source for this story is Roy Hattersley.
232. T. Benn, *Out of the Wilderness: Diaries 1963–67* (London: Hutchinson, 1987), p. 475.
233. Cited in S. Crosland, *Tony Crosland*, op. cit., p. 184.
234. C.A.R. Crosland, notebook entry, n.d. [probably early 1970s], in CP 16(7).
235. Ibid.
236. Crosland, in *The Politics of Education*, op. cit., p. 149

3. The World of the Revisionist

1. C.A.R. Crosland, 'Leftover Left to Kill', *The Spectator*, Vol. 201, 24 October 1958, p. 555.
2. Ibid.
3. B. Gould, *A Future for Socialism* (London: Jonathan Cape, 1989), p. 5.
4. C.A.R. Crosland, Letter to P. Williams dated 22 May [probably 1941], in CP 3(26), Pt. i.
5. Ibid. Crosland leaves the question open.

3.1 The World of the Future

1. See Central Statistical Office, *Economic Trends* (*Annual Supplement*) (London: Her Majesty's Stationery Office, 1992).
2. The phrase is that of Harold Macmillan in 1947. Cited in A. Horne, *Macmillan*, Vol. I (London: Macmillan, 1988), p. 308.
3. Cited in ibid., p. 301.
4. *Social Insurance and Allied Services* (the Beveridge Report), Cmd. 6404 (London: His Majesty's Stationery Office, 1942), para. 456.
5. To be fair, Butler was on the left of one party while Gaitskell was on the right of the other: see *The Diary of Hugh Gaitskell 1945–56*, ed. by P.M. Williams (London: Jonathan Cape, 1983), pp. 307, 395 for evidence that Gaitskell believed Butler to be 'on the extreme left of the Tory Party', that Crosland (with Wyatt and Jenkins) described Gaitskell as situated on the 'Right-wing' of the Labour Party. Also, the two chancellors were united by the unusual attribute of an intellectual's approach to problem-solving. The scope for innovation was in any case severely circumscribed by the small size of the respective Government's majority – 5 when Gaitskell was Chancellor, 17 at the time of Butler. It should also be noted that Butler was later to make more intensive use of monetary policy, raising Bank Rate in 1955 to $4\frac{1}{2}$ per cent, the highest level it had reached in over 20 years. Labour would probably have looked mainly to fiscal policy for the requisite deflation; and would presumably have wanted to skew the burdens in such a way as to spare the poor. These points should be borne in mind in evaluating the closeness of the convergence. The difference that they would have made to the economic history of a period of substantial underlying consensus is, however, not likely to have been very great.
6. See R.H.S. Crossman, 'The Spectre of Revisionism: A Reply to Crosland', *Encounter*, Vol. 14, April 1960. The article to which he is replying is Crosland's 'The Future of the Left', published in *Encounter* in March 1960 and reprinted as Chapter 8 of *The Conservative Enemy*.
7. Cited in M. Foot, *Aneurin Bevan*, Vol. II (London: Davis-Poynter, 1973), p. 505.
8. Cited in ibid., p. 574.
9. R. Jenkins, 'Leader of the Opposition', in Rodgers, ed., *Hugh Gaitskell*, op. cit., p. 123.
10. S. Haseler, *The Gaitskellites* (London: Macmillan, 1969), p. 197. Crosland's attitude to the United States is discussed in more detail in Reisman, *Crosland's Future*, op. cit., Ch. 4.3.
11. K. Marx and F. Engels, *Manifesto of the Communist Party* (1848), in D. Fernbach, ed., *Karl Marx: Political Writings*, Vol. I: *The Revolutions of 1848* (Harmondsworth: Penguin Books, 1973), p. 68.
12. C.A.R. Crosland, 'New Moods, Old Problems', *Encounter*, Vol. 16, February 1961, in CE, p. 238.
13. Cited in Horne, *Macmillan*, Vol. I, op. cit., p. 308.
14. C.A.R. Crosland, *Can Labour Win?*, Fabian Tract 324, 1960, in CE, p. 159.
15. Ibid., p. 151.
16. Crosland, 'Radical Reform and the Left', in CE, p. 128.
17. Crosland, *Can Labour Win?*, in CE, p. 153.

18. Ibid., p. 160.
19. Cited in Haseler, *The Gaitskellites*, op. cit., p. 163.
20. M. Young, *The Chipped White Cups of Dover* (London: Unit 2, 1960), p. 11. The Fabian Society having declined to publish the pamphlet, the author published it himself. Michael Young later became the founder–president of the Consumers' Association.
21. Ibid., p. 19.
22. Cited in *Orientation: Socialism Today and Tomorrow* (Amsterdam: Dr. Wiardi Beckman Stichting, 1960).
23. FS, p. 353 (520).
24. Cited in P. Jenkins, 'Intellect with his finger on the common pulse', *The Guardian*, 21 February 1977.
25. C.A.R. Crosland, 'Preparing for the Next Election', *The Observer*, 21 January 1973, in SN, p. 104.
26. Ibid., p. 105.
27. Ibid.
28. SN, p. 50.
29. C.A.R. Crosland, 'British Labour's Crucial Meeting', *The New Leader*, 3 October 1960, p. 8.

3.2 The Mixed Economy

1. A. Smith, *The Wealth of Nations* (1776), ed. by E. Cannan (London: Methuen, 1961), Vol. I, p. 477.
2. Ibid., p. 475.
3. Ibid., Vol. II, p. 209.
4. A. Marshall, 'Some Aspects of Competition' (1890), reprinted in A.C. Pigou, ed., *Memorials of Alfred Marshall* (London: Macmillan, 1925), p. 275.
5. A. Marshall, 'Social Possibilities of Economic Chivalry' (1907), in ibid., p. 336.
6. A. Marshall, *Principles of Economics*, 8th. ed. (1920) (London: Macmillan, 1949), p. 33.
7. Ibid., p. 34.
8. Ibid., p. 16.
9. Ibid., p. 392.
10. R.L. Hall, *Earning and Spending* (London: Centenary Press, 1934), p. 82.
11. Ibid., p. 37.
12. R.L. Hall, *The Economic System in a Socialist State* (London: Macmillan, 1937), pp. 26–7.
13. Ibid., p. 74.
14. R.L. Hall, 'The Place of the Economist in Government', *Oxford Economic Papers*, Vol. 7, 1955, p. 119.
15. A.C. Pigou, *The Economics of Welfare*, 4th. ed. (London: Macmillan, 1932), p. 89.
16. H. Dalton, *Call Back Yesterday* (London: Frederick Muller, 1953), p. 58.
17. A.C. Pigou, *Socialism versus Capitalism* (London: Macmillan, 1937), p. 138. Crosland read this book when he was a student at Oxford. See his

exercise book on Marxism & Socialist Theory, n.d. [probably 1940s], in CP 2(17).

18. J.M. Keynes, 'The End of Laissez-Faire' (1926), in *Essays in Persuasion* (1931) and *The Collected Writings of John Maynard Keynes*, Vol. IX (London: Macmillan, 1972), pp. 287–8.

19. Ibid., p. 290.

20. J.M. Keynes, *The General Theory of Employment, Interest and Money* (1936), in *The Collected Writings of John Maynard Keynes*, Vol. VII (London: Macmillan, 1973), p. 374.

21. J.M. Keynes, 'A Short View of Russia' (1925), in *Essays in Persuasion* and *The Collected Writings of John Maynard Keynes*, Vol. IX, op. cit., p. 258.

22. J.M. Keynes, 'Am I a Liberal?' (1925), in ibid., p. 297.

23. Keynes, *General Theory*, op. cit., p. 376.

24. J.M. Keynes, 'Economic Possibilities for our Grandchildren' (1930), in *Essays in Persuasion* and *The Collected Writings of John Maynard Keynes*, Vol. IX, op. cit., p. 326.

25. R. Jenkins, *Pursuit of Progress* (London: William Heinemann, 1953), pp. 62–3. This short book (184 pages, widely spaced) bears the ambitious subtitle 'A critical analysis of the achievement and prospect of the Labour Party'. Roy Jenkins presumably intended it as his contribution to the philosophy of revisionism. Many hypotheses are left unexplained, evidence (especially statistical evidence) is seldom cited, and the references suggest an exaggerated reliance on Dalton's *Practical Socialism* and Jay's *Socialist Case*. The book puts Crosland's *Future* into perspective by showing how difficult it can be to make a serious statement about the belief-system of the Centre-Left.

26. J.M. Keynes, 'Liberalism and Labour' (1926), in *Essays in Persuasion* and *The Collected Writings of John Maynard Keynes*, Vol. IX, op. cit., p. 311.

27. H. Spencer, *The Man Versus The State* (1884) (Harmondsworth: Penguin Books, 1969), p. 100.

28. T.H. Green, *Liberal Legislation and Freedom of Contract* (1880), reprinted in R.L. Nettleship, ed., *The Works of Thomas Hill Green*, Vol. III (London: Longmans, Green, and Co., 1891), p. 371.

29. P. Clarke, *Liberals and Social Democrats* (Cambridge: Cambridge University Press, 1978), p. 163.

30. Cited in J. Harris, *William Beveridge* (Oxford: Clarendon Press, 1977), p. 424.

31. Cited in ibid., p. 420.

32. F.A. Hayek, *The Road to Serfdom* (1944) (London: Routledge and Kegan Paul, 1976), pp. 22–23.

33. W. Beveridge, *Full Employment in a Free Society* (London: Allen and Unwin, 1944), p. 199.

34. Cited in Harris, *William Beveridge*, op. cit., p. 436.

35. Cited in ibid., p. 431.

36. Cited in J. Rae, *Life of Adam Smith* (1895) (New York: Augustus M. Kelley, 1965), p. 62.

37. Cited in Horne, *Harold Macmillan*, Vol. I, op. cit., p. 79.

38. H. Macmillan, *Winds of Change* (London: Macmillan, 1966), p. 511.

39. Ibid., p. 209.

40. Ibid., p. 367.
41. Ibid., p. 502.
42. H. Macmillan, 'The Middle Way: 20 Years After' (1958), reprinted in his *The Middle Way* (1938) (London: Macmillan, 1966), p. xx.
43. D. Marquand, 'Has Social Democracy a Future?', *The Spectator*, Vol. 243, 29 September 1979, p. 14.
44. Macmillan, *The Middle Way*, op. cit., p. 231.
45. Ibid., p. 64.
46. Cited in Horne, *Harold Macmillan*, Vol. I, op. cit., p. 296.
47. Cited in ibid., p. 105.
48. K. Hardie, *Labour Politics* (London: Independent Labour Party, 1903), p. 8.
49. G.D.H. Cole, *Self-Government in Industry* (London: G. Bell and Sons, Ltd., 1917), p. 7.
50. Ibid., p. 53.
51. Ibid., p. 5.
52. G.D.H. Cole, *The World of Labour* (1913) (Brighton: Harvester Press, 1973), p. xi.
53. Ibid., p. 332.
54. R.H. Tawney, *The Acquisitive Society* (1920) (London: Collins, 1961), p. 78.
55. Ibid., p. 57.
56. Ibid., p. 171.
57. Ibid., p. 142.
58. Ibid., p. 27.
59. Ibid., p. 149.
60. R.H. Tawney, *Equality* (1931), 4th. ed. (1952) (London: George Allen and Unwin Ltd., 1964), p. 205.
61. Tawney, *The Acquisitive Society*, op. cit., p. 146.
62. Tawney, *Equality*, op. cit., p. 43.
63. Ibid., p. 144.
64. Ibid., p. 145.
65. R.H. Tawney, 'Social Democracy in Britain' (1949), reprinted in his *The Radical Tradition* (Harmondsworth: Penguin Books, 1966), p. 158.
66. Cited in Williams, *Hugh Gaitskell*, op. cit., p. 368.
67. See on this ibid., p. 631.
68. Cited in R. Terrill, *R.H. Tawney and His Times* (Cambridge, Mass.: Harvard University Press, 1973), p. 115.
69. R.H. Tawney, 'A Note on Christianity and the Social Order' (1937), in his *The Attack and Other Papers* (London: George Allen and Unwin Ltd., 1953), p. 170.
70. H. Gaitskell, 'An Appreciation' (1962), reprinted in Tawney, *The Radical Tradition*, op. cit., p. 221.
71. Dalton, *Practical Socialism for Britain*, op. cit., p. 319.
72. Ibid., p. 320n.
73. Ibid., p. 105.
74. Ibid., p. 121.
75. Ibid., p. 142.
76. Ibid., p. 17.
77. Ibid., p. 149.
78. Ibid., p. 243.

79. Ibid., p. 234.
80. Ibid., p. 245.
81. Ibid., p. 332.
82. D. Jay, *The Socialist Case* (London: Faber and Faber, 1937), p. 1.
83. Ibid., p. 2.
84. Ibid., p. ix.
85. Ibid., p. 3.
86. D. Jay, *Socialism in the New Society* (London: Longmans, Green and Co. Ltd., 1962), p. 6n.
87. Ibid., p. 23n.
88. Jay, *The Socialist Case*, op. cit., p. 33.
89. Ibid., p. 3.
90. Ibid., p. 4.
91. Ibid., p. 237.
92. Ibid., p. 252.
93. Ibid., p. 236.
94. Ibid., p. 238.
95. Ibid., p. 321.
96. Ibid., p. 278.
97. Ibid., p. 321.
98. Ibid., p. 350.
99. Ibid., p. 316.
100. Ibid.
101. FS, p. 2n (20n).
102. E.F.M. Durbin, *The Politics of Democratic Socialism* (London: George Routledge and Sons Ltd., 1940), p. 75.
103. Ibid., p. 31.
104. Ibid., p. 145.
105. Ibid., p. 86.
106. Ibid., p. 296.
107. Ibid., p. 301.
108. Ibid., p. 120.
109. Ibid., p. 260.
110. Ibid., p. 144.
111. Ibid., p. 294.
112. Ibid., p. 136.
113. Ibid., p. 129.
114. Cited in Foot, *Aneurin Bevan*, Vol. II, op. cit., p. 612.
115. E. Shinwell, *I've Lived Through It All* (London: Gollancz, 1973), p. 215.

3.3 Gaitskellite Economics

1. R.H.S. Crossman, 'Towards a Philosophy of Socialism', in Crossman, *New Fabian Essays*, op. cit., p. 2.
2. Ibid., p. 27.
3. Crosland, 'The Transition from Capitalism', loc. cit., p. 68.
4. P. Pugh, *Educate, Agitate, Organize: 100 Years of Fabian Socialism* (London: Methuen, 1984), p. 230.
5. 'Next Stage on Road to Socialism', *The Times*, 27 June 1952.

6. T. Balogh, 'Fabians at Sea', *Tribune*, 30 May 1952, p. 6.
7. 'The Fabians', *The Manchester Guardian*, 23 May 1952.
8. J.K. Galbraith, contribution to 'Fabianism Revisited', *Review of Economics and Statistics*, Vol. 35, 1953, p. 206.
9. Ibid., p. 208.
10. A. Schlesinger, Jr., in ibid., p. 202.
11. S.H. Beer, in ibid., p. 206.
12. D.M. Wright, in ibid., p. 209.
13. Ibid., p. 208.
14. A. Bevan, *In Place of Fear* (1952) (London: MacGibbon and Kee Ltd, 1961), p. 106.
15. Ibid., p. 100.
16. Ibid., p. 23.
17. Ibid., p. 35.
18. Ibid., p. 143.
19. Cited in Foot, *Aneurin Bevan*, Vol. II, op. cit., p. 648.
20. Foot, in ibid., p. 634.
21. J. Campbell, *Nye Bevan and the Mirage of British Socialism* (London: Weidenfeld and Nicolson, 1987), p. 264.
22. Ibid., p. 271.
23. G. Foote, *The Labour Party's Political Thought* (London: Croom Helm, 1985), p. 281.
24. D. Howell, *British Social Democracy*, 2nd. ed. (London: Croom Helm, 1980), pp. 190, 240.
25. Cited in Campbell, *Nye Bevan and the Mirage of British Socialism*, op. cit., p. 372. Charles Curran was a Conservative Member of Parliament. The passage is taken from his obituary of Bevan in the *Evening News* of 7 July 1960.
26. Cited in Williams, *Hugh Gaitskell*, op. cit., p. 266.
27. Cited in ibid., p. 261.
28. See on this Foot, *Aneurin Bevan*, Vol. II, op. cit., p. 452 and the footnote on that page.
29. Cited in ibid., pp. 622–4.
30. Pimlott, *Hugh Dalton*, op. cit., p. 586.
31. C.A.R. Crosland, Letter to P. Williams dated 21 April [probably 1946], in CP 3(27).
32. Ibid.
33. R. Miliband, *Parliamentary Socialism*, 2nd. ed. (London: Merlin Press, 1972), p. 344. The first edition of this influential work was published in 1961.
34. Ibid., p. 347.
35. Crosland, *Can Labour Win?*, in CE, p. 162.
36. Foote, *The Labour Party's Political Thought*, op. cit., p. 15.
37. Howell, *British Social Democracy*, op. cit., p. 241.
38. Cited in Crossman, *Backbench Diaries*, op. cit., pp. 280–1.
39. Cited in ibid., p. 768.
40. Crossman, 'The Spectre of Revisionism', loc. cit., pp. 26–7.
41. R. Jenkins, 'Labour's Most Exciting Leader Since Gaitskell', *The Times*, 23 July 1994, p. 14.

3.4 Crosland and Gaitskell

1. S. Crosland, *Tony Crosland*, op. cit., p. 88.
2. Cited in Williams, *Hugh Gaitskell*, op. cit., p. 81.
3. Cited in ibid., p. 27.
4. R. Hoggart, *The Uses of Literacy* (London: Penguin Books, 1958), p. 188.
5. Ibid., p. 325.
6. S. Crosland, *Ruling Passions*, op. cit., p. 83.
7. Cited in Crossman, *Backbench Diaries*, op. cit., pp. 769–70.
8. Williams, *Hugh Gaitskell*, op. cit., p. 375.
9. D. Wood, 'The Inheritance', in Rodgers, *Hugh Gaitskell*, op. cit., p. 155.
10. Crossman, 'Towards a Philosophy of Socialism', loc. cit., pp. 4–5.
11. Wood, 'The Inheritance', loc. cit., p. 155.
12. Ibid., p. 154.
13. Jenkins, *A Life at the Centre*, op. cit., p. 110.
14. Cited in Pimlott, *Harold Wilson*, op. cit., p. 229.
15. Cited in ibid., p. 235.
16. Jenkins, *A Life at the Centre*, op. cit., p. 1.
17. Cited in Pimlott, *Harold Wilson*, op. cit., p. 262.
18. Cited in ibid., p. 255.
19. A. Howard, *Crossman: The Pursuit of Power* (London: Jonathan Cape, 1990), p. 261.
20. Cited in Pimlott, *Harold Wilson*, op. cit., p. 244.
21. Cited in Williams, *Hugh Gaitskell*, op. cit., p. 594.
22. Cited in ibid.
23. Cited in ibid., p. 563.
24. Jenkins, *A Life at the Centre*, op. cit., p. 197.
25. Haseler, *The Gaitskellites*, op. cit., p. 235.
26. Cited in Pimlott, *Harold Wilson*, op. cit., p. 255.
27. Cited in ibid., p. 256.
28. Ibid., p. 259.
29. H. Gaitskell, 'The Ideological Development of Democratic Socialism in Great Britain', *Socialist International Information*, Vol. V, No. 52–3, 24 December 1955, p. 949.
30. Crosland, *Can Labour Win?*, in CE, p. 156.
31. Cited in Williams, *Hugh Gaitskell*, op. cit., p. 69.
32. Cited in ibid., p. 357. This speech recalls that of Crosland at the South Gloucestershire selection-meeting six years before.
33. Cited in ibid.
34. Cited in ibid., p. 67.
35. Cited in Elizabeth Durbin, *New Jerusalems: The Labour Party and the Economics of Democratic Socialism* (London: Routledge and Kegan Paul, 1985), p. 128.
36. Cited in Williams, *Hugh Gaitskell*, op. cit., p. 357.
37. Cited in Elizabeth Durbin, *New Jerusalems*, op. cit., p. 128.
38. Cited in ibid.
39. H. Gaitskell, *Socialism and Nationalisation*, Fabian Tract 300 (London: Fabian Society, 1956), p. 3.
40. Ibid., p. 6.

41. Ibid., p. 3.
42. Cited in Williams, *Hugh Gaitskell*, op. cit., p. 388.
43. Cited in ibid., p. 468.
44. Cited in ibid.
45. Gaitskell, *Socialism and Nationalisation*, op. cit., p. 4.
46. Cited in Williams, *Hugh Gaitskell*, op. cit., p. 387.
47. Cited in ibid., p. 392.
48. Cited in ibid., p. 391.
49. Gaitskell, 'The Ideological Development of Democratic Socialism in Great Britain', loc. cit., p. 944.
50. Gaitskell, *Socialism and Nationalisation*, op. cit., p. 5.
51. Ibid., p. 23.
52. Ibid., p. 36.
53. See on this Williams, *Hugh Gaitskell*, op. cit., p. 449.
54. Cited in ibid., p. 659.
55. Gaitskell, *Socialism and Nationalisation*, op. cit., p. 36.
56. Ibid., p. 15.
57. Crosland, 'New Moods, Old Problems', in CE, p. 241.
58. Crosland, 'Radical Reform and the Left', in CE, p. 127.
59. CE, p. 7.
60. Ibid.
61. Crosland, *Can Labour Win?*, in CE, p. 163.
62. Ibid.
63. Cited in S. Crosland, *Tony Crosland*, op. cit., p. 107.
64. Cited in S. Crosland, *Tony Crosland*, op. cit.,p 229. Roy Hattersley, who thought as Crosland did on a number of issues, refused to vote for Jenkins in the 1976 Leadership election. Supporting Callaghan in order to keep out Foot, Hattersley is known to have been upset by Jenkins's statement in a television interview that democracy was under threat where more than 60 per cent of national expenditure originated in the public sector. (See on this ibid., p. 315). Crosland, who never specified an *a priori* limit to public spending, would almost certainly have shown an equal resistance to the qualifications as a socialist of a politician who was prepared to set a maximum to the services that were at the heart of the campaign for equality and welfare.
65. Leonard, 'In Memoriam: I', loc. cit., p. 12.
66. Crosland, *The British Economy in 1965*, op. cit., p. 2.
67. Crosland, 'Radical Reform and the Left', in CE, p. 128.
68. C.A.R. Crosland, 'In Praise of Hugh Gaitskell', *Socialist Commentary*, March 1973, p. 13. The phrase was first employed in a BBC television statement in 1963, on the night Gaitskell died. The original text may be found in CP 13(26).
69. Haseler, *The Gaitskellites*, op. cit., p. 245.
70. Crosland, 'Preparing for the Next Election', in SN, p. 107.
71. Cited in S. Crosland, *Tony Crosland*, op. cit., p. 104. See also S. Crosland and P. Williams, 'What Crosland would tell Callaghan today'. *The Sunday Times*, 29 June 1980, p. 16.
72. Ibid., p. 105.
73. Benn, *Against the Tide*, op. cit., p. 598.

74. 'Curtain-Raiser to Blackpool', *The Times*, 1 October 1956.
75. Lord Altrincham, 'The Crosland Version', *National and English Review*, November 1956, p. 239.
76. P. Elliott, 'Mr Crosland and Socialism', *New Epoch*, 1957, p. 23. The magazine circulated internally at Ruskin College, Oxford.
77. W. Pickles, broadcast review of *The Future of Socialism* for the European Service of the BBC, unpublished text, n.d., [presumably 1956], in CP 13(9).
78. H. Dalton, *High Tide and After* (London: Frederick Muller, 1962), p. 267.
79. Ibid., p. 412.
80. H. Dalton, review of *New Fabian Essays*, *Fabian Journal*, June 1952, p. 7.
81. Ibid., p. 9.
82. F. Packenham, 'The Future of Socialism', *Fabian Journal*, November 1956.
83. R. Jenkins, 'Down with the class barriers', *Forward*, 5 October 1956.
84. Jenkins, 'Anthony Crosland', in *Roy Jenkins' Gallery of Twentieth Century Portraits*, op. cit., p. 65.
85. W.T. Rodgers, Foreword to M. Summerskill and B. Brivati, *The Group 1954–60: A Time of Hope* (London: M. Summerskill and B. Brivati, 1993), p. vii.
86. D. Marquand, 'Basic Texts for the Left', *The Guardian*, 15 November 1962.
87. Ibid.
88. G. Hutton, 'A Lamp for Labour', *The Spectator*, Vol. 197, 12 October 1956, p. 505.
89. See Will Camp, 'Socialism? How Dare He Use the Word!', *Tribune*, 5 October 1956.
90. 'What is the future of socialism now?', *Daily Mail*, 21 February 1977.
91. N. Birnbaum, 'Ideals or Reality?', *Socialist Commentary*, September 1959, p. 6.
92. Crossman, 'The Spectre of Revisionism', loc. cit., p. 26.
93. R. Hinden, 'A Different Animal?', *Socialist Commentary*, November 1956, p. 28.
94. Kogan, in Boyle and Crosland, *The Politics of Education*, op. cit., p. 19.

4. Ownership

1. Jenkins, *A Life at the Centre*, op. cit., p. 111n.
2. C.A.R. Crosland, *Social Democracy in Europe*, Fabian Tract 438 (London: Fabian Society, 1975), p. 2.
3. Crosland, interview with Llew Gardner, loc. cit.
4. C.A.R. Crosland, *Britain's Economic Problem*, op. cit., p. 220.

4.1 Looking Backward

1. Tawney, *Equality*, op. cit., p. 186.
2. G.B. Shaw, 'Transition', in G.B. Shaw, ed., *Fabian Essays in Socialism* (1889) (London: Fabian Society and George Allen & Unwin Ltd., 1931), p. 169.
3. L. Benjamin, *The Position of the Middle-Class Worker in the Transition to Socialism* (London: Labour Party, 1935), p. 20. Crosland's own copy of this publication may be consulted in CP.

4. Elizabeth Durbin, *New Jerusalems*, op. cit., p. 74.
5. Ibid., p. 200.
6. C.A.R. Crosland, Letter to P. Williams dated 5 July 1940, in CP 3(26), Pt. i.
7. Macmillan, *The Middle Way*, op. cit., p. 258.
8. Ibid., p. 232.
9. Ibid., p. 230.
10. Ibid., p. 185.
11. C.A.R. Crosland, 'Function of Private Enterprise', *Socialist Commentary*, February 1950, p. 28.
12. *Labour and the New Society* (London: Labour Party, 1950), pp. 19–20.
13. *Challenge to Britain* (London: Labour Party, 1953), pp. 2, 3.
14. Cited in Foot, *Aneurin Bevan*, Vol. II, op. cit., pp. 500–1.
15. Cited in ibid., pp. 258–9.
16. Bevan, *In Place of Fear*, op. cit., pp. 144, 145.
17. Ibid., p. 45.
18. Cited in Foot, *Aneurin Bevan*, Vol. II, op. cit., p. 648.
19. Bevan, *In Place of Fear*, op. cit., pp. 37–8.
20. J. Strachey, *Contemporary Capitalism* (London: Gollancz, 1956), p. 292.
21. J. Strachey, 'The New Revisionist', *New Statesman*, Vol. 52, 6 October 1956, p. 397.
22. Ibid. Noel Thompson believes that passages such as this one (revealing as they do 'the lasting legacy of Strachey's inter-war Marxism') demonstrate just how much of a gap there still was between the author of *Contemporary Capitalism* and his contemporary who wrote *The Future of Socialism*: 'It is here that those who have put Strachey and Crosland in the same revisionist camp are fundamentally in error.... While Strachey's perception of the nature and lineaments of post-war capitalism was similar in many respects to that of Crosland this did not lead him on to the view that capitalism had ceased to exist. For Strachey the economic and social arrangements which prevailed in post-war Britain remained capitalist and they were so because a substantial part of the economic surplus was still privately appropriated by those who owned the means of production.' Agreeing with Crosland on the efficacy of Keynesian macroeconomic stabilisation and the separation of management from property, Strachey in 1956 continued to believe that the profit-motive survived as a major determinant of economic activity – and that private property was an obstacle to the revisionist's redistribution: 'Such views', Thompson writes, 'put Strachey closer to the fundamentalist camp of Bevan than to the open-air cafés of Croslandite revisionism.' See on this N. Thompson, *John Strachey: An Intellectual Biography* (London: Macmillan, 1993), pp. 191, 192, 220. The fact that a fellow reformer like Strachey could assign so much importance to the traditional constructs of economic basis and capital-ownership serves as a useful reminder that the Marxian categories were by no means extinct when Crosland was citing them as the *past* of socialism that he did not wish to perpetuate.
23. Pimlott, *Harold Wilson*, op. cit., p. 218.
24. Crossman, 'The Spectre of Revisionism', loc. cit., p. 27.
25. Ibid.
26. Ibid., p. 28.
27. Ibid.

28. R.H.S. Crossman, Letter to C.A.R. Crosland dated 23 October 1956, in CP 13(10).
29. Crossman, 'The Spectre of Revisionism', loc. cit., p. 28.
30. Cited in Foot, *Aneurin Bevan*, Vol. II, op. cit., p. 647.
31. Ibid., p. 646.
32. Ibid.
33. Haseler, *The Gaitskellites*, op. cit., p. 226.
34. Ibid.
35. FS, p. 66 (102).
36. C.A.R. Crosland, 'The Role of Public Ownership', *Encounter*, Vol. 16, May 1961, in CE, p. 49.
37. FS, p. 323 (475).
38. C.A.R. Crosland, Letter to P. Williams dated 21 April [probably 1946], in CP 3(27).
39. Ibid.
40. Ibid.
41. C.A.R. Crosland, 'The Black and White Decade', *The Observer*, 4 September 1960.
42. Crosland, interview with Llew Gardner, loc. cit.
43. Ibid.
44. Benn, *Against the Tide*, op. cit., p. 38. Benn is referring specifically to remarks made in 1973.
45. C.A.R. Crosland, Speech to the Oxford Union, Hilary Term 1946, unpublished manuscript, in CP 13(21).
46. Ibid.
47. Ibid.
48. FS, p. 254 (340).
49. FS, p. 72 (108).
50. SN, p. 42.
51. FS, p. 55 (91).
52. FS, p. 72 (108).
53. FS, p. 55 (91).
54. Crosland, Speech to the Oxford Union, Hilary Term 1946, loc. cit.
55. C.A.R. Crosland, Speech to the Oxford Union, n.d. [probably 1946], unpublished manuscript, in CP 13(21).
56. C.A.R. Crosland, Letter to P. Williams dated 30 November 1941, in CP 3(26), Pt. i.
57. C.A.R. Crosland, 'The Private and Public Corporation in Great Britain', in E.S. Mason, ed., *The Corporation in Modern Society* (Cambridge, Mass.: Harvard University Press, 1959), p. 274.
58. CE, p. 91.
59. Crosland, 'The Private and Public Corporation in Great Britain', loc. cit., p. 274.

4.2 Looking Forward

1. Cited in Benn, *Against the Tide*, op. cit., p. 34.
2. C.A.R. Crosland, 'The Future of Socialism', *Bulletin of the International House of Japan*, October 1963, p. 16.

3. See, for example, Crosland, 'Radical Reform and the Left', in CE, p. 142.
4. Crosland, Letter to Williams dated 21 April [1946], op. cit.
5. Crosland, 'The Private and Public Corporation in Great Britain', loc. cit., p. 274.
6. Crossman, 'The Spectre of Revisionism', loc. cit., p. 26.
7. Cited in Benn, *Against the Tide*, op. cit., p. 38.
8. Cited in ibid., p. 240.
9. Crosland, *Britain's Economic Problem*, op. cit., pp. 219–20.
10. C.A.R. Crosland, 'Socialism, Land and Equality' (Rita Hinden Memorial Lecture), *Socialist Commentary*, March 1974, p. v.
11. Crosland, 'The Transition from Capitalism', loc. cit., p. 64.
12. Crosland, 'The Private and Public Corporation in Great Britain', loc. cit., p. 274.
13. C.A.R. Crosland, Letter to P. Williams dated 29 January [probably 1946], in CP 3(27).
14. Crosland, Letter to Williams dated 21 April [1946], op. cit.
15. Crosland, *Britain's Economic Problem*, op. cit., p. 220.
16. Ibid., p. 107.
17. FS, pp. 349, 350 (508, 509).
18. FS, p. 336 (481).
19. FS, p. 336 (492).
20. C.A.R. Crosland, interview with George Gale, London Broadcasting Radio, 25 April 1974.
21. C.A.R. Crosland, *Towards a Labour Housing Policy*, Fabian Tract 410, 1971. Extract in SN, p. 117.
22. Ibid.
23. C.A.R. Crosland, 'A New Deal for Council Tenants', The *Guardian*, 16 June 1971, in SN, p. 131.
24. Ibid., p. 130.
25. Ibid.
26. Crosland, 'Socialism, Land and Equality', loc. cit., p. v.
27. Crosland, interview with George Gale, loc. cit.
28. C.A.R. Crosland, Letter to P. Williams dated 19 January [probably 1941], in CP 3(26), Pt. i.
29. C.A.R. Crosland, *The New Socialism*, Dissent Pamphlet # 1 (Melbourne: Dissent Trust, 1963), p. 12.
30. Crosland, 'Socialism, Land and Equality', loc. cit., p. iv.
31. Ibid.
32. Ibid.
33. See, for example, CE, p. 194.
34. Shaw, 'Transition', loc. cit., p. 167.
35. Ibid., p. 186.
36. Gaitskell, 'The Ideological Development of Democratic Socialism in Great Britain', loc. cit., p. 928.
37. Tawney, *The Acquisitive Society*, op. cit., pp. 97–8.
38. J.K. Galbraith, 'What Comes After General Motors' (1974), in his *Annals of an Abiding Liberal* (Boston: Houghton Mifflin, 1979), p. 81.
39. Evan Durbin, *The Politics of Democratic Socialism*, op. cit., p. 135.
40. Jay, *The Socialist Case*, op. cit., p. 238.

41. Ibid., p. 237.
42. Strachey, 'The New Revisionist', loc. cit., p. 397.
43. Crosland, *Social Democracy in Europe*, op. cit., p. 2.

4.3 Performance and Politics

1. FS, p. 324 (476).
2. Crosland, 'A New Deal for Council Tenants', in SN, p. 132.
3. Crosland, 'The Role of Public Ownership', in CE, p. 44. Roy Jenkins makes the same point in his *Pursuit of Progress*, op. cit., p. 106, arguing both for a heterogeneity of non-capitalist modes of ownership (the central government, but also 'municipalities, cooperatives and other bodies') and for the selective nationalisation of individual firms (in whole or even in part) rather than, necessarily, of whole industries.
4. FS, p. 334 (489).
5. Crosland, 'The Private and Public Corporation in Great Britain', loc. cit., p. 270.
6. SN, p. 38.
7. Ibid.
8. Shaw, 'Transition', loc. cit., p. 172.
9. Crosland, 'The Role of Public Ownership', in CE, p. 42.
10. SN, p. 39.
11. FS, p. 325 (479).
12. C.A.R. Crosland, 'Prices and Costs in Nationalized Undertakings', *Oxford Economic Papers*, Vol. II, 1950, p. 55.
13. Crosland, *Britain's Economic Problem*, op. cit., p. 214.
14. Crosland, 'Prices and Costs in Nationalized Undertakings', loc. cit., p. 66.
15. Ibid.
16. CE, p. 90.
17. CE, p. 88.
18. CE, p. 91.
19. SN, p. 42–3.
20. FS, p. 11 (30).
21. Crosland, Speech to the Oxford Union, n.d. [probably 1946], op. cit.
22. FS, p. 73 (109).
23. FS, p. 41 (74).
24. SN, p. 41.
25. SN, p. 34.
26. Crosland, 'The Private and Public Corporation in Great Britain', loc. cit., pp. 270, 271.
27. SN, p. 34.
28. FS, p. 339 (495).
29. SN, p. 39.

5. Control

1. Crosland, 'Function of Public Enterprise', loc. cit., p. 30.
2. Crosland, 'Radical Reform and the Left', in CE, pp. 138–9.
3. Crosland, Speech to the Oxford Union, n.d. [probably 1946], op. cit.

5.1 The Principles of Control

1. Hayek, *The Road to Serfdom*, op. cit., p. 94.
2. FS, p. 343 (500).
3. Tawney, 'Social Democracy in Britain', loc. cit., pp. 170, 172.
4. R.H. Tawney, 'We Mean Freedom' (1944), in his *The Attack*, op. cit., p. 94.
5. Ibid., p. 97.
6. Crosland, Speech to the Oxford Union, n.d. [probably 1946], op. cit.
7. Ibid.
8. C.A.R. Crosland, 'The Nature of Capitalist Crisis', unpublished paper [1950], in CP 13(23).
9. CE, p. 67.
10. J.S. Mill, *On Liberty* (1859), ed. by Gertrude Himmelfarb (London: Penguin Books, 1974), p. 68.
11. FS, pp. 346–7 (504–5).
12. J.K. Galbraith and Nicole Salinger, *Almost Everyone's Guide to Economics* (Boston: Houghton Mifflin Co., 1978), p. 50.
13. J.K. Galbraith, *The New Industrial State* (1967) (Harmondsworth: Penguin Books, 1969), p. 77.
14. J.K. Galbraith, *The Affluent Society* (1958) (Harmondsworth: Penguin Books, 1973), p. 154.
15. C.A.R. Crosland, 'Production in the Age of Affluence', *The Listener*, 25 September 1958, in CE, p. 99.
16. C.A.R. Crosland, 'Mrs. Thatcher's Vote Snatcher', *New Statesman*, Vol. 88, 27 September 1974, p. 407.
17. G.B. Shaw, 'Economic' (The Economic Basis of Socialism), in *Fabian Essays*, op. cit., p. 21.
18. Ibid.
19. Ibid., p. 22.
20. Crosland, *The British Economy in 1965*, op. cit., p. 8.
21. R.L. Hall, Letter to C.A.R. Crosland dated 24 January 1956, in CP 13(8).
22. Bernstein, *Evolutionary Socialism*, op. cit., p. 100.
23. FS, p. 346 (503).
24. FS, pp. 345–6 (502–3).
25. Crosland, *Social Democracy in Europe*, op. cit., p. 13.
26. FS, p. 272 (358).
27. FS, p. 271 (357).
28. Cited in Williams, *Hugh Gaitskell*, op. cit., p. 68.
29. Cited in Foot, *Aneurin Bevan*, Vol. II, op. cit., p. 628.
30. Hayek, *The Road to Serfdom*, op. cit., p. 31.
31. Tawney, *The Acquisitive Society*, op. cit., p. 122.
32. S. Holland, *The Socialist Challenge* (London: Quartet Books, 1975), p. 26.
33. Ibid.
34. Crosland, 'The Private and Public Corporation in Great Britain', loc. cit., p. 264.
35. Ibid.
36. CE, p. 55.
37. CE, p. 57.
38. Crossman, 'The Spectre of Revisionism', loc. cit., p. 27.

234 Notes and References

5.2 Industrial Policy

1. H. Morrison, *An Easy Outline of Modern Socialism* (London: Labour Party, 1938), p. 9. Emphasis added.
2. J.A. Schumpeter, *Capitalism, Socialism and Democracy* (1942) (London: George Allen and Unwin, 1976), p. 196.
3. Pigou, *Socialism versus Capitalism*, op. cit., p. 102.
4. Ibid., p. 118.
5. I.M.D. Little, *A Critique of Welfare Economics*, 2nd. ed. (Oxford: Oxford University Press, 1957), p. 271.
6. Ibid., p. vii.
7. FS, p. 343 (500).
8. FS, p. 346 (504).
9. Crosland, 'The Nature of Capitalist Crisis', op. cit.
10. Jay, *The Socialist Case*, op. cit., p. 303.
11. Crosland, 'The Transition from Capitalism', loc. cit., p. 64.
12. Crossman, 'The Spectre of Revisionism', loc. cit., p. 27.
13. Crosland, paper to a Fabian Society conference, Oxford, January 1950, op. cit., in CP 13(23).
14. Ibid.
15. Ibid.
16. See on this C.A.R. Crosland, 'Legislating against Monopoly', *Socialist Commentary*, January 1951.
17. C.A.R. Crosland, 'Curbing the Trade Associations', *New Statesman*, 9 July 1955, p. 34.
18. Ibid.
19. C.A.R. Crosland, 'Tomatoes and Cucumbers', *Tribune*, 28 July 1950, p. 4.
20. SN, p. 238.
21. Schumpeter, op. cit., p. 106.
22. Ibid.
23. Galbraith and Salinger, *Almost Everyone's Guide to Economics*, op. cit., p. 39.
24. J.K. Galbraith, *American Capitalism* (1952) (Harmondsworth: Penguin Books, 1967), p. 106.
25. C.A.R. Crosland, 'The Arrogance of Austerity', *The Listener*, Vol. 54, 8 December 1955, p. 976.
26. SN, pp. 235–6.
27. C.A.R. Crosland, Statement in the House of Commons, 30 April 1968, *Parliamentary Debates (Hansard)*, Vol. 763, Cols. 1006–7.
28. SN, p. 239.
29. SN, p. 236.
30. Crosland, Statement in the House of Commons, 30 April 1968, loc. cit., Col. 1006.
31. Crossman, *Diaries of a Cabinet Minister*, Vol. III, op. cit., p. 186.
32. C.A.R. Crosland, 'Advertising: Is It Worth It?', *The Listener*, Vol. 55, 13 December 1956, p. 977. In view of the fact that Crosland's *Listener* papers of 1955 and 1956 appear so directly to be answering Galbraith, it is important to remember that they appeared after *American Capitalism* (1952) but before *The Affluent Society* (1958) and long before *The New Industrial State* (1967).

33. Ibid. This passage is particularly close to *The New Industrial State*, as is that cited in n.25, above.
34. Ibid.
35. CE, p. 50.
36. SN, p. 53.
37. Crossman, *Diaries of a Cabinet Minister*, Vol. II, op. cit., p. 464.
38. Crosland, *The British Economy in 1965*, op. cit., p. 8.
39. Ibid., p. 10.

5.3 The Environment

1. C.A.R. Crosland, 'A Riposte to Galbraith' (original title: 'The Anti-growth Heresy'), *New Statesman*, 8 January 1971, in SN, p. 95.
2. Crosland, *A Social-Democratic Britain*, in SN, p. 85.
3. C.A.R. Crosland, 'Protecting the Environment', *The Sunday Times*, 25 June 1972, in SN, p. 155.
4. Crosland, *A Social-Democratic Britain*, in SN, p. 72.
5. Crosland, 'Socialists in a Dangerous World', in SN, p. 70.
6. Crosland, 'A Riposte to Galbraith', in SN, p. 95. Galbraith seems to have been in England when *A Social-Democratic Britain* was published. Concerned that Crosland had misinterpreted *The Affluent Society* and his other writings, Galbraith sought to clarify his views on growth (a guarded defence if accompanied by the correction of State-sector poverty). His statement, 'Galbraith Answers Crosland', appeared in the *New Statesman* of 22 January 1971. Before sending it to the editor, he showed it to an academic at Kings College, Cambridge, who promptly reported the matter to Crosland. See Letter from Robin (perhaps Robin Marris) to C.A.R. Crosland dated 16 January 1971, in CP 13(13).
7. E.J. Mishan, *The Costs of Economic Growth* (Harmondsworth: Penguin Books, 1969), p. 142. Mishan apparently did not wait to secure a copy of *A Social-Democratic Britain* before he fired off an angry letter to its author: 'If *The Times* reported you correctly then it appears to me that your arguments are dis[ing]enuous, and if you did read my book I can only say that you understood it very imperfectly.' Letter from E.J. Mishan to C.A.R. Crosland dated 12 January 1971, in CP 13(13). Three days later Mishan wrote again, saying that he wanted to substitute 'mistaken' for disingenuous'. It is not clear what had upset him: perhaps it was Crosland's reference to his more extreme (arguably tongue-in-cheek) solutions such as the reinstatement of the horse-drawn carriage. Like *The Affluent Society*, *The Costs of Economic Growth* is not above exaggeration for effect. If Mishan and Galbraith were indeed misunderstood by Crosland, it is tempting to say that the fault was in part the authors' own for cutting corners in an attempt to appeal to a non-academic audience.
8. Crosland, *A Social-Democratic Britain*, in SN, p. 78.
9. SN, p. 53.
10. Crosland, *A Social-Democratic Britain*, in SN, pp. 77, 85.
11. CE, p. 183.
12. Crosland, Speech to the Oxford Union, n.d. [probably 1946], op. cit.
13. CE, p. 187.

14. CE, p. 183.
15. Crosland, 'The Future of the Left', in CE, p. 124.
16. C.A.R. Crosland, interview with J. Whale and N. Taylor, published as 'Mr. Environment', *The Sunday Times*, 25 January 1970, p. 12.
17. F. Hirsch, *Social Limits to Growth* (London: Routledge & Kegan Paul, 1977), p. 5.
18. Ibid., p. 173.
19. 'Mr. Environment', op. cit.
20. C.A.R. Crosland, Speech to GLC election meeting, Hampstead, 3 April 1973, unpublished manuscript, in CP 13(26).
21. C.A.R. Crosland, Fiftieth Anniversary Address, *Ancient Monuments Society's Transactions*, Vol. 21, 1975–76, p. 17.
22. CE, p. 183.
23. Crosland, Fiftieth Anniversary Address, loc. cit., p. 19.
24. Cited in E. Jacobs, 'Chief of Staff (Environment)', *The Sunday Times*, 19 October 1969, p. 24.
25. Crosland, 'Mr Environment', loc. cit.
26. CE, p. 185.
27. C.A.R. Crosland, 'The Right Machinery of Government', The *Guardian*, 23 July 1970, p. 10.
28. C.A.R. Crosland, Speech in the House of Commons, 18 February 1970, in SN, p. 174.
29. Ibid., pp. 178–9.

5.4 Macroeconomic Policy

1. Keynes, *General Theory*, op. cit., p. 220.
2. Crosland, 'The Transition from Capitalism', loc. cit., p. 40.
3. Ibid., p. 50.
4. C.A.R. Crosland, Speech at the Festival of International Cooperation, Greenwich, 1 July 1972, unpublished manuscript, in CP 13(24).
5. Ibid.
6. SN, p. 54.
7. FS, 1956 edition only, p. 448.
8. C.A.R. Crosland, 'Wage/Price Reactions Further Scrutinized', *The Times Review of Industry*, August 1958, p. 35.
9. A.W. Phillips, 'The Relation between Unemployment and the Rate of Change of Money Wage Rates in the United Kingdom 1861–1957', *Economica*, New Series, Vol. 25, 1958, p. 299.
10. Crosland, Speech at the Festival of International Cooperation, loc. cit.
11. Crosland, *A Social-Democratic Britain*, in SN, p. 83.
12. Crosland, Address to the Trade Union Public Services International, in SN, p. 248.
13. Crosland, *A Social-Democratic Britain*, in SN, p. 83.
14. Crosland, *Social Democracy in Europe*, op. cit., p. 11.
15. C.A.R. Crosland, 'Manpower', *Socialist Commentary*, April 1947, p. 604.
16. Crosland, Speech at the Festival of International Cooperation, op. cit.
17. Crosland, 'Manpower', loc. cit.
18. C.A.R. Crosland, 'My Budget', *News Chronicle*, 28 February 1952.

19. C.A.R. Crosland, 'Curbing Price Rises', *Socialist Commentary*, October 1951.
20. Crosland, Speech at the Festival of International Cooperation, op. cit.
21. Crosland, Address to the Trade Union Public Services International, in SN, p. 249. Emphasis added.
22. C.A.R. Crosland, Speech to a Fabian meeting, Brighton, 4 September 1974, unpublished manuscript, in CP 13(29).
23. C.A.R. Crosland, Speech in Grimsby, 7 October 1974, unpublished manuscript, in CP 13(29).
24. Ibid.
25. Castle, *The Castle Diaries*, op. cit., p. 542.
26. Crossman, *Diaries of a Cabinet Minister*, Vol. I, op. cit., p. 591.
27. C.A.R. Crosland, Speech to the North Lincolnshire Society of Quantity Surveyors, 21 February 1975, unpublished manuscript, in CP 13(31).
28. Cited in S. Crosland, *Tony Crosland*, op. cit., p. 296.
29. Crosland, Speech to the North Lincolnshire Society of Quantity Surveyors, op. cit.
30. Ibid.
31. FS, p. 263 (349).
32. C.A.R. Crosland, 'Industrial Democracy and Workers' Control' (original title: 'What Does the Worker Want?'), *Encounter*, Vol. 12, February 1959, in CE, p. 218.
33. SN, p. 29.
34. C.A.R. Crosland, 'Labour and "Populism"', *The Sunday Times*, 4 April 1971, in SN, p. 99.
35. Crossman, *Diaries of a Cabinet Minister*, Vol. III, op. cit., p. 501.
36. Cited in Pimlott, *Harold Wilson*, op. cit., p. 525.
37. G. Radice, 'Labour and the Unions', in Lipsey and Leonard, eds., *The Socialist Agenda*, op. cit., p. 125.
38. Benn, *Against the Tide*, op. cit., p. 61.
39. Crosland, *A Social-Democratic Britain*, in SN, p. 83.
40. Crosland, 'Preparing for the Next Election', in SN, p. 104.
41. Crosland, *Social Democracy in Europe*, op. cit., p. 11.
42. Benn, *Against the Tide*, op. cit., p. 61.
43. Ibid., p. 47.
44. Ibid., p. 329.

5.5 The Principles of De-control

1. C.A.R. Crosland, 'A Reply', *Socialist Commentary*, September 1959, p. 9.
2. FS, p. 354 (521).
3. FS, p. 357 (524).
4. FS, p. 354 (521).
5. FS, p. 355 (522).
6. C.A.R. Crosland, 'Pilkington and the Labour Party', *Socialist Commentary*, August 1962, p. 6.
7. FS, p. 355 (522).
8. FS, p. 355 (522).
9. FS, pp. 355–6 (522). Appropriately enough, it was a fellow revisionist – Roy Jenkins – who, as Home Secretary under Wilson in the 1960s, was

instrumental in the liberalisation of regulations in morally-charged areas such as this.

10. See Crossman, *Diaries of a Cabinet Minister*, Vol. III, op. cit., p. 837.
11. CE, p. 210.
12. C.A.R. Crosland, 'Policies for the People, by the People', *Socialist Commentary*, November 1971, p. 4.
13. CE, p. 209.
14. CE, p. 205.
15. Cited in S. Crosland, *Tony Crosland*, op. cit., pp. 214–5.
16. Crosland, 'Pilkington and the Labour Party', loc. cit., p. 5.
17. C.A.R. Crosland, 'Patterns of Revolt', *New Statesman*, Vol. 62, 6 October 1961, p. 477.
18. CE, p. 206.
19. Cited in C. Stuart, ed., *The Reith Diaries* (London: Collins, 1975), p. 510. See also I. McIntyre, *The Expense of Glory: A Life of John Reith* (London: HarperCollins, 1993) and Crosland's chapter on 'The Mass Media' in CE, esp. pp. 207–8.
20. CE, p. 208.
21. CE, p. 211.
22. CE, p. 211.
23. FS, p. 356 (523).
24. Cited in S. Crosland, *Tony Crosland*, op. cit., p. 47.
25. Crosland, 'The Nature of Capitalist Crisis', op. cit.
26. C.A.R. Crosland, unpublished manuscript [circa 1950], in CP 13(21).
27. Ibid.
28. 'The Grimsby Gent', *Daily Mirror*, 21 February 1977.
29. Crossman, *Backbench Diaries*, p. 199.
30. B. Walden, 'A Critique of Revisionism', *New Statesman*, 25 June 1971, p. 874.
31. C.A.R. Crosland, notebook entry (1974), in CP 16(8).
32. Jenkins, 'Anthony Crosland', loc. cit., p. 68.
33. S. Crosland, *Tony Crosland*, op. cit., p. 62.
34. Crosland, 'The Nature of Capitalist Crisis', op. cit.
35. Cited in S. Crosland, *Tony Crosland*, op. cit., p. 47.
36. FS, p. 355 (521–2).
37. FS, p. 361 (529). These are the concluding words of the book.
38. See, for example, FS, p. 355 (522).
39. FS, p. 355 (522).
40. W. Deedes, 'Party records', *Sunday Telegraph*, 31 March 1974.
41. Crosland, 'Radical Reform and the Left', in CE, p. 131.
42. C. Fletcher-Cooke, 'War on two fronts', *Crossbow*, Jan–Mar. 1963.
43. C. Randall, 'A British Socialist on Ground Thought Reserved to Capitalism', *Chicago Tribune*, 10 March 1963.
44. 'Growth is not a four-letter word', *New York Times*, 17 February 1972.
45. H. Schmertz, Letter to C.A.R. Crosland dated 4 February 1972, in CP 13(25).
46. Keynes, 'The End of Laissez-Faire', op. cit., p. 294

6. Conclusion

1. A. Briggs, 'Socialism and Society', *The Observer*, 30 September 1956.
2. L.A. Coser, 'Visions and Revisions', *Commentary*, August 1963, p. 178.
3. Pimlott, *Hugh Dalton*, op. cit., p. 587.
4. Cited in ibid.
5. FS, p. 347 (505).
6. C.A.R. Crosland, 'Out of the Rut', review of W.A. Lewis, *The Theory of Economic Growth*, *The Observer*, 6 November 1955, p. 10.
7. Ibid.
8. R.H.B., 'Reshaping Socialist Doctrine', *Financial Times*, 1 October 1956.
9. B. Crick, 'Socialist Literature in the 1950s', *Political Quarterly*, Vol. 31, 1960, p. 362.
10. C.A.R. Crosland, notebook entry (1976), in CP 16(18).
11. Crosland, Letter to Williams dated 13 March 1945, in CP 3(26), Pt. ii.
12. Crick, 'Socialist Literature in the 1950s', loc. cit., p. 368.
13. S. Haseler, Letter to *The Guardian*, 3 March 1977. Writing at the time of Crosland's death, Haseler, then Secretary of the Social Democratic Alliance, was clearly rather pessimistic about the future of the Labour Party's Centre-Right.
14. Vaizey, in Young *et al.*, 'Memoir', loc. cit., p. 87.
15. Young, in ibid., p. 84.
16. C.E. Lindblom, *Politics and Markets* (New York: Basic Books, 1977), p. 8.
17. It is presumably the freedom of manoeuvre that growth facilitates that led Crosland in Venezuela to observe of his *Future* that it was '100 per cent correct everywhere exc. in UK': 'Much easier to see what Soc. means in poorer country: my definition precisely fits Ven.' See C.A.R. Crosland, notebook entries (1976, 1975), in CP 16(8). Evidently he did not regard the lower profile of the boarding schools and the absence of a Clause IV to reform as a significant impediment to the transfer of his revisionism.
18. Crosland, *Social Democracy in Europe*, p. 13.
19. D. Marquand, *The Unprincipled Society* (London: Fontana, 1988), pp. 97–8.
20. Welch, 'Crosland Reconsidered', loc. cit., pp. 83, 84.
21. Cited in S. Crosland, *Tony Crosland*, op. cit., p. 390.

Index

AC refers to Anthony Crosland throughout.